# The Life and Times of Hammerin' Hank Ward:

The Kentucky Park & Highway Commissioner Who Chased
Riverfront Loan Sharks, Tangled with Arsonists in the Parks,
& Banished Run-down Dump Trucks

Sharon Roggenkamp

Copyright © 2024 by Sharon Roggenkamp. All rights reserved.

This book or any portion thereof may not be reproduced or used in any manner whatsoever without the express written permission of the publisher except for the use of brief quotations in a scholarly work or book review. For permissions or further information contact Braughler Books LLC at: info@braughlerbooks.com

Cover design: Paul Curtis

Printed in the United States of America
Published by Braughler Books LLC., Springboro, Ohio

First printing, 2024

ISBN: 979-8-89390-034-7

Library of Congress Control Number: 2024921883

Ordering information: Special discounts are available on quantity purchases by bookstores, corporations, associations, and others. For details, contact the publisher at:
    sales@braughlerbooks.com
    or at 937-58-BOOKS

For questions or comments about this book, please write to: info@braughlerbooks.com

Unless otherwise noted, photos are from the Henry Ward Family Collection by permission of Patricia Ward Willis. Images from Kentucky Park Brochures from Author's collection.

***Advance Praise for THE LIFE AND TIMES OF HAMMERIN' HANK WARD:***
***The Kentucky Park & Highway Commissioner Who Chased Riverfront Loan Sharks, Tangled with Arsonists in the Parks, & Banished Run-down Dump Trucks***

Henry Ward, a hard charging newspaperman and state legislator from Paducah, left a major mark on Kentucky over twenty years at mid-century. Roggenkamp's much needed biography details his legacy as father of an outstanding park system, and as architect of the Commonwealth's modern road and interstate highway system under four mid-century Kentucky governors. Roggenkamp tells his story with considerable energy and humor. Although he lost the race for governor in 1967, "Hammerin' Hank" deserves more recognition for his accomplishments and Roggenkamp delivers that!

> GEORGE G. HUMPHREYS, Kentucky historian, and author of *The Fall of Kentucky's Rock: Western Kentucky Democratic Politics Since the New Deal (2022)*.

Sharon Roggenkamp's persistence brings to us an exceptional Kentuckian's saga, long overdue. Yet, Hammerin' Hank's name would never be sited at the first floor Capitol office where governors preside.
Henry Ward was my friend, and his citizenship lessons and ability to trust his own instincts became invaluable gifts. Readers will find notable examples of Henry's vision, intellect, steadfast fortitude and ability to manage. Modernizing Kentucky's highways, building the finest state park system in America, and slamming brakes on improper governmental deal-making were but a few of his achievements, as you will learn.

> THOMAS L. PRESTON, Founder & CEO of ForeseeNow

Henry Ward—an honorable and progressive public servant—has for too long been overlooked by Kentucky history. Sharon Roggenkamp corrects that oversight with her extensive research and well documented exploration of his tireless efforts to improve the Commonwealth.

> DIANA TAYLOR-GRAY, Taylor-Gray Associates; former Lexington Herald-Leader Bureau Chief, Frankfort, Kentucky; Chief of Staff for Kentucky Governor Brereton Jones, (1991-1993)

**In Memory of**

*Martha E. Oster (1923-2001)*
"I'll get going again…"

*John Robert Oster (1923-2003)*
"Ceiling and visibility unlimited…"

## Acknowledgments

The author would like to thank Patricia Ward Willis, Henry Ward's daughter, for her time, and her father's photographs, files, professional and personal papers to advance this manuscript; and Ellen Winkler, Henry's granddaughter, for her assistance and encouragement. Thanks to Diana Taylor-Gray for her editorial skill shaping this biography. Kentucky historian George C. Humphreys and Thomas L. Preston generously gave their guidance, time and encouragement. Special thanks to my husband Bill for his support along the way to the finish line on this project.

# Table of Contents

| | |
|---|---|
| Dedication | iii |
| 1 End of Damn Story, I Guess... | 1 |
| 2 Explosion and Tears | 13 |
| 3 A Crusader Goes to Frankfort | 23 |
| 4 Rip Roaring Speeches and the Sales Tax Revolt | 37 |
| 5 Reformer Reformed | 45 |
| 6 Dousing the Kerosene Lanterns | 51 |
| 7 A Deplorable Situation | 59 |
| 8 Victors and Victim | 67 |
| 9 A "Decent Fella" | 77 |
| 10 "They'll Build that Dam or Bust" | 83 |
| 11 First Rate Candidate—Third Place Finish | 95 |
| 12 Following in Their Footsteps | 101 |
| 13 The Beautiful Old House & The Moonbow | 113 |
| 14 Roosevelt's "Tree Army" | 125 |
| 15 Ready, Set, Go... | 135 |
| 16 Let's Make A Deal | 145 |
| 17 No More Pioneer Stuff | 153 |

| | |
|---|---|
| 18 A Firebugs' Playground | 161 |
| 19 Speeding Backward | 169 |
| 20 Run Down Dump Trucks | 181 |
| 21 Stranger in the Kingdom | 191 |
| 22 Flashing Yellow Lights | 205 |
| 23 End of Damn Story | 215 |
| 24 Notes on Sources | 225 |

# 1 End of Damn Story, I Guess...

"Henry was a very fine public servant, very stubborn, at times very unmovable, but he put his public service together with his newspaper background so his integrity never came into question. That was what put him head and shoulders above many public officials."

MARLOW COOK, Republican U.S. Senator, who represented Kentucky from 1968-1974

In 1986, retired *Louisville Courier-Journal* public affairs columnist John Ed Pearce interviewed Henry T. Ward for the Kentucky Oral History Commission. This biography is framed by that interview and a second oral history project, exploring the life of a "triple threat man"—a newspaper columnist, state legislator, and Kentucky park and highway commissioner admired for his fierce integrity.

Nicknamed "Hammerin' Hank," he was best known as the father of Kentucky's modern park system. He managed the Kentucky campaigns of U.S. Senator and Vice-President Alben Barkley, worked as a U.S. Senate assistant to Earle Clements, who was a close friend and advisor to President Lyndon B. Johnson, and ran for Kentucky Governor. Yet he earned an unfortunate reference in the *Kentucky Encyclopedia* as an outlier.

### The Man Who Made Kentucky Modern

In 1967, Republican Louie B. Nunn defeated Ward for Governor. That upset in a traditionally Democratic stronghold, registered as a bad omen for the party nationally. The last Democratic loss to a Republican in a Kentucky governor's race occurred during World War II in 1943.

This disappointing and final chapter of Ward's career followed decades of achievement.

He began his career as crusading reporter in Paducah. Elected to the state legislature in 1934, Ward became a fierce advocate for public power programs—the Rural Electrification Administration and Tennessee Valley Authority—that brought affordable electricity to Kentucky. He modernized the parks in 1948, and reformed the Highway Department in 1960. Demanding "more engineering and less politics," he stayed six years—the longest tenure of any previous Highway Commissioner, supervising an unprecedented and historic road building spree during the "go-go" years of interstate highway construction. Political cartoonist Hugh Haynie drew Ward as one of his own bulldozers, while *Courier-Journal* editor David Hawpe praised him as the "man who made Kentucky modern."

Yet the public knew very little about the man behind that progress, an oversight Pearce hoped to correct with his project.

Although *Courier-Journal and Times* editor Barry Bingham Jr. once called newspapers the "last dinosaur in the swamp," Ward and Pearce thrived happily there on a newspaper beat for decades. As they chatted in Ward's home with a tape recorder running, Henry's story begins in Paducah in 1928, as the shy 17-year-old high school graduate anxiously took his seat behind a battered wood desk at *The Evening Sun*.

### An Eventful Beginning

Editors casually tossed new assignments his way–a tried and true method of weeding out timid souls and poor spellers in two weeks. In 1933, he exposed a thriving bootleg liquor and slot machine racket controlled by McCracken County constables. Breaking those stories under his byline on the front page, he also submitted a column under an anonymous pen name—"The Rambler." As trusted informants shared their tips with Henry, he felt obligated to share the information with the county attorney. Ward was subpoenaed to testify before a grand jury, and the reporter, barely out of his teens, was forced to admit he was the Rambler. Indictments followed, and he admitted he carried a pistol to protect himself from angry threats, while nervous officials scanned his column searching for their names.

## A Reputation for Unselfish Public Service

Ward took a pay cut each time he agreed to help the Governors of Kentucky and serve the taxpayers, but he never complained. Asked for his opinion, he delivered it—backed by a torrent of research, facts and detail. *Louisville Times* reporter Rob Kasper observed that Ward's opinions were often "...treated like small puddles of water—something of a nuisance, not worthy of much notice. But other times, Ward's opinions, like powerful waterfalls, have cut into the rock of federal and state policy."

As he moved between jobs in Kentucky and the U.S. Senate in Washington D.C., his reputation for competence, honesty and straight talk drew him into the orbit of some powerful politicians, including President Lyndon B. Johnson. With a reporter's eye for detail and an editor's skill for analysis, his oral history brings politics into sharp and entertaining focus.

## A Presidential Relationship

Ward retired from public life in 1967, near the end of Lyndon Johnson's presidency. Johnson's legacy included his fulfilled promises to deliver the Civil Rights and Voting Rights Acts, bookended by his failed policy in Vietnam.

After winning Kentucky's 1967 primary for governor in a landslide, Ward visited Washington D.C., and the President asked to see him. "Johnson wanted to ask me what I felt ... what I really thought about the public feeling." Yet the President's powerful physicality and Texas bravado did not intimidate the 5' 7" blunt-talking Commissioner.

"'What is the situation in Kentucky? What are they saying about me?'" Johnson wanted to know. And I said, 'Well, I'm sorry, but you asked. I guess you want me to tell you the truth.' 'Well, I do'" Johnson replied, and Henry gave it to him.

*The New York Times* once dismissed Henry as a "colorless organization Democrat," but governors, U.S. Senators, state park lodge clerks and highway engineers did not see it that way. Ward's deep, rumbling baritone was hard to ignore, especially when he flung open a door and growled "Let's get this *damn place organized*!"

## Milestones

His death made front page news in 2002, and the oral history documents why he deserved the headlines:

- Ward sponsored the public power bills enabling Kentucky to accept Rural Electrification Administration loans to form electric cooperatives, and to buy power from the Tennessee Valley Authority. Despite bitter opposition from private utility executives who testified against it, Ward's leadership during contentious negotiations succeeded, bringing affordable TVA power to west Kentucky. Increased access to affordable power served as just another example, Henry declared, of how the New Deal raised spirits *and* Kentuckians' standard of living.
- In 1946, state senator Ward sponsored the bill allocating more than half a million dollars to upgrade Kentucky's park system. Two years later, he accepted the job as Conservation Commissioner. Beginning with an initial appropriation of $450,000, he spent all of it and more. As the post-war boom in tourism accelerated, record numbers of visitors vacationed in Kentucky, a success story featured in *The Saturday Evening Post* in 1955, the year park receipts exceeded two million dollars.
- In 1960, he reformed the Highway Department following a scandal over what he called "a fleet of beat-up trucks." He eliminated purchasing abuses, streamlined the process for receiving prompt disbursements from the federal government, ended the diversion of highway money into the general fund, introduced a formula for rural road funding still in use today, and convinced the Bureau of Public Roads to fund restrooms for interstate rest areas. By 1964, Kentucky outpaced Texas in miles of completed state highway projects

U.S. Vice-President Hubert Humphrey and Ward, National Highway Conference of the Associated General Contractors of America, Washington, D.C.

- After anxious residents and outraged preservationists protested the extension of Interstate 64 through Cherokee Park in Louisville, Henry waved them off and directed engineers to blast a tunnel for the road underneath it. The Cochran Road tunnel later won a national design award integrating the roadway into a natural setting of native rock, stone and landscaping.

## A Former Assistant Remembers

Billy Joe Hall, his Executive Assistant in Highways recalled: "One of the things I learned about Mr. Ward was formal education is nice, but it wasn't necessary. And up until then I had been in an educational community where it was felt that formal education was a great thing, and it is a great thing, but it's not an all and all. And so, Mr. Ward taught me, very quickly, that—that not only he taught me by saying it, he taught me by *being it*. That an individual who applies himself, whether or not he went to college or whatever he did, a person could achieve at a very high level.

"And he had already achieved at a high level, at that time, because ... I looked at his background and learned about his background, and learned about his time not only in a management position, with a newspaper, but his General Assembly, his personal General Assembly background, his experience in Washington as Executive Assistant to Earle Clements, who at that time was a United States Senator, and the hands-on experience of government that he had not only in Kentucky. But an interesting fact that some people knew, I am sure and I heard him discuss on more than one occasion, was that at the time Lyndon Johnson, who was majority floor leader of the United States Senate, had a heart attack, he was substituted for by Earle Clements.

"Consequently, Mr. Ward was the Chief Executive Assistant for the individual who was essentially handling legislation on the floor of the United States Congress for Lyndon Johnson. And the contacts that were made at that time with persons who would ultimately become parts of the White House staff when Lyndon Johnson became President became very significant in Mr. Ward's ability to move the highway program in Kentucky.

"...And so Mr. Ward was able to move things because of his ability to work with the U.S. Bureau of Public Roads because he had contacts and, I might say, muscle in Washington. So there is a very significant factor there that will be forgotten in future generations about how Kentucky was so far ahead of its border states in things like building the major interstates such as Interstate 75 and I 65, [and] ...those are the two major north—south routes for more than 75% of the United States population.

*West Virgina Highway Commissioner Burl Sawyers and Henry Ward, Washington, D.C.*

Hall also tied Henry's love for conservation into Kentucky's national leadership in highway design and beautification. "... (Y)ou get into the construction stage, and Mr. Ward went so much farther than most any other state in the nation has ever gone by having a Division of Roadside Development, which added the natural beauty back to an old construction site. ...And, if you don't mind, I would like to go back to my feeling about why Mr. Ward was such a strong person.

"His background was such that he—he was just a mighty person in terms of strength. He was short of stature, but very muscular, very strong. He had been raised primarily without a father, and he had a limited amount of formal education ... but Mr. Ward developed this tough kind of a reputation which he used very strategically as an administrator, and my judgment is and this is purely my opinion—my opinion is that his own stature and his own make-it-yourself situation, because of not having a father to doing it for him, and his lack of formal education made him tough.

"And so he was a fighter, everywhere he went he was a fighter, he was tough because he had to overcome what he perceived to be shortcomings, and that naturally made him this kind of administrator which was the greatest thing that Kentucky could hope for. In that connection, in that connection because of his toughness, his knowing exactly what needed to be done, knowing how to do it, knowing how to direct people to do it, the nature he developed as a result of all that would result in a shortcoming as a candidate because he wasn't going to give up, he wasn't going to give in, he was not going to be bought."

"And I watched Mr. Ward have groups, people turn against him because he would not sell out. And the consequence was we had a great upset in the 1967 governor's race as a result of that. Although Mr. Ward had more votes in the primary election than 10 candidates combined, he did not win in the general election in a heavily Democratic state. So that has to tell you something, and so what it tells you is that here is a man who has principles, who has leadership ability, and would not—would not give that up, would not give up his principles for an election."

## Multiple Impacts During His Career

A state legislator for 15 years, Ward also coordinated Alben Barkley's U.S. Senate and Vice-Presidential campaigns.

In 1938, Governor Albert "Happy" Chandler challenged Barkley, the majority leader of the U.S. Senate, for his seat. Barkley won, but their campaigns were the subject of a Pulitzer Prize winning series written by Thomas Stokes, who revealed how both candidates traded state and Works Progress Administration jobs for votes.

After the election, Henry viewed it as yet another shameful example of the difference between the way government *should work*, and how partisan politics corrupted it.

In 1948, Governor Earle Clements asked him to lead the Department of Conservation. Henry protested that he voted against Clements in the primary, and everyone knew it. Besides, he explained to Earle, *if he* accepted, he needed total authority to replace the "political bums" drawing state paychecks, with a professionally trained staff. Thanking Clements, he declined the offer, but Clements refused to take no for an answer.

A year after Henry accepted the job *and* a pay cut, long time operators of the hotel at Cumberland Falls State Park, disgruntled by strict oversight by the state, burned down the Moonbow Inn, a pre-civil war national landmark, removing it from the state's control, forever.

But Henry never looked back. By 1955, Kentucky's parks collected over $2 million in revenue and earned accolades as one of the nation's finest park systems.

Halfway through his career at this point, *Courier-Journal* columnist Alan Trout described his "...genius for rubbing people the wrong way. But with it, he has a genius for getting things done. Somehow, he resembles one of his own bulldozers."

Forty years after leaving the Highway Department, employee B.L. Stamper easily recalled his former boss. "His smile was forced. No sense of humor. Stern. An everlasting memory. Devoted to duty. A human dynamo. He had a great capacity for knowledge and was always eager for more. He worked the living tar out of me," said Stamper, who struggled to compose himself during the interview, noting that the years working alongside "Hammerin' Hank" were some of the best he'd known.

## A Trusted Assistant to U.S. Senators

In the late 1950s, Ward joined U.S. Senators Barkley and Clements in Washington D.C. as a floor assistant specializing in conservation and flood control legislation. In 1959, he returned to Kentucky, happily settling into a new job as area development director for the Jefferson County Chamber of Commerce. But soon after, Governor Bert Combs appealed to him for help, and Henry's wife, Gladys, threatened to divorce him if he accepted another state job.

*The Courier-Journal* broke a story that Earle Clements, now Kentucky Highway Commissioner, approved a contract to lease dump trucks from a corporation owned by a prominent Louisville automobile dealer, Governor Combs' former campaign finance chairman. Did the Governor know, they asked, the battered trucks were registered in Alabama, and their weight limits exceeded the Department's own specifications?

Clements was hard to locate and slow to respond, and finally, Combs, stung by relentless coverage of what newspapers called the "malodorous truck deal" publicly cancelled the lease himself. Clements suddenly resigned, announcing his return to Washington to help coordinate the Kennedy-Johnson presidential campaign. Henry received a telephone call from Clements, urging him to take the job if Combs asked him.

Yet, Henry was not interested. *The trouble with the damned Highway Department*, Ward exclaimed, was that it entangled intelligent and powerful people like Earle Clements into scandals over "run down dump trucks." Caught between his fuming wife and the Governor, he talked it over with Combs: "Bert, you're in trouble—your administration's in trouble over purchasing. And I've got my reputation to maintain. Because I expect to go back over to the Chamber of Commerce, and I'm not going to come over here and *ruin my reputation* about participating in any kind of deal regarding purchasing! And if you name me Commissioner of Highways, *by God*, it's going to be wide open to competitive bidding—Everything we buy!'" Combs agreed to Henry's terms, then shrugged off the complaints that followed—no one, not even the Governor, it seemed, could tell Henry Ward what to do.

## A Newspaperman's Legacy

In 2002, Henry's front page obituary was accompanied by a photo of a frail, elderly man with a warm, gentle smile on his face. The "father of Kentucky parks" was profiled as an extraordinary public servant who proved it was possible to govern *and* keep your principles and integrity intact. Those tributes and the Ward oral history projects are linked by another common thread—how a man so stubborn, tactless and driven drew such fierce affection and loyalty.

"Henry Ward was incorruptible," said former Governor Edward "Ned" Breathitt, and his reputation for being "mean," or "tough" preceded him. Yet he reserved that side of his temperament for incompetent or inflexible bureaucrats he accused of wasting his time. Robert Bell, his assistant in the Highway Department remembered "He never directed an unkind word to me, but he raised unshirted hell with people he thought deserved it."

"Henry Ward was no charmer," Paducah newspaper publisher Fred Paxton acknowledged, but Paxton admired him for his commitment to doing the right thing, no matter the cost. Newspaper editor Preston Kennedy remembered the day a reporter, "the most mannerly, sweetest young man" informed him he was quitting the newspaper to work for Henry in the Highway Department. Declaring "I would go *to hell and back for Mr. Ward*," Kennedy distinctly remembered their conversation—because he was one of the few reporters Preston ever met who had yet to utter a single curse word in the newsroom.

An experienced reporter often has a mind like an encyclopedia. Henry was no exception, recalled Kennedy, and "You just *knew* you could *count* on what this man was saying to be *true*."

People seeking information often called Henry Ward, who until the day he resigned as Highway Commissioner, liked to answer his own phone. If during a casual conversation, you mentioned you hit a dead end for answers, a few days or weeks later, a gracious letter or package arrived. Signed by some official 500 miles away, it explained that following a conversation with their good friend Henry Ward, some helpful material was enclosed—and don't hesitate to call if you need more.

Ward often poked fun at himself, and his wry comments did not register until several minutes after you parted company. Reporters are often the best storytellers, and when Henry describes the Blackstone Hotel in Chicago, you realize he was sitting *in the room* with Senator Alben Barkley and Harry Truman, the night an anxious Truman warned Barkley he heard rumors Roosevelt planned to choose Truman for his running mate.

Ward described sitting inside the crowded press box at the 1932 national Democratic convention, staring in awe at Will Rogers. "There I had a chance to learn that his wit and humor were as natural as his shock of hair that insisted on falling toward his eyes. ... He talked with any and everyone in the press box, and he always had an audience. Heywood Broun, Robert W. Scripps, and many other nationally renowned newspapermen were in the press box, but none of them attracted the attention that Rogers received."

It was true, people nodded, Hammerin' Hank was stubborn, and one newspaperman called him "the Edward G. Robinson of politics." Yet many remembered his humor and warmth. Another prominent Kentucky newspaperman, Tom Wallace, recalled how Ward's sincerity and command of the facts appealed to audiences. At an American Planning and Civic Association conference, Henry and conservationist Louis Bromfield were the featured speakers. They "were at the finish neck and neck as entertainers; that both kept the audience on its toes more constantly than other speakers. That was, of course, due in part to the fact that Mr. Ward used his well-known talent as a humorist to drive home his points in uttering a heart cry..." Ward spoke off the cuff, and "he made his argument of interest to his audience because of his earnestness of purpose."

Ward was a character all right, and it was a *damned shame* he lost the election in 1967. He won the nomination in a landslide in May with 72% of the vote, but by October, Louie Nunn's campaign gained dangerous momentum.

He blamed himself. Campaign workers recalled he refused to cross a street to shake hands with potential voters—sighing that campaigning was just a waste of time. The voters knew who he was and what he had done—all the laws he passed and the parks, roads and bridges he built, he protested.

Above all, "Henry Ward was a walking civics book writer," remembered Preston Kennedy. "It struck me, and my mind never changed, it struck me that he knew more about state government, how it operated and knew how it ought to be operated, above and beyond anybody I was ever around." Ward understood how government worked, and how it *should work*, and that's when the trouble often started.

## Motivated to Work for Progress—Not Power

Up on the 10th floor of the Highway Department, when county "contact men" strolled into Henry's office to discuss free gravel deliveries, state jobs for relatives or no bid contracts, they watched in disbelief as he pulled the cigar out of his mouth long enough to order the "sons of bitches" to clear out and go cry on the Governor's shoulder. They did—then patiently waited until the next election.

After his defeat, the winner, Louie Nunn, later set the historical record straight. Ward's legacy as a crusading reporter, legislator and public administrator earned him his rightful place in Kentucky history without ever being elected, Nunn asserted—calling Henry "the greatest man who never was governor."

The man who made Kentucky modern accepted responsibility for his defeat, ending a brutal self-analysis of his failed campaign in a long sigh and a low exclamation: *"end of damn story, I guess."*

That *damn story* is a portrait of a newspaperman convinced cynicism weakens our democracy, and that voters should demand public officials be held accountable for their actions. Naysayers and obstructionists infuriated him. Close associates backed away when Ward cornered someone who shrugged "nothing could be done" to "change the system."

Sharply interjecting "I just happen to know a little about..." cities of the first class, the wholesale rate of a kilowatt hour of electricity, negotiating a three-state compact reducing pollution in the Ohio River Valley, or the proper depth of gravel for a solid road bed, it was a dangerous phrase coming from a man who knew "a little" after decades of experience in journalism, the state legislature and Washington D.C.

For every excuse something could not be changed, Ward explained *in exhaustive detail* how it could, and closed off further objection by exclaiming *"For god's sake—let's get busy!"*

Try as he might to convince you he was tough as nails, whether you were a U.S. Senator or the desk clerk at a state park lodge, his family and friends confirmed that once you earned his trust, he would do anything to help you—a loyal, steady and lifelong friend. Above all, Ward's idealism never faded—he insisted we can and should do better. That passion and hard-edged integrity, remembered Senator Cook, is linked to Ward's coming of age as a newspaperman.

## 2 Explosion and Tears

"When I was a boy in Lone Oak, long years ago, my chums decided to dub me 'Guinea,' for the very simple reason that one of my chief pleasures was chasing a flock of Guinea hens which resided in the neighborhood ... and I remembered how, as a boy, I was always ready to fight when anyone called me 'Guinea,' which simply meant that I was in a fighting mood all the time."

Ward's story unfolds against the backdrop of the Great Depression. "I was a nobody ... just a damned kid who had to go to work for a living and couldn't go to college," he said. "Tried to find someplace that had a scholarship, but there were just none available. ..."

He was "lucky, that's all" to work for two west Kentucky publishers who taught him a "fine philosophy about what the responsibility of a newspaper was to the public." Pearce opens the interview asking: "When were you born?" and the stories flow.

"I was born in McCracken County in a little community called New Hope. ... My father believed in education, and because they had only a very small little school at New Hope, when I was only two years old, we moved to Lone Oak, which had a much better school. And he operated a dairy. And when I was five years old, he was burned fatally in a fire."

Decades later, Ward's daughter, Pat, recalled his panic after she stumbled too close to their fireplace and her robe burned. Henry lunged to pull her back, shaken. "I can see my father all over again!" he exclaimed, the flash and explosion still vivid in his memory.

On a cold November morning in 1914, 52-year-old Gus Ward and his oldest son Earl carried a can of fuel into his farmhouse and entered the bedroom where two of his younger sons lay sleeping.

As he lit the match, the gasoline-contaminated kerosene exploded. Despite being badly burned, they extinguished the fire. Earl survived, but his father lay suffering with serious burns on his face, chest and legs until his death two weeks later.

"You can imagine how desolated my mother and seven kids were," Ward recalled. "I have only vague memories of my father. He must have been a kind and patient man. ... The first bottle of soda pop I ever had was at the county fair. ... I can see him now, in the grandstand at the fairgrounds, digging down in his pocket for a nickel to buy me that bottle of pop. It also was at the fair, of course, that I had my first ride on a merry-go-round, saw my first clowns."

Henry accompanied his father in a horse-drawn wagon delivering milk door to door, and, "Those trips to Paducah to sell milk are the best of memories," he recalled.

Ward's mother, Beulah, and his older brothers operated the dairy, while the younger children took comfort in the simple routine of a country childhood.

"I set traps for rabbits and waded in a neighbor's creek. I got a gray sweater and an orange for Christmas. I ate a lot of gravy and biscuits for breakfast. Eggs were rare. I went to the Highland Cumberland Presbyterian Church a lot," Ward remembered.

Small and green-eyed, Henry resembled his mother, sharing the same "twinkly expression," Ward's daughter recalled. In 1918, Mrs. Ward purchased a boarding house in town.

"I learned early how to wait on tables and also learned early that if you wanted to eat, you'd better grab it if it was there because other people would get it before you did." The move upset the eight-year-old, and after teachers held him back a grade, "I was miserable."

He skipped school often, playing in the marsh along the river until a truant officer marched him back to school. But the champion hooky player settled down, performing so well he was promoted ahead of his classmates during $6^{th}$ and $8^{th}$ grade.

Families paid for school books back then, and Henry earned his book money carrying coal into his neighbors' houses. New folk heroes emerged as bootleggers and moonshiners captured the nation's imagination. During Prohibition, 13-year-old Henry worked as a drugstore delivery boy. Whiskey was sold by prescription only and, hopping onto his bicycle, "I delivered *a lot* of prescriptions. I worked at night and had a lot of time to study between deliveries. I gradually advanced to soda jerking and even did some clerking. I recall that to buy condoms a customer had to go to the back of the store and whisper to the pharmacist."

Henry saved $125, and his mother insisted he quit working and enjoy his senior year. "I did that with enthusiasm. I tried out for the football team, but at 135 pounds, I was too small. I was in two musical plays, even singing in a co-starring role. I was on the debate team which went to the state tournament, where a couple of damn girls beat us. I was a member of the school's honor society and won the history medal. I was on the staff of the high school paper. When my senior year ended in 1928, I was surprised to be named salutatorian. A girl beat me out by one point for valedictorian. The story of my life—losing to a female."

After graduation, "The only job I got I could find was a soda jerker. I gave up after a couple of months because I just wanted something better than that." Walter Jetton, Ward's high school principal, learned Lloyd Robertson, the editor of the *Paducah News-Democrat*, needed a reporter. Robertson hired Henry, who survived his two-week probation. Paid a starting salary of $12 per week, that industry-wide rate remained unchanged since 1847.

A photograph shows the thin recruit seated in a slat-backed swivel chair. Wearing a tie and a suit coat too large in the shoulders, he barely clears the top of the heavy wood desk. Calm and composed in the photo, he later admitted he questioned why Robertson hired him in the first place. "I had a little experience on the high school paper, that's all, and I couldn't type except for the hunt and peck system and I was also shy. But I stuck to it."

*Cub reporter, (1928) The Paducah Sun*

By 1928, the newspaper's publisher, George Goodman, had owned the paper for a decade. After Prohibition forced him to sell his mail-order whiskey distribution business in 1918, he bought the *News-Democrat,* and invested immediately in a new Cox tubular press, linotype and monotype machine.

Subsequent anniversary editions of the paper praised Goodman, noting he breathed "more life into the paper than it had ever had before." Described as a "fighting influential force" for Paducah, he had to be, because Goodman's chief rival was a Paducah 8th grade dropout, the indefatigable Edwin J. Paxton, publisher of *The Evening Sun.*

Goodman later recalled how the jump from shipping liquor to buying linotype machines tested his confidence: "I'd only been through the eighth grade and I didn't know anything about newspapers. Irvin Cobb, who used to be editor, told me to stick to the local news. I read a lot, and wasn't afraid to take sides (we drove the Ku Klux out of Paducah) and in seven years the circulation grew from 4,000 to 12,000," he recalled.

Somewhere on a desk or shelf in news room, a well-thumbed copy of the *Handbook for Newspaper Workers* guided the staff as they skirmished over new subscribers. It warned editors to avoid glorifying crime, because "criminals ... like actors and politicians, crave publicity. ..."

That high-minded admonition meant little to Paducah readers who snapped up daily extras tracking suspenseful manhunts for "thugs," "bandits," or "half-wit slayers" driving "death cars."

Henry later learned his ancient wood desk belonged to one of Paducah's local heroes, the nationally acclaimed author and humorist, Irvin Cobb. Cobb earned recognition by becoming one of the country's youngest newspaper editors at the age of 19.

"Mr. Cobb, what would you say is the greatest difference between the journalism of your day and the journalism of today?" the popular war correspondent and author was later asked. "Well," Cobb answered thoughtfully, "I guess in my day we weren't so hampered by fact." Henry's editors laughed, but he remembered their rigid standards ordering facts and details, and that a proof reader's judgment unassailable. Initially overwhelmed by that responsibility, Henry, a voracious reader, was better prepared to strike out on his own than he gave himself credit for.

"I had a lonely childhood. Mother was busy feeding boarders. Homer was too old for me, and Bob too young. I built myself a hideaway over the garage and spent a lot of time there."

Popular boys' books during the 1920s included "Men of Iron" and "Captains Courageous," and no one cajoled him to read or rewarded him for good grades.

Writer Ray Bradbury described how this generation landed steady white-collar jobs without earning a college degree.

"Libraries raised me," Mr. Bradbury said. "I don't believe in colleges and universities. I believe in libraries because most students don't have any money. When I graduated from high school, it was during the Depression and we had no money. I couldn't go to college, so I went to the library three days a week for ten years."

Ward echoed Bradbury's point. "Looking back, I do not consider the lack of a college education to have been a handicap," Ward recalled. "I knew I had to work for a living. Not thinking I already knew it all, I made a practice of continuing to study, to learn all I could of the subject I faced, to dig for the facts myself. In the newspaper world at that time, it definitely was not a handicap, because the editor wanted to teach the reporters to do things his way—not as some professor in school has instructed him. In today's world, things are different. A college degree is a practical necessity. But I'm not yet sure it produces any better newspaperman than the old way."

As Ward thumped Royal typewriter keys against a ribbon of satiny black cloth, "The old way" (according to *The Handbook*), tested his "...grammar, punctuation, English, diction, journalistic structure, typographical style and accuracy. ..." Retired editor Preston Kennedy recalled a single guideline on word count: "The length of a story is when you have told the story. And when you have told the story...*shut up*! Don't embellish it, don't color it. *Be fair*!"

As Ward packed details into a single sentence: "The Ladies' Society to the Brotherhood of Locomotive Fireman and Engineers will meet at 2:00 in the Odd Fellows Hall," his editors praised copy "so tight you can't cut a word out of it." After every press run, the galleys were destroyed, melted down in what machinists nick-named the "hell box." Henry endured some hell of his own, each time his copy was returned covered in proofreader's marks.

In 2009, the *New York Times* public editor lamented, "How Did This Happen?" after the newspaper's "...facts got mangled when [Walter] Cronkite died." It happened because generations of persnickety proofreaders retired or died.

As corporations acquired small family-owned presses in the 1980s, community newspapers were classified as "debts" on an asset sheet. Staff cuts, attrition and content reduction ballooned profit margins and shareholder returns, a trend Kennedy sternly judged to be "One of the bad turns that journalism took".

Proofreaders, replaced by spell check and employees juggling four jobs at once, were the first to go. "The most *valuable* people who *ever lived*!" exclaimed Kennedy, some reporters "just *hated* them for messing with their material." Yet the Latin and Greek marks, symbols and crosses, produced material judged to be "factually correct and error free," he noted.

Kennedy smiled broadly as he recalled his apprenticeship: it consisted of an editor shuffling up to his desk and casually asking if he ever covered a City Hall meeting. Replying "No sir," he was instructed to go anyway and submit a feature before deadline. Both Henry Ward and Kennedy remembered racing out of the building in a cold sweat of fear.

During Kennedy's first week on the job in 1946, Henry asked Kennedy if he ever covered a criminal trial. "And I said 'No'. "And he says "I've got to send you over to cover a murder trial. So, I went. And I said you'll have to guide me when I get back. And he said, 'No problem. You write the verdict in the first paragraph and you write below it what you feel was pertinent to the circumstances that led to the verdict.' So, I go over and I cover this trial and I was lost all morning. I didn't know what I was doing. But, along sometime or the other, the jury returned its verdict and I wrote it down, and I came back and wrote the story and he accepted the story and it was in Sunday's paper."

"And on Monday morning when I came in a tiny Black man was seated there on the chair and in those days, Black people referred to white people as 'Boss.' "And he stood up and said, 'Boss, I don't want to cause you any trouble. You just put my dead brother in prison for 21 years.' I said, 'What?' He said, 'Yes sir, you did. So, I panicked.

"And I go to Ward. And I told him what this man was saying. And Ward says "*By God*, you ought to know more about his brother than we do! You go back over there and you tell him that we'll look into the thing and *we'll correct it this afternoon!*

"So, I go back over to the courthouse. Ward sends me back over to the courthouse to the Circuit Clerk's office. The fella goes and gets the copy of what the jury had written down, and the jury had gotten it backwards—gotten the wrong name. Had reversed it. And the foreman of the jury had shown it to the judge and he didn't catch it and I was dumb I didn't catch it, but I learned a big lesson of my life on that Monday morning. You can't take a piece of paper and accept it to be the gospel truth. You better do you a little checking if you want to be right about it."

The news routine organized a jumble of mundane details covering births, deaths, marriages, sports scores, garden club meetings, storms, accidents or other misfortunes into a portrait of daily life that captured the unique rhythm of life in every town.

Before the invention of the World Wide Web, when people needed answers, they called their telephone operator, local librarian or the newspaper office, and Henry assured his readers that "...if you don't think newspapers try to tell the truth, ask any reporter what sort of instructions he has about getting facts, all the facts, and nothing but the facts."

*Sun Democrat* reporters pulled on coveralls and rode derricks to the top of the world's largest locomotive roundhouse and explored the giant lower lock gates of the TVA dam at Norris Lake.

"Spillways and Powerhouse at Norris [Dam]-Down Into Its Bowels Went a *Sun-Democrat* Reporter," one headline read. Much like today's World Wide Web, newspapers of 80 years ago transported people from their living room into every corner of the world.

Instead of clicking a mouse to scroll down a screen, readers shook out the creases and drooping corners formed by the tall, narrow newspaper pages. You could spend hours thumbing through bulky Sunday editions, and grandparents or parents engrossed in a story often shooed their children away—"Leave me alone—I'm reading my paper!"

A typical edition of the *Democrat* in the late 1920s and 1930s, arranged in dense columns of fine print, fills the page: a ribbon cutting celebrating a $2 million dollar bridge linking Paducah to Illinois; the opening day for the "sparkling new Irvin Cobb Hotel at 6th and Broadway;" the death of Wyatt Earp and Lily Langtry; and news Universal Air Line showed a 10-reel motion picture to a dozen passengers on a flight from Minneapolis to Chicago.

Henry's mother took a break from balancing her rent ledger and peeling potatoes to study exotic travelogues describing how a "Vast Dam Near Sukkur Desert Transforms a Fertile Valley," followed by the latest dispatch from Mrs. W.R. Peterson. The socialite shot bear and moose with her husband and traveled to Palm Beach to capture tropical fish. Shootings were "malicious;" Congressmen "berated" one another in "floor tilts," and the "woodlands inside the city playground" felt "the axe."

Editor Karl Harrison called Paducah a "happy madhouse of commerce and robust life." Major employers included the International Shoe plant, Beasley Marble and Granite Co., Wallerstein's Department Store and the Illinois Central railroad shop, built at the turn of the century.

In 1925, the railroad shop expanded on 100 acres south of Kentucky Avenue. Inside, skilled union millwrights and machinists repaired 400,000-pound locomotive cars on the world's largest locomotive turntable.

Popular restaurants included the Peacock Garden and Twinkling Star. At the Irvin Cobb Hotel, orchestra tunes drifted into the air during rooftop dances. Streetcars carried passengers to the riverfront to enjoy a paddle wheel steamboat ride. Vaudeville shows were popular, and the average cost of a movie ticket was twenty-five cents. Five Paducah movie houses sold tickets to fans enthralled by the latest action-adventure drama or movie serial ending in a weekly cliff-hanger.

On the heels of the silent comic masterpieces starring Buster Keaton or Charlie Chaplin, came Walt Disney's first animated short feature—*Steamboat Willie*. In 1927, audiences flocked to *In Old Arizona,* the first full-length talkie shot outdoors on location.

In one column, Henry described hometown reaction to a movie scene in *George White's Scandals:*

> "...a gal rushed into the old homestead just as the be-mustached sheriff was dispossessing her old pa and ma. From a Claussner Hosiery Mill stocking (do they still call them that), which did its duty in enhancing the lovely lines of a lovely lower limb, she drew a roll of bills, $3000 of the royal green of this great nation. Disdainfully she tossed the money at the sheriff, and thereby the mortgage was lifted from the old family home.
>
> But when the sheriff had stalked away, her Pa turned, and in trembling tones, wanted to know: "Daughter, where did you get $3000? "In Paducah," was her reply. "All of $3000 in Paducah? Daughter, have you been a good girl? Pa insisted. "You've got to be good to get $3000 in Paducah," the merry lassie answered, as the audience howled with glee."

In his interview of Ward, John Ed Pearce continued: "Now the Depression was starting to hit Paducah, wasn't it?" "It was very rough," Ward replied, and he recalled being paid with scrip instead of cash for a time.

Eight thousand Kentuckians fought in World War I, but after it ended "... whatever small share of prosperity Kentucky enjoyed faltered in 1929-30," wrote historian George Blakey.

A year after Robertson hired Ward, Goodman sold the *Democrat* to his competitor, Edwin Paxton. Paxton paid Goodman $100,000 cash and $125,000 in bonds, and kept him on the payroll as an advisor. After Ed Paxton, Jr. married Goodman's daughter, Evelyn, Paxton joked, "That completed the merger."

"It was merged with the *Sun* and became the *Sun-Democrat*, an evening paper. And I was merged right out of a job," Ward recalled. "Following Horace

Greeley's advice to 'go west, young man,' two friends and I bought an old Ford Model T and started west."

As the collapse of the stock market, and impact of the Dust Bowl triggered an unprecedented economic crisis, Ward slept on the ground at night. "That old Ford barely made it to Oklahoma City. And I spent about two months out there looking for jobs and couldn't find one because 1929 was getting into the Depression, and there were simply no jobs available. I survived by working at anything I could find, and the findings were scarce."

"But after about two months of it, they called me from Paducah and said come back, the *Sun-Democrat* had a job for me. They had started a bulldog edition. The *Paducah Sun* was an evening paper and the *News Democrat* was a morning, so they started a bulldog edition to keep the morning subscribers and they wanted somebody working on the desk. It was a two-man job. One man, and a young kid to run errands..." Ward hurried back to his mother's boarding house and started working the two to midnight shift.

# 3 A Crusader Goes to Frankfort

> Calling town officials "scheming crooks, grasping politicians and grafting individuals," Ward declared " ...(I)t is a desire to eliminate this situation, to sweep the slate clean, to assist in giving Paducahans a new deal that has prompted the Rambler to take action against fraud and to aid in sponsoring movements that will make Paducah a better place to live. That is a definite answer to the gamblers who have been angered by the Rambler's discussions of their games and tactics. And here's a merry 'ha-ha' for their threats of vengeance."

Edwin Paxton, Sr., the newspaper's publisher, became a role model for Henry. Paxton was "a lot like (publisher) George Goodman in his sense of responsibility to the community and encouraged his reporters to take an active interest in civic affairs," Henry remembered.

Retired *Paducah Sun* executive editor Preston Kennedy recalled his first encounter with Henry and "the old Mr. Paxton" in 1946. He dropped out of the University of Kentucky after a single semester ("It was so big there—and I was just so lost,") and applied for a newspaper job.

Arriving for his interview, employees directed him to the drugstore next door. Paxton, Sr., stopped there each morning to drink a Coke. "I learned later on that was his first chore of the day. His eyesight was bad, his hearing was bad. And he had Henry Ward with him."

They hired Kennedy on the spot. His second week on the job, managing editor Joe LaGore returned from vacation, furious someone was hired in his absence. Yet it all worked out—Kennedy stayed for 38 years, retiring as the paper's first executive editor in 1984.

"You see these people, these people were people of character ... But, but you run a newspaper, you know. Or you're out in a public position, and people are going to take pokes at you. But this elder Mr. Paxton was such a gentleman, and so gentle, that he would come into your presence ... he would remove his hat, he would extend his hand, he would smile, and he would be gracious. And if there was ever a time anywhere or at anyplace, he was not gracious, I never knew it."

It was generally known that if you landed a job with the Illinois Central Railroad or the *Sun-Democrat,* you were lucky because it meant you "had a job for life," said Kennedy.

Henry grew close to the elderly publisher and his son, Edwin Paxton, Jr., bonds that compensated for the loss of his father. In 1942, friends arranged a testimonial dinner honoring Henry. Paxton could not attend but sent a letter of praise to be shared with the crowd. "I never saw a man of any age who could see all sides of any question like Henry Ward. I know no man who tries to be fairer to everyone than he. He will show you at once how a thing will affect the other fellow, and if it is unjust, he will promptly tell you so...He will fight hard, but fair. If he inflicts a hurt, he is hurt, too very deeply, but he drives on to make his point, attain his goal...Henry is truly a triple-threat man: a newspaper man, an ideal civic worker, and as eager a laborer for the good of the commonwealth as Kentucky possesses..."May he be with us for many years to perform his labors of love is the prayer of one who loves him like a son."

Years later his son Fred remembered his business school curriculum at the University of Notre Dame did not analyze case histories of self-made men like his father. The elder Paxton once casually mentioned it took 18 years to turn a profit.

Fred recalled another crucial lesson his father taught him—"Either you change or you die." Paxton revived his dying hometown newspaper in 1900; and by 1957, "WPSD-TV went on the air...after a three-year struggle at the FCC (Federal Communications Commission) to win the license in a contested hearing. He was the first—and I believe the only- newspaper owner to win a television license for which there were competing applicants. The FCC gave demerits to a newspaper owner because they wanted diversity of ownership. His record was so strong, however, that the FCC chose him as the better applicant," recalled Paxton. That waiver, granted under stringent conditions, permitted simultaneous ownership of the *Democrat*, and television station WPSD.

Edwin Sr.'s optimism, work ethic and persistence increased the newspaper's circulation. Stories recounting his struggles to keep the paper solvent became the stuff of legend in the city room.

At the 1931 annual meeting of the Kentucky Press Association, Urey Woodson recounted the Association's 100-year-old history in a lively speech describing the trials, tribulations and achievements of its membership. Citing Paxton's irrepressible energy, he declared "That boy [Edwin J. Paxton] was and is a live wire. He bought up every mushroom sheet in this town he couldn't put out of business otherwise." Some luck and Paxton's tenacity ensured the paper's survival under brutal business conditions, a colorful history that began with a winning lottery ticket.

In the 1880s, W.F. Paxton won $20,000, purchased a grocery store, then promptly went broke. After a stint as a traveling salesman, he became a U.S. Marshal, then founded Citizens Bank & Trust Company in Paducah.

In 1896, W. F. and his partners purchased the assets of a faltering paper called the *Paducah Standard*. Renamed *The Paducah Sun*, four years later, the masthead's prospects were still dimming. His son, Edwin, an $8^{th}$ grade dropout and former railroad clerk, currently worked as an assistant cashier in his father's bank.

He occasionally filled in for the *Standard's* society editor, and W.F. asked his son if he wanted to take over as publisher. Paxton eagerly accepted, introduced himself to his foreman and star reporter, then brushed past to watch a flat-bed press create a four-page newspaper six columns wide and 20 inches long.

Paxton composed editorials in longhand, sold advertising, kept the books, stewed over circulation numbers, and bartered with advertisers strapped for cash. He covered the daily wire, too, 7 days a week, at ll:oo a.m. and 2:oo p.m.

In April 1906, he got a message to hurry back to the desk –an earthquake, measured at 8.0 on the Richter scale, struck San Francisco at 5:13 a.m. "I stayed with it so long that I could close my eyes and see the buildings crumble and the people die," he said. The next day, he led a drive that raised $3000 for the survivors. He stayed again in April 1912, bringing news of 1,503 lives lost on the Titanic to doorsteps and front porches in town.

He negotiated contracts with the typographers' union, and during the bank panic of 1907, the *Sun* printed currency backed by the assets of the local banks. He acquired smaller papers: *The Leader, Voice of the People, Register* and *Labor Journal*; when the cost of newsprint soared to $1000 per rail car during World

War I, family members urged him to quit. Yet Paxton played the long game, and pushed through it.

By 1928, his health was suffering. His son managed the paper, but Paxton checked in with him daily. *"West Kentucky's Greatest Newspaper"* etched on its masthead; its employees labored under the weight of that expectation on a daily basis. At the impressionable age of 20, Henry listened to Paxton, Sr., describe the paper's responsibility in forceful terms: "Many are the problems that come up in a newspaper organization and many are the serious problems of outsiders, individuals of the city, county, state and nation that are dumped into a newspaper office for criticism or for sympathetic treatment and counsel. They are daily, almost hourly occurrences, and they are a 'he man' task, too!"

*Edwin Paxton, Sr., (center), Ward, and* Paducah Sun-Democrat *staff*

In 1929, on the night his son, Ed, Jr., finalized the merger with Goodman, Paxton Sr. collapsed. After 30 years, the man whose restless energy paralleled the driving pace of the nation's machine age, needed rest. Doctors issued a stern warning for him to slow down, and he moved to Florida to recuperate.

Henry returned to Paducah to cover the "bulldog" (earliest, or often advance) edition. It was sent to out-of-town subscribers and used for street sales. *"The*

*Paducah Sun* was an evening paper, and *The Sun-Democrat* was a morning, so they started a bulldog edition to keep the morning subscribers, and they wanted somebody working the desk. It was a two-man job: one man and a young kid to run errands to put out that bulldog edition. ...It went to press generally about twelve o' clock. I don't recall-I must have worked on that, let's see, the rest of '29 and '30. I must have worked on it at least about two years, before I was transferred to the day side."

He covered local government, and crime. "I have seen 19 men executed in the electric chair at the Eddyville penitentiary, and some strange experiences have been connected with those electrocutions." Assigned to cover one particularly notorious rape trial, the jury convicted the defendant, who was sentenced to hang in Smithland. Henry covered the gruesome spectacle, repelled by the circus atmosphere and picnic lunches spectators brought.

He persuaded his editors to add a column he suggested they call "...'Ramblers Rambling' by the Ramblers,' and the idea was to let other reporters contribute to it. Write items that they picked up. It lasted about a month that way. Finally, I was the only one making contributions to the column. But I was what you call a little bit of a crusading reporter. We had eight magistrates and constables and three of them ran rackets."

Creed Black, former publisher of *The Lexington Herald-Leader*, started his career at the *Democrat*, and witnessed firsthand how Henry's crusading streak formed Ward's approach to life and public service. "The smaller the town, the tougher that kind of newspapering is, because you are likely to meet your targets." Henry did, and they tried to intimidate him. One of his cars was stolen and wrecked, and he scuffled with a gambler in downtown Paducah. But the 20-year-old enjoyed the danger and excitement, cultivating a tough and fearless image along the way.

He exposed a corrupt gang of constables nicknamed the "Raiding Knights of Canaan." "They'd raid places that had slot machines, take them to the magistrate's office, take the money out of the machines, make the owners pay a fine, then give the slot machines back to them. I conducted a campaign on gambling. To break that up, and because I was convinced that they were bribing the officials. In magistrate's court, the owners were pronounced guilty and fined."

In court, Henry inquired about the fines and fees Magistrate C. M. Black collected from slot operators for witnesses who failed to appear. "Can you explain the difference between a 'witness fee' and 'kickback?' he innocently asked.

"If you'd attend to your business, we would be all right," Black warned him "I'm making your business, my business now, and very much so, too. Just friendly playmates, that's all we are," Henry shot back.

Along with the slots, prohibition enforcement was lax, and locals dubbed one particular train the "Whiskey Dick." In early 1933, the Rambler heard rumors that East St. Louis gangsters intended to take control of bootlegging operations in McCracken County.

"So I used a fellow who was a notorious drunk. We went around to several bootleggers and he drank their rotgut liquor, and I encouraged them. Of course, I did not tell them who I was and I encouraged them to talk about how the fellows came in, and threatened them if they did not buy their whiskey from them, they would be shot up. I went and wrote stories about all that."

His column triggered a grand jury investigation, and the District Attorney subpoenaed Ward and the bootleggers to testify. "And they were reluctant to do so. And I said 'You need to testify about these birds threatening your outfits about you selling whiskey.' So they did testify and these bootleggers were indicted. I received several threatening phone calls, of course. I was a very courageous reporter, (laughing). At that time, I bought me a .22 pistol and carried it around. The threats never came to anything of course. They left town after the trial."

The story broke January 12, 1933: "3 Indicted in Racket, 4 in Slot Machine Cases" detailing charges against the Commissioner of Public Safety, a magistrate and two former constables

Soon after, a gambler named "Red" from Metropolis Lake tried a different tactic. "You're kind of stupid writing about all this stuff," he chided Henry. "Just be easy about it and I'll see to it you're well paid for it." He offered Henry sixty dollars a week—a lot of money in those days—to keep quiet. A "yes" or "no" question, Ward walked away, but the details of their chat appeared in the next edition of the newspaper.

"The next Sunday, I remember, I was downtown, had a straw hat on, sailor tie. . .and I started around the corner to Irving Cobb Hotel. He came out of the hotel, dashed up, threw a fist at me, and we started. ... tried to have a good fight. Knocked my derby off! He tried to whip me. We shadow-boxed to a draw. The cops came, and by that time I was mad about it, and they wanted to know if I wanted to prosecute him, and I said 'Hell, no! Prosecuting takes too much fun out of it.'"

His adventures continued, and a few of his columns read like chapters in a *Hardy Boys* mystery or a scene from the Hollywood blockbusters *Little Caesar* or *Scarface*.

Awakened by a 2:00 a.m. phone call, a whispered voice alerted Ward the constables detained a bewildered truck driver inside Magistrate Black's home. Henry arrived at Black's house and pounded on the front door, demanding entry.

In his column, he described the scene: "... the magistrate inside his office, a smoky lamp casting a soft light over the room, flanked by his henchmen, questioning the victim, "Bill Priddy, a Lexington, Tennessee, man in the clutches of 'the law'. And seated in another chair, facing Magistrate Black, with a law book in his hand and arguing technical features of the Acts of the General Assembly on truck laws, was The Rambler."

He *was* having too much fun; at the same time, he exposed a pervasive culture of blackmail, extortion, and violence that threatened the public safety and damaged the county's reputation.

In July 1933, Ward announced what many already guessed: "You may notice that there is a new byline heading this column. The reason is this: The Rambler has been doing a lot of talking about himself. I have tried to persuade him to restrain himself, but to no avail. Now I can talk about him, telling you his bad points as well as some of the good things he has been passing on to you. In addition to that, it has been rumored that the Rambler was afraid to reveal his true identity. So here I am. But, regardless of what byline is used, I assure you that this column will continue to contain the truth, the whole truth and nothing but the truth, regardless of the personal consequences or the threats of bodily damage."

Henry described a second profitable "racket:" "Paducah was then a big railroad center. ... [T]he average employee in the shops and in other industries were not paid handsome salaries in those days. It was a happy hunting ground for loan sharks. So we launched another campaign," he wrote in his unpublished memoir.

"Our newspaper retained a lawyer to sue the loan sharks on behalf of those who had been defrauded, but it quickly became apparent that the old law on usury did not provide an effective remedy. The victims had no written records to prove their arguments, and the operators were not required to keep them and to the borrower a receipt for payments."

25 loan shops operated in Paducah, and Con Traig, a local businessman, complained to Henry that he "... couldn't get the fellow who was now the representative to change the law and something ought to be done about it. I said, 'Hell, a lot of things ought to be done about it. There ought to be some modern laws, municipal law. ...'" Traig's response surprised him. 'Run for the legislature yourself,' he said. 'I think you could be elected.'"

"I said 'All right, that's ridiculous. I'm twenty-three years old, just a kid—don't know anything about it, about politics at all'."

After some thought, he changed his mind, acknowledging his "insatiable desire to correct these evils." But his crusading zeal collided with an unprecedented crisis blocking emergency relief in Kentucky.

Four years after the stock market collapsed, the *Sun Democrat* encouraged citizens to ". . . cease complaining, lift up their chins and roll up their sleeves. This is a time to put all we have into the task of building up Paducah. Only by individual determination and hard work can there be a complete restoration of confidence. As confidence comes back, timidity will vanish and the bugaboo of depression will become as the mists of the morning, breaking with the sun."

Before "Black Friday" of 1929, 2,246 Kentucky industries employed 77,000 production workers; by 1933, half those businesses closed, and 21,000 people lost their jobs. 120 banks failed between 1930-32. "These industrial collapses gradually took down with them retail and commercial businesses; 245 Kentucky firms declared insolvency in 1930, a larger number the following year, and in 1932, 356 businesses failed," historian George Blakey wrote.

In Washington, D.C., Harry Hopkins, a former social worker, led the newly created Federal Emergency Relief Administration. It took several years and nine billion dollars in aid from that agency to vanquish that "bugaboo of depression."

As the Depression deepened, job seekers traveled hundreds of miles, congregating on street corners or at railway depots. Desperate for work or food, anxious residents eyed them with fear or suspicion.

"One of the earliest eyesores of the depression, transiency was everywhere deplored, though seldom understood. Feature writers, finding good copy in the hitch-hiker and the jungle dweller, aroused public interest in the subject" Hopkins wrote in his book, *Spending to Save*.

Thousands of laborers, many uneducated beyond the sixth or eighth grade, fled to Arizona and California to escape harsh weather and look for jobs. "...By January 1933, whole sections of American business had all but closed up shop, leaving brilliant, talented and able men without a job. Ninety per cent of New York architects alone were unemployed."

Hopkins' staff documented the steady climb in unemployment: 1930: 4,065,000; 1931: 10,614,000. In early 1933, at the American Federation of Labor, the Chief of the National Income Section, a brand-new graduate from the Wharton School of Business, tried to grasp the human toll behind the rising jobless rate, as the numbers jumped from 12,000,000 to 14,597,000.

On an icy February morning in 1933, Henry glanced out the city room window. A stranger in a filthy coat appealed to passersby for spare change. His co-workers joked none of them looked respectable enough to be approached, so Henry grabbed his hat and coat, and crossed the street to find out.

"The man had been stopping only the more prosperous-appearing gentlemen who passed him, so the Rambler was somewhat surprised when he was hailed as he came near, with the plea, "Mister, give me a nickel for a cup of coffee.' That was an opening, so the Rambler began questioning the man."

Ward offered to buy him some coffee and a bowl of soup. Inside the warmth of the drugstore, the stranger explained he hitched 750 miles from Minnesota looking for work.

"I'm a married man, but I can't make enough to support my wife...Yeah, it's pretty hard on us," he acknowledged. "I won't lie to you, though, by saying I am looking for work. There ain't no such thing anymore. I'd take a job if I could find one, of course, but I've been all over the country looking for one and I'm still bumming around...You see a lot of families on the freights now, men with their wives and children. On the freight from Fulton this morning there was a man, his wife and three small kids. They were going to the home of relatives up north."

Ward asked about the possibility of violence or riots, but hunger, not politics, forced him from town to town. "Men like me, out of work and with nothing, won't start any trouble as long as we can find something to eat. Everybody's hoping that conditions will improve."

Finishing his soup, he returned to the corner, and readers met the man from Minnesota in Ward's column the next day.

During the Hoover administration, the President believed that the responsibility for local relief belonged to churches, families, and neighbors, but by the winter of 1933, those resources were exhausted.

On Saturday, March 4, 1933, anxious Americans listened as new President Franklin D. Roosevelt pledged to end this suffering "with vigor." He summarized "Our common difficulties... "[T]he withered leaves of industrial enterprise lie on every side; farmers find no markets for their produce; and the savings of many years in thousands of families are gone. More important, a host of unemployed citizens face the grim problem of existence, and an equally great number toil with little return. Only a foolish optimist can deny the dark realities of the moment..."

For years, Roosevelt confronted a dark reality of his own. He contracted polio in 1921, and remained permanently paralyzed. His mother Sara, urged him to return to a quiet life on their family estate, while his wife, Eleanor, argued the opposite. She insisted he would recover and return to politics. He willed himself through suffocating episodes of depression, adept at hiding his despair, but on that day his victory reflected their shared commitment to public service.

His struggle forged his empathy for the "forgotten men" whom Roosevelt insisted needed more than sympathy from the do-nothings who counseled patience. It seemed this man, who battled chronic and debilitating pain, drew energy and strength from restoring purpose to their lives again. During his campaign, he delighted the crowds with his vigor, humor and warmth. It created a strong bond with ordinary Americans that few presidents can lay claim to.

At that moment in time, perhaps no one was more ideally suited to lead the nation forward and restore hope. Nothing can be accomplished, he declared, by "merely talking about it. We must act. We must act quickly." Roosevelt called a special session of Congress within 24 hours, and Congress convened to stabilize the economy.

As Kentucky Senator Alben Barkley responded courteously to letters fuming "I shall never vote for FD Roosevelt, not even for the dogcatcher of Podunk Village," Henry Ward admired President Roosevelt's ability to put his ideals and ideas into immediate action.

"Millions of men and women were on the verge of starvation. Roosevelt and men of the caliber of Senator Alben W. Barkley took steps to meet the crises. . . The New Deal's program typified the principle of Thomas Jefferson that we should be united in common efforts for the common good," Ward wrote.

At the Library of Records and Archives in Frankfort, nearly 100 files packed tightly inside grey cardboard boxes show how Roosevelt put Jefferson's principles into play in Kentucky. Compiled by workers from the Civilian Works Administration and the Works Progress Administration, the reports document Depression—era conditions in housing, sanitation, education and public health in every Kentucky county.

The forms, some hand written in pencil or typed on onionskin paper, contain vivid descriptions of rural isolation and poverty.

"The housing on the entire western portion of the county, which is in the Cumberland Forest range is nothing more than shacks, and is lacking in sanitation, repairs and are far too small for the family who occupy them. There is one doctor for every 2,638 people at very high ratio, which probably reflects the fact that the income of many people in the county is too low to obtain medical services when needed."

There were 296,000 farms in Kentucky, yet only 3 per cent used electricity. In one, two and three-room schoolhouses, teachers earned $83.50 per month. Lacking sanitary toilets or playgrounds, children acquired self-reliance at an early age and hauled up dip buckets from outdoor wells for a drink of water.

In Washington, Harry Hopkins sent field researchers to evaluate economic and living conditions in the states. Reports described the daily lives and conditions of potato farmers in Maine, Blacks walking 8 miles a day searching for "a little cleaning to do," a six-year-old beet picker in Colorado, and unemployed musicians and miners in West Virginia and Kentucky.

In Texas, two small boys refused to go to school, ashamed of the striped, hand me down clothing they were given to wear. A dead giveaway they were on relief—they feared their classmates would laugh at them.

Hopkins' instructed writer Lorena Hickock to "...go out around the country and look this thing over... Go talk with preachers and teachers, store businessmen, workers, farmers. Go talk with the unemployed, those who are on relief and those who aren't. And when you talk with them don't ever forget that but for the grace of God you, I, any of our friends might be in their shoes. Tell me what you see and hear. All of it. Don't ever pull your punches."

As social workers and FERA employees canvassed Kentucky, Henry finished his newspaper shift and knocked on doors, handing out black and ivory campaign cards printed "Pledged to a Course of Reform in State and County Government." He hoped to pass two new laws -a bill granting cities the right to operate municipally owned utilities, and to put the loan sharks out of business.

In August, 1933, as frustration mounted over job losses and desperate living conditions, fierce political rivalries escalated into violence. The Associated Press reported Kentucky voters "... poured out in near record-breaking numbers in most parts of the state". 14 people died during confrontations, and in east Kentucky, grudges over ballot boxes and campaign posters were settled using rifles, machine guns and dynamite.

In Harlan County, "...about 500 bullets were fired at them and a stick of dynamite was thrown to the edge of the porch and exploded." State troops rushed to the scene, but "...no further trouble was reported."

In west Kentucky, the Rambler's popularity worked in his favor: "Ward Captures Seat in House by 359 Margin—Paducahan Will Be Without Opposition in November General Poll" read the front page of the *Sun-Democrat*.

Two weeks later, Kentucky defaulted on its matching share of funds required for eligibility for Federal Emergency Relief Aid (FERA) funds. Aid workers reluctantly locked the doors of the county relief offices, and reassured hungry families, wilting in the heat, the Governor would do something soon.

Traveling through the east Kentucky coalfields, Lorena Hickock observed that as much as she admired the mountain people's patriotism and rigid code of honor, they had no food and were too physically weak to start a riot.

After the state's default, Hickock met Caroline Boone, a field supervisor with the Kentucky Relief Board. Responsible for ten counties in her region, she estimated about 28,000 families drew relief. That number represented nearly 150,00 people because, "nobody heard of a family of five in those mountains." Statewide, 22% of the state population now drew relief, Hickock was told.

"Pasted up on the doors of the relief offices to which those people until August 12 came for their work slips and food orders are typewritten notices stating that for the present there will be no more help for them. Every morning, little groups of people –those who still have enough strength to walk anywhere from one to ten miles—come straggling in and stand staring helplessly at those notices. Many of them cannot read."

'Every morning,' the head of the relief staff in one of those towns told me, 'I take the morning paper and go out on the steps and read aloud to them what's happened at the special session of the legislature in Frankfort. 'Every morning what's happened is—nothing. They listen dumbly, and then they go away.'"

On her final day in the Bluegrass, an extension agent accompanied Hickock as she interviewed residents in Knox County. "You travel as far as you can over roads that only a Ford…in the hands of an expert could go. Then you get out and walk. On one of the trails, we met an old woman. They called her "Aunt Cora'. Half-dead from pellagra, she stumbled along on her bare, gnarled old feet, clutching under her arm a paper bag containing a few scraggly string beans she begged off somebody. I stopped and talked with her. As I started on, she reached out and laid her hand on my arm and said in a voice that was hardly more than a whisper: 'Don't forget me, Honey! Don't forget me!'"

In September, while Aunt Cora whispered and prayed, Governor Ruby Laffoon called the General Assembly into an emergency session. "Kentucky Must Not Fail!" he thundered, to raise additional revenue to restore federal assistance. Legislators listened politely, levied a "little tax on whiskey and a little tax on beer," adjourned and fled back home.

Legislators estimated taxes would raise between two and a half or three million dollars, but receipts totaled little more than six hundred thousand. The elderly judge was furious, forced to wait until the next session convened in January, 1934.

As the Governor resolved to pass a controversial new sales tax, Henry promised voters he would "accept the votes and influence of any clique, clan, faction or organization that desires to support me, but I will accept the dictates of no organization."

Years later, he admitted "At 24, I was too young, inexperienced, naïve and meek to cope with the professional politicians who dominated the state legislature." In

January, he moved into a Frankfort hotel, unpacked his typewriter, and mailed a column home every day.

During the winter of 1934, the state budget was on the brink of collapse and a battle underway over a proposed new sales tax. The brand new representative read stacks of telegrams imploring him to vote "yes" to restore relief and re-open the schools. Henry's foolish pledge to increase government services without raising taxes a lie, it taught him a harsh lesson in public service he never forgot.

# 4 Rip Roaring Speeches and the Sales Tax Revolt

> Is it not a hard matter to tell where the pig leaves off and the hog begins? ... Why should not every citizen of the Commonwealth of Kentucky bear his proportion of the burden of state government? ... I am tired of playing politics upon the miseries of the people of this state.
>
> GOVERNOR RUBY P. LAFFOON JANUARY, 1934.

As Kentucky's youngest representative entered the House of Representatives' chamber, newspaper reporters pestered Henry: "Shall we put you down in our little black books as progressive or insurgent?" Ward joked he was neither—"just radical," and he ignored warnings from senior legislators that newcomers "harden their heart for consideration of revenue measures...in the dark days ahead."

More than 700 bills awaited disposition, including Henry's loan sharking bill. Previous attempts to regulate payday lending languished in the House for more than 20 years.

In his column, he reported a $10,000 slush fund used to influence representatives' votes proved effective, but no one approached him. "I'll go even further than that. I have not been offered any part of any slush fund or any legal tender of any sort. Maybe my honest and open face warns the bribers to avoid me."

"Ward Compels Reading of his Loan Fee Bill," a headline announced on the front page of the *Sun-Democrat:* "Paducah is infested with loan sharks," Ward declared, adding the city "is a railroad center and loan sharks love to prey on railroad men." He predicted that "...public sentiment ... and an intensive fight by a group of legislators and others interested in the solution of this problem" would force them out of business.

His bill required lenders to be licensed by the state banking commissioner, and provide borrowers with a copy of their loan contract, enforcing penalties for violating the proposed bill.

Veteran legislators shooed him away. "Now comes Representative Chris Gottschalk, of Covington, to hurl Yankee rocks at Paducah's crown. 'Aw, Ward, that loan shark bill won't affect your little country town,'" Gottschalk chuckled. Ward retorted "... (I)t's more than an even money bet that there are as many or more loan sharks in Paducah per square foot as in any other city in the Commonwealth, Covington, included!"

Trained by *Sun Democrat* editors to prove it, Henry submitted bankruptcy petitions listing Paducah railroad workers carried average loan balances of $200 at an interest rate of 28.57 per month, or more than 240% per year.

During the committee hearing, Chairman Rhodes Myers interrupted Henry to protest current law permitted recovery for usurious rates, and the loans provided a service to people without a history of credit. Yet Myers intentionally omitted a key fact, underscoring *why* Ward's bill required written contracts.

Henry explained the current law *did* provide recovery—*if* someone could prove they paid interest of greater than 6 percent. "The trouble was that without records or witnesses, the victim of usury could not prove his case. I remember that one man testified that he had borrowed $150 to pay his wife's medical bills when his son was born. He had paid on the loan every month, yet the lender said he still owed the $150. The only way he had to show how long he had been paying on the loan was that his son was now 11 years old."

As House members listened, Myers warned them overriding the Rules Committee set bad precedent. Henry stood his ground, urging members "not to let the committees dictate to us." By a vote of 53-27, the bill passed both readings to became law.

A huge win for a novice legislator, the *Sun-Democrat* ran a lengthy feature Ward submitted explaining how the new law protected workers. Kentucky was one of the last states to cap usurious rates and Louisville had one of the highest bankruptcy rates in the country. Ward predicted that workers in the cities of Paducah, Louisville and Covington, "the centers of the small loan business in

Kentucky," would benefit most from the bill, and "...the business of making loans in the amount of $300 or less might be likened to the long fight of a people to escape from tyrannical slavery and oppression. If the new law solves the problems for which its sponsors intend it, the battle to drive loan sharks from the state of Kentucky will be finished, and a campaign which started more than 20 years ago will be concluded in triumph."

After the bill passed, a chance meeting in a downtown restaurant in Frankfort made a deep impression on Henry. A young man recognized him, and made his way over to thank him. He recently signed a note to borrow $10, with $12 due back in 30 days. But he lost his job, and couldn't pay for three months. He signed it before the new law passed, at a monthly interest of 20%—totaling 240% if he carried the loan for a year. He thanked Henry for fighting back. If he borrowed money again, the interest was capped at 3.5% per month, and 6% annually. The encounter convinced Henry it was one thing to write about solving problems; as state representative his actions had a positive, direct impact in the daily lives of Kentuckians.

Yet industry lobbyists fought back, and filed a restraining order against the law. Courts issued a stay, permitting lenders to charge interest at rates between 240% to 500%. Eventually the Kentucky Supreme Court ruled against the appeal.

Inside the Capitol Press Club, newspapermen tipped their hats to Henry for leading a rebellion against the Rules Committee. They moved his name in their little black books to the "anti" column, which stood for "anti-administration" man.

Majority Leader Dr. A.L. Hill sternly criticized Henry, their new ringleader. "These young fellows in the House do not know our system. They have broken precedent several times," Hill complained. *The Union County Advocate* labeled Ward the worst offender. He violated the "sacred rule" of the House by securing enough votes to override the Rules Committee. He should be "ashamed of himself," Hill scolded, and Ward agreed. He *was* ashamed of himself—he wrote, for failing to "shout from the rooftops" he was *fed up* with colleagues who lacked "guts" and let "unscrupulous politicians control them".

Ward's next bill permitted municipal ownership and operation of water and/or electric utility services. A right referred to as "home rule," Paducah owned its water company, and the *Sun-Democrat* long supported local ownership of utilities. Henry had reported and followed both federal and local policy on public utility ownership. A complex subject, his column helped the average reader understand the differences between a public and privately operated utility, how the rates were set and how rules of operation affected customers. In Henry's mind the critical difference meant publicly owned utility companies were accountable to their customers; privately owned companies had a duty to maximize shareholder returns.

After a city franchise expired, private companies often bid for ownership. Small cities with limited budgets could not afford attorneys to defend their bids against corporations with generous legal budgets, and attorneys filed appeals causing long delays. The tactic often forced them to give up bidding for control of the franchise. The companies also maximized the talents of a public relations staff to bombard the public with radio and newspaper ads designed to persuade potential customers their rates would increase and quality and service suffer under municipal ownership.

In the Kentucky Senate, the Rules Committee rejected a companion bill for home rule filed by Covington Senator Jack Murphy. Henry described Murphy's reaction: he "started howling," accused the utility lobby of controlling the committee, and threatened to call for a grand jury investigation of the vote.

Throughout his life, people variously described Henry as "principled," "hardheaded," or "sanctimonious." In 1934, the freshman representative was obnoxious *and* cocky—he declared that Murphy's bill was "putrid" and "ridiculous" compared to his version of a bill, one that he praised as "ideal." It survived the first reading in the House, and was tabled during the second. Now it was Henry's turn to howl as he demanded the Committee publicly admit they were controlled by the private utility lobby. "Are we going to be dictated to by interests that are private? ..." "I don't think we are."

Chairman Robert Beatty "cut my throat from ear to ear and clear through to the backbone," he wrote in his column. "Without any explanation they voted to table my bill to give cities of the first, second, fourth, fifth and sixth classes the right to acquire their own municipal light, heat and power plants. And the table is a mighty bad place to have a bill, for tabling a bill is about the same as putting a man in the electric chair and letting him sizzle for a half hour. It never looks the same again."

The *Sun-Democrat* rushed to Henry's defense; the editorial reads like a draft of a Frank Capra film script for *Mr. Smith Goes to Washington*: "Henry Ward, raised here, acquiring his knowledge on this newspaper, challenges the Utilities commission and seems to have lost. Henry Ward is not much more than a boy. He left here with the understanding that his employers would be behind him in anything he did that was right. He has fulfilled the obligation and the employers are still behind him. He is possibly broken-hearted by the cheap attitude of the people at Frankfort, because he will not concur in all of their evident efforts to take money from the commonwealth and put it to their own account, he is not popular. When a kid like this goes up there with honesty of purpose, with resolute desire to help this state and its people, and then is confronted with a situation which makes it impossible for him to do what he thinks is the right thing, it is too bad. I would not give a continental damn for anything Frankfort had or is supposed to have, against the honesty of a man who is trying his best to put things on a decent, honest level."

In his memoir, Henry supplied the historical context. Public versus private ownership of a utility "...was a major issue in Kentucky politics. The private versus public utilities issue was similar to the railroads versus trucks battle that influenced political campaigns over a long period. The private utilities and railroads were dominant during the early years of the Commonwealth. They elected a majority of the legislature, and their friends controlled the administrative branch."

In the oral history interview, Pearce asked Ward about the quality of the legislature back in those days:

"I'd say not more than ten percent of them really knew much about what was going on back then. After all, it—you had to work at it if you expected to understand the legislature. One advantage I had not running back home every time they had sessions for it, I had time then to study. And because I always felt that because I hadn't gone to college I had to work harder—and keep on studying and learning all the time. It was a very valuable thing because I didn't think I knew it all and I had to work at it. I did work at it. But the average legislator didn't. Didn't read their bills ... were pretty easily influenced then, particularly by the governor at the that time, the governor controlled the legislature.

The General Assembly adjourned in March, but rumors spread Governor Laffoon planned a special session in May to pass a general sales tax.

After property values plummeted in 1933, legislators suspended Kentucky's property tax. A quick and popular fix, the exemption covered 73% of all taxpayers, and state education spending dropped to an all-time low of $6 per student.

Henry complained that the "hard and fast administration boys who controlled both houses of the General Assembly" lacked the will to tackle the relief crisis and should have acted earlier. A general sales tax was now inevitable, Henry concluded, because Thom Rhea, next in line to become Governor, supported it.

"But we probably will return to Frankfort within a month, pass a sales tax, an income tax and anything else the administration wants. And when the special session is over, it has been suggested that those who cooperate in carrying through the program which already is outlined gather in a body and give three cheers of "Rhea, Rhea, Rhea."

Ward studied revenue proposals spinning round and round like carousel horses. Legislators proposed new taxes on amusements, soft drinks, cosmetics, jewelry, radios, pianos *and* incomes—yet all the spinning was a sideshow, and Ward knew it. He counted the votes, and 60 members were pressured by the Kentucky Merchants Association to vote "no."

Sorting through letters and telegrams pouring in, some supported the tax, others demanded he lower them more: "Why don't you get some action on? You all do the things that should be done for us. You know we need relief—taxes high as [a] cat's back and nearly 50% of the taxpayers on the delinquent tax list." His former high school principal, Mr. Jetton, reminded Henry he faced a choice between "raising hell" or keeping the schools open. "What is actually *done*, not what is *said* ," will count, wrote Jetton.

At times, the registered Democrat and loyal New Dealer echoed President Hoover. "Personally, I am not in favor of new state taxes for any purposes," he wrote. Responsible officials should "...let the local communities take care of their own needs. ..."

He took that hard line and announced his no tax pledge before he arrived in Frankfort. In the House chamber, a large chart stood at the front. Each day, the clerk regularly updated the tally of Kentuckians applying for food or relief. Those numbers soared, and so did the pressure on legislators to restore emergency aid.

In March, Henry polled readers about which taxes to vote for. "Do you want a sales tax—nuisance taxes on everything from baby bottles to fishing tackle and pianos to an income tax or what? In other words, if you want me to vote for a new tax, then tell me which one to vote for. Be consistent. Don't ask for a reduction of taxes, and then turn right around and demand something that will necessitate new taxes."

Following a four-day round of negotiations with Republican legislators, Laffoon was hospitalized. Despite his exhaustion, the Governor called a Special Session for May 9, 1934.

Spectators packed the gallery, dressed in Sunday church attire. Suits, ties and sweater vests for the men, and frilly hats and brightly patterned dresses for the women. Governor Laffoon arrived, strode to the lectern, and methodically disposed of the legislators' objections, one by one.

Ten years into the future, he promised, a general sales tax spread evenly and fairly would become law in every other state in the nation.

For legislators stung by threats from shopkeepers and merchants, he reminded them the protests were hypocritical and self-serving: "He says, [the merchant] 'For God's sake, don't put any burdens on the poor fellow.' My Friends, they are willing to put it anywhere, just so you take it off them." Forget trying another whiskey tax, he warned, because a tax increase on distillers would drive them out of the state.

Pausing briefly, he acknowledged, "I haven't had time to sleep or eat, much less write a speech that might have been more attractive than the one I am delivering to you."

Shifting from his frustration to flattery, he declared "I have bragged on this Legislature when I was out of its presence and feel I am justified in doing so in your presence, and I say again that this present General Assembly of Kentucky is composed of the most outstanding representatives of the people that I have ever seen assembled in this Capitol.

"They can call you wild jackasses if they want to, but I shall say that you are conscientious men that want to do your duty, and there is no compliment, gentlemen, that I could pay you that you do not deserve."

Contrasting the dedication of schoolteachers to the greed of the Merchants' Association, he stared up into the gallery. "So, my friends, you see it is whose ox is gored as to how they look at public questions." Laffoon's forceful appeal to put duty ahead of politics convinced Henry it was time to join the "sales tax crowd."

On May 16, the House restored the ad valorem property tax and added an income tax. Their courage prompted a call for more bodyguards: "House Passes Income Tax, Capitol Guarded" read the bold, black two-inch newspaper headlines.

Rumors spread the success of both taxes paved the way for the third—the sales tax. Public reaction mirrored the split in the General Assembly. A riot squad of steel-helmeted National Guardsmen carrying clubs, pistols, rifles and sub-machine guns circled the Mansion after Governor Laffoon opened several letters written in blood, threatening to "blow the old Governor to hell" with dynamite. Waiting for the final roll call vote, Ward filed regular updates on the chaos in the Capitol.

One hundred and fifty jobless men arrived from Northern Kentucky, petitioning the Governor for $5 million in relief. "Last night the jobless were still hungry. Tuesday, they rode all day through the rain, and arrived here late, cold and hungry. One of them declared: 'We are almost ready to start eating the grass on the hillsides,'" Ward reported.

The public demonstrations peaked in late May. "5000 Merchants Expected to Meet Legislators" read *Sun-Democrat* headlines. Crowds waved signs, marched on the grounds and then invaded the Chamber, climbing on top of the desks and shouting slogans.

Ward's story angle played up the music, marching and his colleagues' conceit: "Many of the legislators referred to their visiting constituents as being 'the cream of Kentucky citizens.' Some of these visitors apparently had been consuming "Cream of Kentucky," or some other brand of liquor, for many were in a jovial mood. It was a beer-drinking crowd, too, in fact, so much so that Frankfort's supply of beer was entirely exhausted."

Eight bands played music on the Capital grounds and the Speaker of the House, W.E. Rogers, Sr., roared at the horn players to keep silent. As legislators huddled in small groups, Laffoon fired the daughter of legislator who voted against the tax from her state job.

Ward wavered once more before roll call. He filed an amendment reducing the tax to 2% by eliminating the percentage returned to the counties. Protesting the formula was unfair and unconstitutional, his amendment failed and he retreated, voting "Aye" for the full 3%.

On June 7, the House voted again. House Bills 37 through 42 levied taxes on appliances, medicines, perfume, gum, playing cards, clothing, golf balls, catchers' masks, and of course, "any other appliance used in the game of baseball, etc." The vote edged up to 47 ayes to 50 nays.

The standoff ended the next day. The "Gross Receipts Tax Law of 1934" plugged a hole in the state budget as big as Mammoth Cave by raising $11 million in new revenue. Released from the sweltering chamber, the "jackasses" reminded enraged merchants the tax expired at midnight, June 30, 1936.

Speaker Rogers' vote secured the constitutional majority, while Ward later lamented that because his name fell last in the roll call, he was blamed for casting the vote tipping it into law. As voices echoed in the chamber in a tight roll call of 51 for to 47 against, Rogers smiled.

"I have heard it rumored that there is such an organization in the state as the Retail Merchants Association." he said. "I want them to get full credit for the passage of this bill, so I vote aye."

The session adjourned, and Henry learned Paducah store owners are "heaping bitter criticisms on me for my vote in favor of the sales tax." On his way home, he detoured through Illinois and Indiana. Both states recently enacted a sales tax, and if the sky was not falling there, he hoped to placate angry shop keepers, who another friend warned, intended to fill Henry's pants with buckshot.

# 5 Reformer Reformed

> "I made a vigorous fight for an act to enable Paducah to acquire a municipal light and power plant, and if I am sent back to Frankfort, I will secure the passage of that act. I challenge the people of McCracken County to make a thorough investigation of me and my purposes and of the opposition to me. I am a young man, I am making my own way in the world, with no one to help me other than my friends. ... I pledge to you that I will fight for your interests, first, last and all the time."

Eager to get back to work at the newspaper, Henry discovered a noose swinging over his desk—and the Yellow Dogs started a betting pool on Henry's odds for winning a second term.

Yet he had much to look forward to—he married, was reelected, and celebrated the birth of his daughter, Patricia in 1935. His break from politics included breaking in new reporters. Creed Black, retired editor of *The Herald-Leader*, recalled how high Ward set the bar for himself and others.

As Creed sat gossiping one day with a co-worker, Ward pinned him to the wall with a look and growled: "You won't find out what's going on just sitting in here...[so] I got out of the office," Black remembered. "[Ward] was not only city editor, he also wrote a daily column and most of the editorials, which added up to a workload I have more than once recalled for the benefit of latter-day employees who complained about having too much to do," he wrote.

Someone else admired Henry, too. Gladys Lindsey worked as a hostess at the Irvin Cobb Hotel and remembered: "I felt like I knew him from the articles he wrote for the *Sun Democrat*."

The newspaper sponsored McCracken County's annual beauty pageant, and Ward bet his coworkers he could woo, win and marry that year's winner.

Gladys was crowned Miss McCracken County in 1935. A front-page photo of the winner shows an elegant, smiling young woman wearing a sash and crown, a large floral corsage draped over her shoulder. Lindsey "is 21 years of age and resides in the Sloan Apartments. She is employed at the Irvin Cobb hotel, is a brunette, with black hair and brown eyes; weighs 117 pounds and is 5 feet 4 one-half inches tall.... A large crowd witnessed the ceremonies at the theatre and the crowning of Miss Lindsey as 'Miss McCracken County,' as Henry Ward, *Sun Democrat* staff writer and contest manager, acted as master of ceremonies and introduced the nominees."

On their way to the state competition in Louisville, Henry stopped in Frankfort, to show off his desk in the House and introduce her to Governor Laffoon.

"By the time we got back to Paducah, I was really smitten. I had been dating a girl in Louisville, in fact I had a date planned with her the night I was to be in Louisville, but by that time I had forgotten all about her," Ward remembered. When they returned to Paducah, the couple saw each other every day. Lindsey—vivacious and intelligent, athletic and opinionated—and the Rambler made an unusual pair.

"The marriage, which comes as a surprise to the friends of the couple, was solemnized Monday evening, September 24, at the parsonage of the Union City Baptist Church, Union City, Tenn.... ..." read the announcement. A second society page item described the private dinner party held for the couple at the hotel, including table decorations "...in green and white with lighted tapers casting a soft glow over the central appointment, a wedding cake topped with a miniature bride and groom."

In 1935, Lieutenant Governor "Happy" Chandler called the legislature back into special session. Chandler, a sales tax opponent, took advantage of a loophole in the state constitution to call a special session to approve a direct voter primary system in Kentucky. Chandler belonged to a faction controlled by Nelson County attorney and political kingmaker Ben Johnson, and currently nominees were chosen during a state party convention.

In early February 1935, Governor Laffoon traveled to Washington, D.C., to meet with Senator Barkley. After his train crossed the state line, Chandler invoked a clause in Kentucky's constitution that transferred power to the Lieutenant Governor in the Governor's absence, and as acting Governor, he put the compulsory primary issue to a vote.

Laffoon rushed back to rescind the call, but it was too late. After Chandler left Kentucky on February 6, *The New York Times* reported that Senate President Robert Humphreys presided as Governor in the Lieutenant Governor's absence.

"Three Governors Confuse Kentucky," the *Times* headline read. "Chandler issues Assembly Call, Laffoon Revokes It, Court Intervenes, Humphreys Sits for a Day."

Legislators stayed in session despite Laffoon's order. "I was among them," Henry remembered. "We insisted that once a call for a special session had been issued, it could not be rescinded by the governor. We took the issue to court, and the Court of Appeals upheld the position of the legislature. A handful of legislators met daily in Frankfort to keep the session alive until the Court of Appeals acted."

The open primary law passed, but Laffoon insisted it include a runoff election between the top two candidates. His last-ditch attempt to derail Chandler failed, and Chandler defeated Thomas Rhea in the runoff.

Henry was reelected by just 300 votes. Chandler supporters opposed him for his sales tax vote, and Laffoon supporters resented his vote for the open primary.

In a 21-inch black-bordered newspaper ad, he admitted: "When I first went to Frankfort, I was inexperienced, and consequently could not do so good a job as I desired. That will all be changed now. I will be one of only about 15 men in the House with previous legislative experience. That is worth more than can be put into words."

He supported freeing Kentucky's toll bridges, a law to permit voter registration at the Courthouse five days a week year-round, and a bill that barred charging state employees "assessments" during political campaigns. He proposed a bill adding McCracken County to the state primary road system, and supporting reforms to the administration and operation of county government. His hard won maturity was reflected in his final and only tax pledge – amending the dog tax law to allow every family to own one dog tax free.

In his personal memoir, "Recollections" Henry recalled that after he switched his vote on the sales tax, "... (O)pponents accused me of getting a new car in return for my vote. The car dealer had proof of the inaccuracy of the charge, because I bought it on credit, but the anti-sales tax element preferred to believe I had sold out. Looking back over the years I participated in politics, I am proud this was the only time that anyone even hinted that I had accepted a bribe, gift or favor in return for my vote or influence. More significant to me is the fact that in all those years I was never approached. I suppose my reputation as a crusading newspaperman was such that anyone who might have considered approaching me was scared off by the possibility that I would rush in and expose them. ... I don't think I ever knew more than one or two crooks at the legislature in the years that I served."

His second term in 1936 was far more productive. He sponsored and passed a bill limiting the jurisdiction of the Public Service Commission over the right of cities to contract for their own power, and enabling Kentucky to accept federal funding through the Rural Electrification Act to form rural electric cooperatives.

Initially, he worked well with Governor Chandler. But over time, as Chandler's confidence increased, Henry accused him of embellishing his record, breaking campaign pledges and putting his personal ambition ahead of his public responsibilities. When Chandler complained, Henry facetiously replied he was just trying to be "helpful" by setting the record straight—over and over again, in his newspaper column, for the next three decades.

In 1939, *Time Magazine* published an admiring profile of Chandler. Headlined *The Happy Man*, news of the death of Kentucky Senator Marvel Logan, "...a quiet, kindly, able Southern judge, baggy-kneed, [and] baggy-faced," opened the door for his successor—Chandler—"the nearest thing to Huey Long since the Kingfish was shot to death in 1935."

The writer described the irony of the scene the day the "bungling" Senator Alben Barkley escorted Chandler, his bitter political enemy, into the Senate. "...Kentucky's happy man is no mere country clown. A swift and educated brain, a vaulting ambition and one of the sharpest instincts in the U.S. lie behind his automatic incandescent smile, his hot-palmed handshake. Prancy as a Blue Grass Colt, 'Happy Chandler' is a natural politician. In politics he has the easy grace of Joe Di Maggio coasting under a long fly-ball, the same talent of making tough ones look easy."

It was no secret that Chandler's political aspirations included running for President of the United States, and he cultivated warm friendships with Huey Long and Virginia Senator Harry Byrd. His image as a conservative populist played well with Kentucky legislators who opposed President Roosevelt, and staunchly resisted increasing the state budget to pay for services or raise taxes.

Chandler's decision to support Henry's REA bill ended hardship for his rural constituents, with much of it paid for by the federal government. REA boosted Chandler's popularity and burnished his image as a man of the people.

Prior to Roosevelt's election, thousands of rural Americans were still literally left in the dark. In the 1930s, the U.S. lagged behind Europe providing universal access to electricity. Public power legislation at the top of FDR's agenda, the Congress and state legislatures remedied the existence of two Americas—one with electricity and one without.

Prior to the 1936 general session, Henry asked Chandler to consider supporting three bills: "...the Rural Electrification Administration measure; the TVA bill; and a proposal to enable the Governor and Highway Commissioner to take steps to free the toll bridges. Of course, I would like you to include all three bills in the special session. If you cannot do that, I prefer the Rural Electrification bill since it is an emergency measure, in view of the fact that a large number of counties are waiting for this legislation before they can take [sic] advance of offers from the Rural Electrification Administration. I wish to assure you that I will cooperate in measures intended for the good of the people of the Commonwealth."

Access to affordable electricity raised spirits and standards of living in towns stretching from Nicholasville to Owenton, and Benton to Pikeville, as electric lights, heat, water pumps and refrigerators ended generations of back-breaking drudgery for Kentuckians.

Working together, Henry and Chandler, backed by pro public power advocates on the Public Service Commission, sped that emergency legislation through quickly.

That session of 1936 marks the beginning of the legacy of the "man who made Kentucky modern." Decades later, people have forgotten or are simply unaware, how awe-struck Americans celebrated the arrival of electricity in the 1930s.

# 6 Dousing the Kerosene Lanterns

> During debates in Congress over funding the REA, one early federal study confirmed "... at the rate of progress shown in the 10-year period preceding 1935, it would have taken about 50 years to make electric service available to half the farms in the United States."

As Ward and Chandler paved the way for REA power, they witnessed the birth of the rural electrification movement, a vibrant portrait of self-determination. It featured stout mules and men dragging 90-foot poles through poison ivy, stinging nettles and tangled vines in rough terrain and isolated hills and hollows. Farmers rode through blizzards and storms to attend the first organizational meetings, and a story about a broken power line evokes the bitter divide in public opinion over FDR's expansion of government programs.

REA *Poster, U.S. Department of Agriculture*

At daybreak, linesmen discovered the "charred remains of an owl and possum locked in a death struggle" at the foot of an electric pole. Like that owl and possum, public and private power advocates grappled over the future of public power in the Tennessee Valley.

Mississippi Congressman John Rankin led the group of "roughnecks" seeking funding for the REA. During one debate, Rankin pointed to the existence of two Americas—one with electricity and one without, but Connecticut representative Schuyler Merritt cut him off, preferring silence to the truth:

> Rankin: *I wonder if the gentleman knows that in New Zealand two-thirds of their farms are electrified, [and] in the United States about ten percent are.*
> Merritt: *In New Zealand, they deal with enormous tracts of land. ... Also New Zealand is a socialistic state. ...*
> Rankin: *I wonder if the gentleman knows that in France and Germany ninety percent of their farms are electrified. Those are not socialistic states.*
> Merritt: *No, they are not socialistic, but they are imperialistic.*
> Rankin: *I wonder if the gentleman knows that Holland and Switzerland are practically 100 percent electrified?*
> Merritt: *But they are no larger than our New England.*

*Rankin: I understand there is no state in New England that has even twenty-five per cent of its rural farms electrified.*
*Merritt: I do not care to give the gentleman more time.*

In May of 1936, Congress, approved the Rural Electrification Act (REA) bill, which distributed federal loans to the states to form rural electric cooperatives.

Morris Cooke, REA's first administrator, emphasized electrification brought rapid progress: it improved living standards, raised literacy rates, and increased agricultural efficiency and productivity.

"In one county in which I have worked, you could count on the fingers of your two hands all of the farmers past 40 years of age who had an education beyond the seventh grade," Cooke wrote. "The greatest extent of the farmers of America had become the forgotten man," he wrote, but after the arrival of electricity, the children of these farmers no longer needed to go to town.

Even better, in 1940, Steven C. Tate, president of the National Association of Rural Cooperatives, credited the REA for saving the souls of Tennessee and Kentucky's "moonshine likker" makers. Some bootleggers switched from distilling alcohol to broiler production, and as they tended chicks chirping inside their electric brooders, "it contributed to the moral uplifting of the nation," said Tate.

Yet Robert Watt, president of Kentucky Utilities, insisted taxpayer funded competition would destroy stockholder-owned utility companies. As a young electrical engineering graduate, Watt began his career with Kentucky Utilities in 1912. One of the company's first five employees, he supervised construction of its generating station in Pineville in Bell County. Six feet three inches tall, Watt was blind in one eye, and walked with a cane. The avid hunter and fisherman chewed tobacco and played poker, interests more in common with Roosevelt's cousin, Teddy, the adventurous outdoorsman, than his wealthy, well-connected cousin from Hyde Park, New York.

His grandson remembered him as a staunch conservative. After President Roosevelt's election, Watt criticized the administration's expansion of government programs and assistance, and "Everything Roosevelt did he was opposed to it, except I guess when he died, he probably wasn't opposed to that," recalled Watt's grandson, attorney Robert Watt, III. "He thought he was an *awful* person."

In Kentucky, the controversy over public power lasted decades. Utility company lobbyists leaned hard on Kentucky legislators to protect the industry's monopoly on electric service. Kentucky Utilities, the state's largest company, owned $71 million worth of electric, gas and water utilities and served more than 70,000 customers in over 80 counties. Its annual profit exceeded $11 million, (maintaining a solid balance sheet despite the Depression) a value close to $210 million dollars today.

What Henry called "the hot fight" over public power began in 1934, after Governor Laffoon created the Public Service Commission. Laffoon asserted it was more efficient for a single agency to regulate utilities, but critics charged he did it as a favor to his cousin, Polk Laffoon, Jr. Polk Laffoon served as chief executive of the Union Heat, Light & Power Co., and the Cincinnati Gas & Electric Company, and the new commissioners were industry insiders.

The "antis," led by Henry, strenuously objected to the Commission, and the *Louisville Courier Journal* published an inflammatory editorial titled *Rape of the Cities*. It denounced the bill creating the PSC as "...the most vicious piece of legislation ever passed and is a real test as to whether the Governor is controlled by an honest desire to serve the people or is influenced by selfish or political interests to serve the power trust and their lobbies."

On the first day of the 1936 legislative session, Henry introduced House Bills 4, 5 and 6. The laws removed cities from the jurisdiction of the Commission, allowed them to own their own water or electric plants, and revised rules under which a city advertised the expiration of its electric franchise.

Governor Chandler bumped into Ward soon afterward. "Henry, some representatives of the utilities have asked for a hearing on your utility bills; do you want to stay for the hearing?" he asked.

"Of course, I wanted to stay, and did. And it was fortunate for the fate of the bills that I remained, too because Robert Watt, of Lexington, president of the Kentucky Utilities Company and Squire Ogden, of Louisville, an attorney for the company, presented arguments to persuade the Governor to veto two of the measures which I had sponsored in the legislature. ... I believe the Governor will sign all three of these bills. . .. I believe that Governor Chandler will sign these measures despite the fact that he is a stock holder in the Kentucky Utilities Company, and despite the fact that the private utilities have the strongest lobby of all other interests here in Frankfort."

Henry learned the value of avoiding fiery speeches, holding his temper in check, and memorizing parliamentary rules. "I got the bills referred to the committee of which I was a member. I got them out of committee immediately. Got them passed real quick. Personally took them to the Senate, and Lee Gibson was senator from Owensboro at the time and got him to sponsor it. And worked on the Senate and did what he could to get them passed. Got them passed early. Took them down to Happy's office personally, and in my own fountain pen asked him to sign it and then I was in pretty good shape."

Protecting "home rule" meant little to thousands of rural Kentuckians living outside the city limits, where a different story unfolded. Residents who lived just yards away from a power company's boundary line looked on with frustration each night, at the cozy glow of their more fortunate neighbor's electric lamp framed inside a window.

The federal REA law was signed in 1935. In 1936, Ben Kilgore, the executive secretary of the Kentucky Farm Bureau Federation, notified Governor Chandler that "Our inability to secure an enabling act from the Kentucky legislature has brought our rural electrification work in Kentucky to a standstill. Other states are going ahead while our state is not only failing to make progress, but is becoming tremendously discouraged."

Morris Cooke notified Chandler that the agency reserved over one million dollars for Kentucky "so that you see a good deal hangs on getting the type of legislation which will make it possible for us to operate."

Henry and Chandler stayed ahead of Cooke, and the General Assembly passed the bill quickly. In the long term, Robert Watt and industry executives hoped to repeal it. In the short term, they could obstruct it, and they immediately petitioned the Public Service Commission for a ruling settling what rates to charge the cooperatives for supplying them electricity, and how to divide up the new service territory.

If Ward was determined, Chandler shrewd and Watt powerful, they were joined by another formidable character, an ex-Kentucky governor, 66-year-old J.C.W. Beckham. Under Chairman Beckham's leadership, the Commission dismissed the industry's shrill protests and hand-wringing and moved the hearings along.

Beckham, according to historian James C. Klotter, "had been more concerned about building and controlling his political base than on enacting great changes in government." Nearing the end of his 36-year career in politics, and mourning the death of his only son, he presided firmly over the negotiations, and coordinated a swift settlement that drew praise from Morris Cooke.

As utility company attorneys and executives nit-picked the figures used to set the cost of a kilowatt hour, Governor Chandler's files grew thick with irate telegrams from electric, telephone and gas companies unhappy with the Commission's pro consumer policy and orders.

"RESOLVED, THAt WHEREAS radical, unusual, unnotified, uncalled-for and unexpected changes have been made by the Public Service Commission under the presidency of Hon. J.C.W. Beckham in the telephone rates heretofore applicable for many years in Hopkins County," fumed one local mayor, who forwarded

Chandler a copy of the resolution his city passed following a subscribers' meeting of Southern Bell Telephone and Telegraph Company.

Kentucky Utilities' service territory covered more than two thirds of the state. Thousands of Kentucky farmers rushed to join cooperatives, deed over property easements and wire barns and houses. Yet their electricity would not be turned on until rates were set.

According to Robert Watt, "If you give things to people then you must first take them away from other people." The "other people" were utility shareholders, deprived of stock income caused by competition from a new federal agency subsidized by the taxpayer.

The comment infuriated Henry. Extending service to rural territory was time consuming, labor intensive, and reduced the industry's profit while rural Kentuckians did without. The REA guaranteed funding for electric service to residents the private industry refused to serve. Their opposition was *"ridiculous!"*—Henry snapped. The new program freed Kentuckians from lives of physical drudgery, and the industry's self-serving obstructionism was transparent.

If rate negotiations deadlocked, (and this was the goal of Kentucky's utility executives) states were forced to spend the government loans building generating stations, causing delays and financial hardship for the cooperatives. REA supporters worried the money set aside for Kentucky would be released to states who completed their applications.

The Commission responded to the industry's tactics in a public statement noting that "... rural electrification, through low-cost projects sponsored by the Federal Rural Electrification Administration, has not progressed rapidly in Kentucky primarily because electric power has not been available at rates which farm organizations can afford to pay for such service" and that if it was necessary to approve new generating stations, they would. "... [T]his is no idle threat" they warned, but attorneys from the Kentucky-Tennessee Light & Power Company filed another appeal, containing a new set of rate calculations for review.

Commissioners quickly ruled that the average cost figures the company submitted "... mean nothing" and issued a binding order setting the new rate. In a press release announcing the new order, the Commission quoted praise from a congratulatory telegram sent by Morris Cooke:

"... the Kentucky Public Service Commission has done more to aid the development of rural electrification in the United States than any other public agency by giving associations the right of way in developing their projects and by keeping the companies from building spite lines, and also by setting a wholesale rate of 1.2 cents per kilowatt-hour to be charged the associations by the private companies."

REA's current administrator, John Carmody, sent his best wishes to Governor Chandler, noting the May, 1937 order "... might well serve as a model for other state commissions. ...You may be sure that such cooperation will be matched here by our best efforts to take electricity to every farm in Kentucky that can be served."

Organizing meetings in Nicholasville, Jessamine and Fayette County quickly followed, and drew 400 people. Toughened by years of hard work, volatile prices and unpredictable weather, farmers scribbled names on membership agreements and signed over rights of way.

In late summer, federal officials, the Commission and representatives from the Kentucky Farm Bureau met at the University of Kentucky College of Agriculture to track progress, while workmen from the A.A. Electric Company of Cicero, Illinois crisscrossed the countryside, setting poles and stringing lines.

The temptation to label their work a towering achievement is too great—the company erected two poles—one 95 feet high on the Jessamine County side of the Kentucky River, the other 85 feet high in Madison County, at Valley View. The pine poles cost $300 each and were buried 10 feet deep.

By October 11 cooperatives received $2.5 million for more than 2,000 miles of line serving 9,000 to 10,000 farmers in 23 counties. On June 15, 1938, the city of Nicholasville hosted a gigantic celebration as the first switch turned on new electric lights. Shops and schools closed, and John Carmody arrived from Washington, D.C., to celebrate this milestone.

As cooperatives spread across the state, proud members praised the miracle of electricity: "The first benefit we received from the REA service was lights, and aren't lights grand? My little boy expressed my sentiments when he said, 'Mother, I didn't realize how dark our house was until we got electric lights.'" said Rose Scearce, who could hardly believe how her life could be changed so dramatically by well pumps, stoves, refrigerators and vacuum cleaners.

Ward's reporting experience on federal and state utility issues proved valuable in the legislature. Colleagues respected the depth of his knowledge, and he remembered that during the 1936 session, "...I gained a reputation as an advocate of utility legislation that almost stamped me with the nickname of 'utility' Ward." At that time, the Kentucky Municipal League lobbied for public power, and critics insinuated Ward acted under their direction, rather than independently.

Returning home, Ward looked forward to spending time with Gladys and Pat, and enjoying the camaraderie in the city room. Instead, Alben Barkley recruited him to handle his statewide publicity for his U.S. Senate campaign. That summer, Ward worked a punishing schedule on nights and weekends, and

Gladys often joined him, typing correspondence and stuffing envelopes at the Seelbach Hotel in Louisville.

As Henry negotiated printing contracts and edited radio scripts, the hotly contested primary between "Ole Alben" and "Sonny Boy" Chandler was the subject of a Pulitzer Prize winning newspaper series exposing how the candidates twisted federal and state employees' arms for contributions and votes.

Henry and Barkley formed a close bond. In 1937, Henry's loyalty fueled a bitter political rivalry between Henry and Chandler that lasted until Happy evened the score, 30 years later, during the Kentucky Governor's race in 1967.

# 7 A Deplorable Situation

"One word more. You have heard charges ... and counter charges of the use of political influence exerted on primary voters. ...Personally, I am not greatly disturbed by these stories because I have an old-fashioned idea, an old-fashioned faith that the voters of Kentucky, no matter whom they employ or by whom they are employed, are going to vote their own personal convictions on Primary Day."

President Franklin D. Roosevelt,
Covington, July 1938.

"The Sheriff of the county told me that due to the economic conditions of most of the voters, they would sell their souls for thirty cents."

Private Investigator's "Report on the
Counties: Adair" July 1938.

Henry's work routine and family life comfortably settled, the major stories of 1936 and '37 included Kentucky's brutal drought, followed by the catastrophic Ohio River flood of 1937. Edwin Paxton, Sr. rushed back from Florida to organize relief efforts—90% of the town lay underwater and 27,000 residents were evacuated to safety.

The biggest story of the decade, the flood caused $250 million in damage in Kentucky, the equivalent of five billion dollars today.

In the summer of 1938, Washington D.C. reporter Thomas Stokes covered a political storm in Kentucky, featuring Alben Barkley and Happy Chandler, and his series was awarded a Pulitzer Prize.

A string of Congressional races that summer threatened FDR's base of power, and in Kentucky, it pitted the federal WPA workforce against Chandler's state government machine. Roosevelt, Barkley, Thomas Stokes, and George Goodman played key roles in the drama. Against that backdrop, Henry coordinated Barkley's publicity campaign in a race that Stokes charged was "a grand political racket in which the taxpayer is the victim."

Calling Chandler a "fair-haired boy among the anti-New Deal element," Stokes reported "Kentucky's smiling, 39-year-old Governor, known by everybody in the State merely as 'Happy,' has become the darling of those who dislike the New Deal and all its works. Governor Chandler, in other words, is a symbol of national significance."

As Chandler raised his national profile, Ward accused Happy of breaking the campaign promises he made to Kentucky voters. After Chandler bragged his tax plan retired a state debt of nearly $29 million, Ward studied the receipts. He whittled Happy's claim down to $17 million, helpfully pointing out the reduction on the correct figure reflected revenue generated by new taxes. More skeptic than critic, he pushed back against Chandler's exaggerated claims, a tactic that infuriated Chandler.

In January 1938, Chandler slammed Ward during his opening address to the 102$^{nd}$ session of the Kentucky General Assembly. While acknowledging the public's "agitation toward freeing the toll bridges," he asserted that some legislators were "selfishly seeking to place themselves in a favorable position in the public eye."

Afterward, Henry caught up with him, thanking him for "taking the crack at me." Chandler's homespun cheer faded. "You have been taking some cracks yourself, and I'm just trying to get even with you. ...I once thought you had something in you, but I have decided that you wouldn't be happy unless you could crack at someone all the time."

Ward admitted he was right. "The trouble is, however, that there are always so many things around to crack about that I can't keep still," he wrote.

Alben Barkley admitted he was caught off guard by Chandler's challenge for the Senate, and he shared a story that reinforced *The Louisville Courier-Journal's* view that Happy remained happiest practicing "the politics of destruction."

In 1935, Barkley and his wife planned to attend the inauguration ceremony of Manuel Quezon as the first president of the Commonwealth of the Philippines. Quezon, "... a very brilliant man," Barkley recalled, invited his guests to stay in the President's mansion to attend that historic ceremony, and the Barkleys were looking forward to the pageantry and celebration. "We had accepted, and our stateroom had been assigned to us on the boat and we packed our bags to go to Manila."

After Chandler defeated Tom Rhea in the primary runoff, it "created a very desperate and ticklish situation in the Democratic Party," remembered Barkley. "And I was urged by Mr. Chandler's friends and his campaign manager not to go to the Philippines, but to stay at home and campaign for him in the race for governor."

Because Barkley and President Roosevelt led national efforts to persuade states to adopt direct primaries, Barkley now felt obligated to support "the fellow who won the nomination in the first compulsory primary election held in Kentucky".

"But I stayed at home and helped to elect the governor, Mr. Chandler, and so forth. Well then, of course, I naturally had a feeling that he ought not to oppose me at my very next election in '38 three years later. He had a perfect right to oppose all that and me, but I felt in all probability he could come to the Senate later anyhow, and maybe as soon as he would if he ran against me, because I didn't think he could beat me. I realize that any young, active and personable governor who is in charge of the state political machinery can give any Senator trouble and I didn't relish any fight of that sort. I didn't think I was entitled to have it. "

In late January, Chandler telephoned the White House. Although Marvin McIntyre, a native Kentuckian and President Roosevelt's secretary was available, Happy declined to speak with him, and was connected to President Roosevelt's son, James.

"I made no request of the President or his son." Chandler said. "I merely told him of the situation in Kentucky and that if I decided to run I would be the next Senator from Kentucky and Senator Barkley would not be."

During Barkley's oral history, his interviewer asked: "How did you handle that?" "I handled it by campaigning harder than I had ever campaigned in my life," Barkley dryly replied.

Henry was all in for Barkley as well, and he explained how he used one of Chandler's favorite strategies against him early in 1938:

"... (S)ome of us were for Barkley and decided to do what we could to try to pin Happy in. Happy had, of course as you recall, run on a platform with repealing the sales tax, so you would replace them with a whole bunch of special taxes—on everything from candy to soft drinks, movies. So in the '38 session, I introduced some bill to repeal all those special taxes he had proposed. And one day Happy's out of the state for some reason, so I couldn't get them out of committee. Of course, he controlled the committee. So, I got up and made a motion to suspend the rules and to take those bills away from the committee in the absence of a committee report and put them on a floor vote. Damn if the motion didn't pass! Happy rushed back to the state and raised hell about it. And I said, 'Happy, I'm just trying to help you keep your campaign promises. ...'"

The stage was set for the "bitter, nasty sort of campaign" Ed Paxton, Jr. predicted. Henry avoided those factional feuds and he concentrated on promoting Barkley's Senate record during the campaign. President Roosevelt's effectiveness and political strength rested on the outcome of elections for an unusually large number of open Senate seats.

That election cycle split the Kentucky General Assembly into two camps. Senator Bob Humphries was the first to declare he would not concede a single county to Barkley. During the winter session of the General Assembly Ward shared a story that underscored how his personal and professional conduct was guided by his integrity.

In February, Ward, at work in a room at the Capital Plaza Hotel on a liquor control bill, overheard Humphries and Chandler supporters planning Chandler's U.S. Senate campaign strategy in a private dining room during a meal. A Barkley supporter, Henry had not joined his campaign staff yet, but even if he had, it would not have changed what he did next.

"They got to talking in rather loud tones, and their voices came right on through the thin wall just as though the thin wall hadn't been there. So, to escape the position of being an eavesdropper, I had to leave my work and this room until they finished their discussions."

As Ward drafted his liquor bill and studied an ominous sounding proposal from the Chandler's administration men called the "voter purgation" bill, two prominent newspapermen tallied the number of U.S. Senate primary contests ahead, and where they were located. Staring at the national map, they zeroed in on a single state—Kentucky.

New York Times columnist Arthur Krock (a Kentucky native) predicted Kentucky's August primary "may be the Gettysburg of the party's internecine strife over national control in 1940." Barkley's fate tested the strength of FDR's popularity and the unity of his own party. Roy Howard, manager of the Scripps-Howard news organization, warned Barkley in April he planned a coordinated attack to defeat Roosevelt. "Well, he said, "That's it. That's all we're--that's what we're interested in. We're interested in beating Mr. Roosevelt. And if we can beat you, we'll slap him between the eyes."

*Albert Benjamin "Happy" Chandler; U.S. Senator Alben Barkley, (left), after winning election as Senate Majority Leader*

"Many big businessmen not only feared Roosevelt, they hated him to a degree rarely seen in American history," observed authors James Burns and Susan Dunn in *The Three Roosevelts: Patrician Leaders Who Transformed America.*

Before Roosevelt returned to politics, he spent much of his time building the Roosevelt Institute for Rehabilitation in Warm Springs, Georgia, in 1927. He designed a car with controls he could operate himself and enjoyed long drives into the countryside. He stopped often, and visited with local residents. That bond, and their common sense and resilience, inspired him to return to public service.

And so later, during his popular fireside chats, when he derided those "calamity-howling executives with an income of $1,000 a day" objecting to an eight-hour day or a minimum wage, he remembered his rural friends on the back roads, their worries and struggles, and they remembered him. Determined to close the gap between the wealthy classes and the "forgotten man," he enlarged the mission of the federal government on an unprecedented scale.

In late 1937, the *Magazine of Wall Street* ticked off reasons why business owners like Howard raged Roosevelt was "piling on" too much at breakneck speed: a Supreme Court decision was pending on which businesses were subject to collective bargaining rules, a new National Recovery Act likely meant new regulations, and the controversial Supreme Court "packing plan" confirmed the President preferred exercising royal, rather than constitutional powers.

"Fiscal policy of administration is in a mess. Deficit, bond prices, tax prospects, spending program, credit control, inflation, deflation, all are mixed together. Subjected to conflicting counsel, Roosevelt probably will not follow definite policy but try to muddle through," editors gloomily predicted.

Newspaper and radio outlets large and small divided along partisan lines. Each new relief agency or government regulation—the Federal Emergency Recovery Act, Farmers' Home Administration, or the National Labor Relations Board-drew praise or damnation.

Taking time away from his efforts to rebuild McCracken County after the flood, Edwin Paxton, Sr. surprised his son by lifting the *Democrat's* policy not to "mess with any elections." The national recovery was still underway, his father explained, and continuity in administration policy was critical to ending the economic crisis.

Editors at *The Louisville-Times* and *The Courier-Journal* broke with the tradition as well, publishing an endorsement July 1:

"*The Courier-Journal* does not customarily take an editorial position in party primaries in Kentucky, but the Senatorial primary in the Democratic party this year transcends all ordinary bounds of importance. It is more vital than any usual party contest, more vital than any usual state election, for on its results hinges a good measure of the national prestige of President Franklin D. Roosevelt."

Ed Paxton, Jr. formally announced the newspaper's opposition to Chandler, and that the *Democrat* stood "100 per cent for Barkley. ...It's going to be a bitter, nasty sort of campaign. ..." the younger Paxton wrote to his father-in-law, George Goodman. "...but I'm taking bets and giving odds of up to 50,000 votes that the Senator will be re-elected."

The winter of 1938 was a prelude to the battle between the two popular Kentuckians. Henry supported Barkley and stood firm. In one column, he accused Chandler of attempting to steal votes for the upcoming election by pushing his purgation bill, and predicted Happy would soon "make a monkey of himself."

Kentucky's attorney general also opposed the bill, and he warned the Senate the administrative costs of paying county boards and workers to wipe voter names off the rolls could cost the counties nearly $3 million. An amendment reducing those costs followed, but the boards retained something of tremendous political value—the power to purge voters right up to the night before an election.

The timing of Happy's decision to "update" Kentucky's system of voter rolls was so blatantly corrupt that Henry reported "Chandler's bill is so manifestly vicious and improper that the docile Senate, which usually can be counted on to bend to the will of the chief executive, refused to accept it."

Ward's blunt commentary should have put him in exile, except it was a measure of his standing in the General Assembly that his colleagues respected his credibility, research skill and knowledge.

"At one time in the session, it was suggested by some administration leaders that any bills I sponsored be squelched because of my opposition to many administration proposals. That the suggestion didn't get far is evidenced by the fact that seven of my bills were passed by the House, which sets some sort of record for independently sponsored legislation for this session," he reported.

As the Purgation Act wound its way into the Kentucky Court of Appeals that spring, Roy Howard dispatched Thomas Stokes from Washington to investigate rumors WPA bosses were conducting a systematic campaign of coercing employees and benefit recipients into voting for Alben Barkley.

# 8 Victors and Victim

Stokes defended his series, stating "... that the WPA there (Kentucky) was deep into politics on behalf of Senator Alben W. Barkley and that the state governmental organization was deep in politics on behalf of Governor A.B. Chandler, his opponent, and that the whole affair was a grand scheme in which the tax payer is the victim."

"My name is Happy Chandler, Governor of Kentucky, 40 years old, married, a life-long Democrat and a victim of the WPA."

"Relief politics" ignited controversy early in Roosevelt's presidency. Democratic control in the White House now extended to state and local party officials administering hundreds of benefit programs, and Republicans and business owners bitterly resented it.

According to Stokes, the contest between Barkley and Chandler was a "grand political racket in which the taxpayer is the victim. ...The tangible prize is a $10,000 a year seat in the United States Senate for the next six years."

Reviewing a flood of citizen complaints, Democrat Morris Shepard of Texas, chair of the Senate Campaign Finance Committee, declared the "deplorable situation" in Kentucky should "arouse the conscience of the country." He sent a federal investigator and three aides to Kentucky on August 3 to monitor the "hotly fought" primary.

Ten and one half billion dollars in federal relief money was allocated to the states between 1933 and 1943. As early as 1934 and 1936, WPA chief Harry Hopkins received complaints from employees in Indiana and Pennsylvania that supervisors abused the system. The Finance Committee, responsible for enforcing legislation to curb Senate corruption, anticipated the 1938 election cycle would bring trouble, and Senator Shepperd sternly warned WPA administrators in 11 states to steer clear of "playing politics."

On June 6 1938, the Scripps Howard newspaper chain published the first installment of Stokes' series exposing how "the dirty hand of local politics" played out in the Bluegrass state.

Headlined "Vote Buying Bared in Kentucky. Funds Poured Out to Help Barkley; Foes' Aids Ousted. Chandler Fights Back with State Pay Roll, Hiring More Vote Getters," Stokes' colleagues described him as a "reliable, disinterested reporter," and they speculated his Georgia accent likely put many of the Kentuckians he interviewed at ease.

A tough and experienced correspondent, he understood Southerners and the South from previous assignments and "other exposes, notably of Southern sweatshop conditions and of Southern efforts to attract Northern industries through tax exemption and labor union freedom."

Traveling 1,400 miles by car, Stokes met with Tom Rhea's precinct organizers in Louisville, turned north into Campbell County, then followed roads east into the mining and mountain towns of Paintsville, then looped south into Harlan County. Next, he meandered north to stop in McKee, zigzagged back to the tobacco fields in Edmonton, then finished in west Kentucky at Madisonville.

In courthouses, cafés, post offices and WPA offices, Stokes asked a single question: Did any WPA official or state of Kentucky supervisor promise a reward (don't worry—you get to keep your job) or threaten revenge (I promise you—you'll be fired) if you did not vote as the bosses directed?

He confirmed that Goodman, "an amiable, vigorous, ruddy cheeked 62-year-old former mail order liquor dealer and former newspaper publisher from Paducah," mailed a written letter to staff in early March, warning that, "No employee of the W.P.A. in Kentucky shall respond to any request for lists of names or other timekeeping information except that specifically permitted by rules and regulations established by this administration."

Stokes interviewed employees who complained their District Directors compiled lists of worker names and voter affiliations for Barkley campaign organizers in 32 counties, who in turn pressured them to vote for Barkley.

His second installment detailed how a WPA District Director in east Kentucky called an employee meeting to announce he recently switched his party registration from Republican to Democrat—an example they all would be wise to follow.

From "top to bottom," Stokes confirmed "...the word has gone down the line that Mr. Barkley must go back to the Senate." The June 7, 8 and 10 installments, a political travelogue across Kentucky, revealed a growing list of complaints from quarry timekeepers and carpenters who resented pressure from supervisors to sign forms verifying their party affiliation or pledge cash contributions to the Barkley campaign.

The Bluegrass, a border state during the Civil War, was once again bitterly divided as kingmakers Tom Rhea and Dan Talbott arm wrestled for control of Barkley's Senate seat.

As Stokes crossed from one county into the next, Henry "started the Barkley publicity office with a borrowed typewriter and mimeograph machine and my wife doing the envelope stuffing. The Seelbach Hotel let us have office space—on credit."

The speed and convenience of digital texting decades away, Ward mailed typewritten instructions to Barkley: "If you can get us your speech, or excerpts, by noon Friday, we can take care of the papers all right. Of course, if that is impossible, we can manage. By all means, however, copies of the speech ought to be available on Saturday at Lexington. The earlier we get the advance, the better chance there is that the Sunday morning papers will give good and complete coverage to it. In case you haven't seen it, also enclosed is a copy of the first issue of *The New Dealer*. We had 200,000 copies printed and sent it to all counties in the state. We also have printed 50,000 posters with your picture and sent to every county."

Henry composed a column called "Today in Kentucky" distributed to newspapers statewide. While Stokes traveled from town to town, visiting restaurants, offices and courthouses, Henry's column focused on Chandler's record, and the "voter purgation" bill he was attempting to ram through the General Assembly.

Skilled at breaking down complex topics in a readable format, Henry sailed through an explanation of key points from a recent Court of Appeals ruling that "went to great lengths to correct glaring defects" in Chandler's bill.

Chandler's intent in the original bill was clear, and Henry explained its impact: "A political machine that desired to win an election by honest or dishonest methods could, through the purgation boards, cancel the registrations of thousands of voters known to be unfriendly to its candidate."

Arrange Henry's column and Stokes' fourth installment—"Fired for Refusal to Back Barkley, Say WPA Workers"—side by side, and the storytelling reveals Kentucky's finely tuned political machines rivaled the professionalism and workmanship of any world-class concert orchestra.

"As the campaign gets hotter-and it will be the hottest in years in Kentucky, where they are all hot, ..." Stokes reported Chandler supporters "frankly admit the political use of State employees and the application of political pressures. 'If I find a man on a State job who's not for Happy, I'll fire him,' snapped J. Dan Talbott, State Finance Commissioner and the real 'brains' behind governor Chandler's political career."

Stokes finished eating lunch at Joe's Place in McKee, and Joe suggested he meet interview Jack Frost, in charge of administering the "old age" pension rolls in Jackson County.

Wearing a button with the smiling face of Happy Chandler on his lapel, Frost introduced Stokes to his brother-in-law, Casper Ratts. They found Ratts (Barkley's Jackson County campaign manager and Frost's brother-in-law) "a slender gentleman, his straw hat cocked back on his head" lounging around inside WPA headquarters.

Stokes asked Ratts if the WPA was playing politics in McKee, and Ratts assured Stokes this was impossible—all but about 30 Jackson County voters were registered Republicans. Besides, he grinned, Jack was clearly playing politics for Chandler.

"They're putting on people in this county who were disqualified by us when I was on the old-age assistance," he said. Frost jumped up quickly to deny it. 'Not while I'm in charge,' replied Mr. Frost."

"There was a federal investigator through here the other day. He said my county was clean. But they've got three or four investigators working in Clay County. Pointing to his brother-in-law's Chandler button, the Barkley manager said: 'You ought not to be wearing that. The old-age assistance is half federal and half state.' (The federal government provides half the funds, while the State furnishes the other half and administers it.)"

'Well, I've got a right to wear half of it.' But the answer dwindled away. It didn't seem quite satisfactory. Abashed, Jack Frost looked down at his button and felt of it. This is politics in Kentucky in this turbulent political year," Stokes concluded.

In Washington, the Senate committee sifted through newspaper clippings, letters and telegrams, including one from a Boston blueblood in Cambridge, Massachusetts named Mrs. Henry Du Bois Tudor.

"The Kentucky mountaineers are not often considered of great importance in political campaigns," she scolded, "but just now their voting significance is being taking into high consideration by both factions of the Democratic party struggling for the senatorial primary election in the Blue Grass State. Senator Alben Barkley and Governor "Happy' Chandler are leaving nothing in the laps of the gods so far as the August 6$^{th}$ primaries are concerned."

Henry believed Barkley's denials he approved any coercion. "I took an active part as an official in the Barkley campaign organization. I know the policies that were decided upon and followed, and I know that the policy most stressed was that no effort to coerce or intimidate the WPA workers be made. Frankly, it was considered 'bad politics' for the campaign."

But Ward's punishing workload—coordinating print and radio deadlines, ad and speech copy, and writing a column kept him locked inside the Seelbach. Stuck behind a desk and typewriter, Stokes was out in the field, watching and listening first hand at how those campaigns were operated.

In June, Henry published a Gallup poll showing Barkley leading Chandler 2-1. He added and distributed a new four-page broadsheet called *The New Dealer—Published in the Interest of Good Government, Henry Ward, Editor.* "Barkley Has Earned Splendid Record, Consistent Supporter of Acts For People," Henry wrote, detailing the highlights of Barkley's 11$^{th}$ year in the U.S. Senate. Now serving as Majority Leader, his record included supporting public power, and a long list of New Deal programs benefiting Kentucky farmers, organized labor, shopkeepers and industry.

Ward believed the choice was simple: elect a selfish, ambitious man who intended to use a U.S. Senate seat as a stepping stone into the White House, or reelect the majority leader of the U.S. Senate, whose close working relationship with FDR benefited Kentuckians. Yet he admired Chandler's audacity—given the sheer weight of Barkley's record, any serious candidate needed an ego the size of Chandler's just to run the distance.

The *Lebanon Enterprise* published a full-page ad titled "The Miracle of the Loaves and Fishes" announcing a 20$^{th}$ Century miracle—a man who appeared out of nowhere. Young Governor Chandler reorganized a defunct state government, balanced the budget, retired the state's debts and "removed our unfortunates from their dungeons and placed them in light and airy asylums and reformatories. ... Why keep a man in office twiddling his thumbs, waiting for his time to expire, when so much is to be done at Washington? Let's show that humanity is capable of gratitude and send him to the United States Senate to help that other great American, Franklin D. Roosevelt, to the glorification of Kentucky, now and forever. Amen."

For Ben Johnson, Chandler's former ally, it was all too much. In a hand-written letter to Barkley, he scrawled "as yet, no one will accept the statement that he is comparable to Christ, but Happy is young yet."

On June 18 Barkley greeted a rain-soaked crowd of 5,000 people in Lexington—"a throng that filled the grandstand at the trotting track here and overflowed into the infield."

The Senator, a voracious reader who found it difficult to put down a book, was nicknamed the "Iron Man" after he barnstormed through every county during the Kentucky governor's race of 1923—and his reckless driving drew more attention than his campaign promises. Still energetic and vigorous, his extensive travel broadened his personal and political perspective.

Popular for his oratorical skills, his autobiography, *That Reminds Me*, aptly described his speaking style. Whether quoting irascible mountaineers or spinning a tale of sinister hell hounds bedeviling a devout Christian, Barkley affectionately embraced the resourceful and resilient spirit of the proud people of his state.

In Harry McPherson's classic book on the Washington political scene of the 1930s, 1940s and 1950s, he shared a story that illustrated Barkley's ability to connect, honestly and simply with his constituents, at times, in a hostile setting.

In the early 1940s, "Barkley was interrupted in the middle of a magnificent town square speech in eastern Kentucky when someone yelled 'How do you stand on FEPC?'"

FEPC, the Fair Employment Practices Act, barred employment discrimination on the basis of race or ethnicity. "Barkley surveyed the crowd. Eastern Kentucky, like Tennessee, had long been divided on the race issue. There were the grandchildren of Unionists and Confederates and copperheads in the audience; no one knew how many of each. At last Barkley quietly replied 'I'm all right on FEPC.' And went on with his speech."

Transport Barkley decades into the future, and it is likely his Facebook or Twitter platforms would have gone viral on a regular basis. The keynote speaker for the Democratic Party's national conventions during the 30s and 40s, he was a crowd favorite. During raucous proceedings in Chicago in 1940, the delegates cheered, stamped their feet, and roared with approval after he asserted that the Republican platform is "written in mud by the migratory feet of a weasel."

On that summer's day in 1938, he stood alone, un-coached and unscripted, backed by years of support for labor rights, aid for farmers, retirement benefits for railroad workers, improved housing, and veteran assistance.

"The record I have made during 25 years as a Congressman and a Senator, Barkley said, 'is written in the legislative history of these years ... it cannot be changed. I shall not seek to misrepresent or magnify it. I stand upon it. If I cannot stand upon it I have no right to stand at all. ..." Each time he mentioned President Roosevelt's name, he paused for the pounding applause to die away.

He did not mention his opponent's name, but he did repeat the official WPA line: "Every pensioner, every WPA worker, every highway employee and every employee of the state and national governments has a God-given right to vote as he pleases."

Yet on the subject of a free and impartial vote, Barkley had no right to stand at all: he killed a bill protecting WPA from politics early that spring, not once but twice.

In 1936, Senator Frederick Van Nuys sponsored a bill prohibiting WPA employees from endorsing political candidates, but it died quickly in the House. In 1937, Democratic Senator Carl Hatch of New Mexico tried again, attaching an amendment to a relief and recovery bill forbidding WPA employees from engaging in any form of political activity or endorsement.

Barkley delivered an impassioned speech against it, reported Washington columnist Raymond Clapper, that "laid bare as cynical a picture of democracy as Hitler could paint, and makes a mockery out of five years of fireside chats. It was a disturbing speech and those who will be most disturbed are the real friends of President Roosevelt."

"They are at liberty," Mr. Barkley said, " to roam around at their will or at the will of their boss or their organization, and indulge in politics to their heart's content, but we are proposing that anybody connected with a job under WPA or PWA or CCC or the AAA, or any other activity for which we appropriate money in this joint resolution, shall be tied with a rope to a tree so that he is helpless and cannot even speak unless he can whisper to the ear of somebody what his intentions are, while all those others who draw pay out of the Treasury of the United States are free to roam at will and play the political game to their heart's content."

Clapper got straight to the point. "[Barkley] explained that it wasn't fair to hog-tie the WPA workers this way when State highway employees were free to play politics."

Three weeks after Barkley's speech in Lexington, Harry Hopkins and George Goodman attacked Thomas Stokes' reporting, accusing him of bias and distorting the facts.

Stokes set the record straight: "... I had no other instructions than to write the facts as I found them. I had no axe to grind. I lay no claims to infallibility. I yield myself to the usual margin of error. I made a careful investigation, in good faith, and I stand on my conclusions."

Ralph Burton, the investigator for the Sheppard Committee, compiled a list of 22 complaints that mirrored Stokes' reporting alleging coercion and intimidation in violation of the Corrupt Practices Act. The Committee forwarded the charges to Hopkins, who denied all but two.

Hopkins was required to respond to the allegations in Washington, and he informed the Senate Committee that James Boddie, Director of WPA District 1, compiled lists of WPA workers who were registered voters and sent them to county campaign chairmen, and he took "appropriate administrative action" against another WPA foreman who "chatted" with an old friend and coworker, after a political rally for Governor Chandler during the Senate primary.

Hopkins released a 15-page statement inferring Stokes' reporting was biased. He acted in good faith and with good intentions, he declared, reiterating WPA workers followed the rules. Hopkins complained it was not possible "in a far-flung organization covering the 3,300 counties in America, with 64,000 projects and 2,700,000 workers" to control "over zealous partisans." Clearly, he resented any insinuation a "planned and organized political campaign" played out on his watch.

But Stokes fired back that the WPA investigators Hopkins sent to Kentucky were under pressure to keep the boss from looking bad, and so "It is only human for them to say 'it isn't so.'" As Hopkins and Goodman issued daily denials, Kentucky newspapers reprinted a lively stump speech delivered by Henry at a picnic rally in New Hope in mid-July.

Surrounded by friends and neighbors, he praised Barkley as "...the biggest man in the United States Congress ... a man whose experience, qualifications and prestige fit him for the position." Never forget, he told them, that many of the supporters cheering Chandler on represented the Roosevelt-haters back East, fueling Chandler's self-serving ambition.

Quoting Chandler's boast "I have kept my promises made in 1935," Henry asserted that "... For the truth of the matter is that Chandler's trail as Governor is completely blanketed with broken promises," and he ticked them off, one by one.

Chandler repealed the sales tax but substituted other taxes in its place, deducted campaign contributions from state employee paychecks, and bragged his state government reorganization saved money and streamlined efficiency, that is, until he announced his candidacy for the Senate, and started adding state jobs again (in exchange for votes.) He padded state payrolls as the August 6 election neared, failed to free the toll bridges and reneged on funding the old age pension.

Finished with facts, Henry piled on the adjectives, declaring: "Happy Chandler has been the most domineering, the most dictatorial, the most ruthless and the most vindictive Governor this state has ever seen."

"Chandler is making a play for the wets and the dries. He double-crossed both at the last session of the Legislature. And he is double-crossing most of the fellows who are supporting him now, because he has promised most of them that he will support them for Governor in 1939. ...Chandler and Dan Talbott will double-cross Fred Wallis. They will double-cross Keen Johnson, because Dan Talbott doesn't like Keen Johnson or Fred Wallis and Dan Talbott is the boss and will pick the state administration's candidate for Governor in 1939."

His speech described the way Kentucky politics *actually* worked, yet he urged the crowd to back Barkley, to ensure a "real government 'of the people, by the people and for the people.'"

# 9 A "Decent Fella"

> Ward told Pearce he was overdrawn at his bank the summer of '38 because "funds were so tight I didn't feel like charging everything I spent to the campaign. ...I well remember how sore I was."

The Sheppard Committee released its final report in January 1938. In Kentucky, state employees contributed over $70,000 to Chandler; the Barkley campaign received $24,000 from WPA workers and employees in four other federal agencies.

They agreed that Chandler's supporters intimidated and coerced state employees for contributions. No evidence was submitted to link Barkley directly to any violations. Noting his denials lacked credibility, they permitted Barkley to retain his Senate seat.

*New York Times* columnist Arthur Krock concluded "There are many persons in this country, aside from Republicans, with selfish interest in discrediting any New Deal effort, who believe the administration, and especially Mr. Hopkins, turned their backs on political activities they knew were going on. But even if these critics have no basis for their belief, the Sheppard report sustains them indirectly. What it says, in effect, is that personal honesty at the top is insufficient to keep off the hand of dirty local politics. That in itself is the requiem of Mr. Hopkins' WPA."

During that election cycle, campaign spending for radio, newspaper and periodical advertising in 11 states revealed Kentucky ranked third—higher than the much larger states of California, Maryland and Pennsylvania.

Near the end of the campaign, Henry recalled one particular meeting with Tom Rhea that stood out in his memory. A week before the primary, Rhea called his team together for final instructions. "And Tom Rhea said, 'I've got to have a hundred thousand dollars set aside for use on election day.' And I said, '*For God's sake*, what are you going to do with a hundred thousand dollars?' And he says –Tom said, 'Well, think about it. 120 counties. That's less than a thousand dollars a county. ...' And I said, '*You* haven't been out politicking. We'll *talk* about it. What *can* you do with less than a thousand dollars a county? ... Well, it was staggering to me..." he trailed off in a disgusted tone. "...I learned later on that they'd saved $35,000 out of the [Barkley] campaign to use on the governor's race next year to start drawing ground as they can. Of course, I was—I didn't support any of them. ..."

Relieved the campaign was finished, Ward's column remained popular. He mixed folksy hometown news with stories about his family life, and shared some amusing episodes he experienced in the House of Representatives.

In 1936, he introduced a bill to increase funding for West Kentucky Industrial College (a Black teachers college at that time), that stalled in the House. Ward sent a letter to every House member, asking them to confirm what their intent was when they voted for the bill, so that he and a co-sponsor could get it moving along again.

He published his favorite reply: "I haven't the faintest idea what my intention was, and can only suggest that you address a letter to Colonel M.J. Brennan, care of Democratic City Headquarters, Louisville, Kentucky, and ask him just what I had in mind when I voted for this bill."

He jokingly admitted: "It's always been my ambition to have a lobbyist present me with a lot of money to use my influence one way or the other so I could get up on floor of the House, wave the money around and make a rip-snorting speech."

He described teaching his daughter, Pat, to ride her bike, and consoling her after the family dog died. He summarized a *Forbes* magazine survey of 15,000 American business executives, that revealed "the business men who voiced their opinions in this poll were 77.1 percent against the New Deal recovery programs," followed by a description of how the oldest municipal water filtering system in the United States operated.

Following the Barkley campaign, Henry happily returned to *doing things*—drafting bills to improve water quality and increase the state park budget. The parks were "my first love and one (in) which I had the deepest personal interest" he told Pearce during the interview.

"I had been very much interested in parks and had worked like hell to get a big increase in appropriations for parks. I don't know why—I'd always been interested in agriculture. I had worked as a newspaperman fairly closely with the Farm Bureau in Paducah. I had—was very close to Bill Johnstone, who was then county agent in Paducah, and we, with the newspapers, sponsored the first soil conservation district in Kentucky in McCracken County.

"And we got it established as a watershed which served, you know, the hometown. So, I was very much interested in following the soil conservation program from its very inception. I became interested in water, as a resource."

At that time, Ward recalled the lack of any local or state sanitation standards, and communities along the Ohio River were growing deeply concerned about the pollution. Residents noticed migratory bird populations declining, and it was no longer safe to fish or swim in the rivers or their tributaries. Beginning in 1936, both Congress and the states understood the need for to improve water sanitation. Meetings and conferences between states and delegates continued for years, and Congress recently approved federal aid for construction of sewage treatment plants to reduce pollution.

In anticipation of that federal action, Kentucky joined 7 states to form the Ohio River Valley Sanitation Compact, a pledge to cooperatively prevent and control water pollution. On January 18, 1940, Henry introduced a bill authorizing Kentucky's membership in the organization, and was later elected chair of the Sanitation Commission in 1952.

A large number of states lacked any minimum public health standard to protect drinking water, or required businesses or homes to dispose of sewage and waste in a safe or sanitary manner. Before 1948, just one percent of residential or industrial waste was treated. Over one-half of the improved navigable waterways of the Ohio River basin flowed into Kentucky—but "La Belle Rivière" (beautiful river) looked and smelled like a cesspool. Runoff that originated from steel mills and coke plants in the upper Ohio Valley sickened people from Pittsburgh to Paducah.

Every year on the first Saturday in May, thoroughbreds pounded down the homestretch at Churchill Downs in a world famous two-minute horse race. Elsewhere in the Ohio Valley, livestock farmers and horse breeders set another record—the Commission announced Cincinnati's daily water contamination load "was equivalent to 720 dead horses -and that this amounted to the discharge of one dead horse every two minutes."

In 1948, delegates (including Henry) formed the Ohio River Valley Water Sanitation Commission, to negotiate a compact to reduce pollution that threatened public health—causing cases of typhoid, illness and rashes and to restore the waterways so that the public could enjoy them for their beauty and recreation.

The questions were complex as they reviewed reports identifying the stew of oil, salt, phenol, acids and raw sewage dumped into the public waterways. There were no simple answers. What action should be taken against a hog farmer, they debated, dumping a dead, diseased carcass in the Ohio River, where it floats into a waterworks intake in Indiana? The recent congressional funding and the compact provided real hope progress could be made preventing pollution and improving public health.

The compact was initially criticized for lacking any effective enforcement powers; in 1966, a *New York Times* article announced a "New Era on Ohio River -Recreation is on Rise as Clean Up Drive Reduces Pollution," as the reporter praised "a river that now looks clean and sparkling, a river that now offers many wide stretches for safe swimming."

Henry often explained that "conservation" meant much more than a park or forest survey. He praised Kentucky for its beauty and abundance of natural resources, and explained it gave him great satisfaction to contribute to laws or policies that promoted clean air, clean water and the state's scenic beauty.

After the 1942 session ended, state politics, Ward concluded, was as exciting as digging a ditch. "To re-draft a bill 71 pages in length and, so far as possible, reconcile the divergent views of numerous persons and groups is no small task. As a member of a sub-committee, I can testify to that."

Another newspaperman and friend, J. Howard Henderson from the *Louisville Courier Journal,* published a column titled *"An Unregenerate Rebel Mourns the Softening of Henry Ward."* Henderson missed the old Henry, the "anti" who steered clear of partisan bickering and whose political independence kept people off balance. He lamented how "a fellow craftsman (had) now turned organization politician. In former years, we gloried in his spunk. He was a newspaperman's kind of legislator, independent in thought and action, not striving for official approval, unmoved by official frowns."

The legislative sessions of 1940 and 1942 proved Henderson wrong. Legislators trusted Ward for accurate facts and information. If he made a promise, he kept it. He traded "raising hell" for sitting through hours of committee meetings or testimony to draft bills that earned enough votes from both sides to pass, and it increased his effectiveness.

What Henderson did not know was that Ward's next crusade—an obsession, both his colleagues and critics charged—was to pass a bill permitting TVA to sell electric power generated by a proposed new dam at Gilbertsville. The Kentucky dam was the capstone for the massive TVA works project that President Roosevelt predicted in 1933 would employ thousands of workers. Henry's interest in the potential of TVA to transform west Kentucky began the day Roosevelt signed the bill into law, and he regularly reported on its progress in his column.

But the private power industry bitterly resisted TVA, and historian David McCraw explained what shaped their opposition: "The power industry...grew from two mutually hostile traditions: a private tradition, which started it and built most of its network of generators and high-tension lines; and a public tradition, which tried to curb private financial and political excesses, sometimes by going into the business itself. On a collision course since the turn of the twentieth century, the two traditions met head-on when Franklin D. Roosevelt entered the White House in 1933."

In 1940, Henry fiercely defended the public tradition, intent on exposing the industry's self-serving objections to the TVA. He hoped to persuade Governor Keen Johnson to accept a TVA enabling bill, because in west Kentucky, the electricity generated by the agency would cut the cost residents paid for electricity in half. Howard Henderson hinted Henry was "selling out" by cooperating with Johnson, ending Ward's "anti-administration" streak. Ward fired back, "Howard, you may be right, but there's one thing I've learned about being in Frankfort. You have a lot of fun being "anti" all the time, but you don't get much done. You can accomplish a hell of a lot more by going on and working with him [Governor Keen Johnson]—he's a decent fella. And I did."

# 10 "They'll Build that Dam or Bust"

> "Do you have to make four or five arguments over T.V.A. every morning and have a fight over it every afternoon?'" complained Representative Sam Milam, Russellville."

In 1933, the business magazine *Forbes* hired writer and poet James Agee to travel to the Tennessee Valley to compose a feature describing the Roosevelt Administration's "great experiment"—the multi state TVA dam project. President Roosevelt created TVA by executive order in 1933. Conceived as an agricultural, flood control and conservation program, the goal was to promote the "unified development of a region."

The 23-year-old Tennessee native returned with a literary masterpiece—tracing the course of a river that roared "like blown smoke through the floodgates of Wilson Dam, to slide becalmed along the crop-cleansed fields of Shiloh, to march due north across the spreading marshes toward the valley's end where finally, at the toes of Paducah, in one wide glass golden swarm the water stoops forward and continuously dies into the Ohio."

Senator Barkley spent four frustrating years seeking Congressional appropriations for the Kentucky Dam, and he used the flood of 1937 as a catastrophic flourish to his plea. Construction and excavation for a "large reservoir with more than 4,000,000 acre-feet of flood storage," started in July 1938.

Common adjectives depicting TVA projects and its scope centered around its size, praising men and machines for carrying out these massive, bold engineering feats first, to relieve unemployment, then to increase power capacity for war production to aid European allies during World War II.

*Photo from National Archives at College Park, Public domain, via Wikimedia Commons*

Yet one elegantly designed Art Deco style booklet likely left west Kentucky residents bewildered by its dismal description of the place they called home: "In the summer of 1933, if a flyer had climbed into his plane at Paducah, and made a leisurely trip following the Tennessee River for 650 twisting miles, he would have seen a sluggish stream, heavy with brown silt, pushing its load down to the Mississippi. ...Had he been an agronomist he would have known that the color of the river meant a freight worth countless millions sweeping itself into the Gulf of Mexico, that the gullies meant land destroyed almost beyond hope of rehabilitation, that no humans, however, industrious, could maintain any reasonable standard of living on this land. Worse still, he would have known that to wring out a miserable existence these farmers were destroying what was left of the land as surely as if they had set out to dynamite away every last foot of fertile topsoil."

*The Kentucky Project,* the final report compiled by the U.S. Army Corp of Engineers, documents the transformation of west Kentucky from an agricultural backwater to a recreational powerhouse. Drillers with explosive charges hiked through the valley searching for a specific type of bedrock strong enough to last: "One range or line of holes drilled across the river at the Kentucky site was completed late in the fall of 1935 and disclosed a continuous rock line from abutment to abutment." Tracing their fingers over the map to the spot where the crews hit rock, they discovered a suitable location, at a place formed from "dense, dark gray, cherty Fort Payne limestone" at river mile 22.4 near Gilbertsville.

The dam served as the capstone of the immense system of nine dams and locks that transformed the Tennessee into a 652-mile-long river highway. "Because of its unusual size, Kentucky Reservoir construction required the purchase of more land than any other TVA reservoir project and the evacuation of more families than any other project except Norris."

As construction workers moved into their new housing at the job site, McCracken County voters re-elected Henry in 1940. In a full-page ad in the *Sun-Democrat* he appealed for their support:

"I have to work to make a living for myself and family, so I cannot devote much of my time to campaigning between now and the Democratic primary on August 5. Furthermore, the office of State Representative pays about enough to take care of expenses, so if a Representative is really going to be honest, he can't spend much money getting elected. ...I am convinced that at the 1940 session I will be in a position to be of far greater service to the people than ever before. . . .If conditions are favorable, I shall ask my fellow members to elect me as Speaker of the House, which will give me an opportunity to render constructive service for the people of this state."

Henry admitted he made "some mistakes...but my heart has been right," even though "I made some enemies, too." Henry believed government's biggest challenge was "...reducing the cost of local government, and [I] ask you to permit me to continue my work."

A veteran of the 1934 sales tax fight, he confirmed he would vote for any necessary and reasonable tax increase. "I realize the enemies of these taxes will fight me because I propose them, but I don't like to kid the people about increasing the benefits of government without telling them where I propose to get the money."

For his 4th term, the *short* list of bills he planned to sponsor including giving cities the authority to build golf courses, consolidating the office of jailer and sheriff, to tax pari-mutuel betting, give the State Railroad Commission authority to hire experts to mediate freight rate disputes, reduce the cost of auto transfers, provide a legal process for removing a city manager, create a Kentucky Division of Markets, reduce pollution in the Ohio River, create a grading system for strawberries *and* exempt municipal recreational projects from state taxes.

Still one of the youngest legislators in the House, (he was 31), his workload increased after local officials, members of the Kentucky Farm Bureau, the Kentucky Municipal League, and its new spin-off, the Kentucky Public Power League, asked Henry to sponsor an enabling bill permitting the state to purchase hydroelectric power produced at the Kentucky Dam.

In January 1942, 40 representatives from the far western corner of Kentucky—Ballard, Calloway, Carlisle, Fulton, Graves, Hickman, Marshall, and McCracken—urged Governor Johnson to support Henry's bill. An enabling bill giving Kentucky the right to resell electricity at a reduced cost benefited residents and attracted new industry.

Educator James H. Richmond, president of Murray State College, warned that "Kentucky was once regarded as a 'detour state' because its highways were not modern. ...there is a danger that we may become a detour state, industrially speaking, if we permit new industries to skip over us because of inadequate electric power supplies."

Proposed TVA service territory included all of Tennessee, parts of Alabama, Mississippi, and, potentially, parts of Kentucky. In west Kentucky, when residents turned on their lamps at night, "The Kentucky rate thus established is 42% higher than the Tennessee rate," a state which had already accepted TVA power.

In an unpublished history of rural electrification in Kentucky, author Gary Luhr explained a key difference between the REA and the TVA acts. "Under

TVA, a state had first claim on any electricity generated within its borders. Four electric cooperatives along Kentucky's southern edge already distributed TVA power, and the Gilbertsville project could supply low-cost electricity for other Kentucky co-ops as well as municipal utilities."

Eager to take advantage of the lower costs, Middlesboro city officials petitioned the circuit court for the right to contract with TVA. But private power company attorneys sued, arguing Kentucky's constitution barred a city from negotiating with a federal agency.

At the dam site, as gigantic earthmovers discharged diesel fumes and thick black smoke into the sky, and laborers wrestled steel pilings into the ground, the court ruled Kentucky's constitution barred the right of cities to contract directly with the TVA to purchase electricity.

Henry acknowledged the pending court case and strength of the power industry's opposition weakened the bill's chance for success. Governor Johnson and Henry met informally to discuss it, but Johnson expressed concern the utility's tax-exempt status reduced city, county and state revenues.

Utility executives launched a well-funded publicity campaign accusing the agency of "forcing" Kentucky to accept TVA power. Legislators' desks were covered with flyers denouncing "Ward Bill 146," because it "demands special privilege legislation," "threatens tax losses to cities, counties and the state," and "denies to the people of Kentucky their inherent state's right to …control…the utilities that serve them."

In full page newspaper ads using bold, black font nearly an inch high, Kentucky Utilities officials painted a grim picture of a dark future clouded by the government overreach: "…an issue that vitally affects every taxpayer…everyone who works in a mercantile business…every doctor and dentist…every farmer… every freeborn American who likes to call his soul his own."

In the Kentucky House and Senate, a majority of legislators simply did not care—because TVA's impact was limited to west Kentucky, far away from their districts.

Yet Henry believed Governor Johnson would support it if the issue of taxes could be resolved. Johnson became Governor in 1939, after the unexpected death of Marvel Mills Logan created a vacant seat in the U.S. Senate. Happy Chandler filled Logan's seat, and Lieutenant Governor Johnson finished Happy's term.

The owner and publisher of the *Anderson News* in Lawrenceburg, and *The Richmond Register*, he easily won a second term in the general election. Long active in state democratic politics, his low-key temperament and executive skill marked a period of measured and thoughtful calm in Kentucky politics.

As Henry worked under the guidance of TVA officials and its attorney, J.C. Fitts, on the draft bill, Johnson sent John Kirtley, chair of the Public Service Commission, on 1500-mile fact finding trip through Tennessee, Mississippi and Alabama, to consult with other states who successfully negotiated for TVA power.

During the 1940 session, Henry's bill never made it out of the House. After a hot debate on the floor, it was defeated by a vote of 53-27. It gave cities the right to buy or build an electric distribution system, and to purchase electricity directly from TVA. The distribution systems, classified as "public works" were financed by revenue bonds approved by the voters, and it exempted TVA from the jurisdiction of the state Public Service Commission.

That exemption provoked strong opposition because it curtailed the private industry's control over the Commission. Afterward, Henry warned the fight was just beginning—"As I see it, the issue is reaching such importance that to oppose it strikes me as being close to treason against the state."

Yet a certain amount of self-interest sparked his frustration. Eight west Kentucky counties stood to benefit from access to TVA's lower rates, and according to historian George Humphreys "...it could be argued that Henry and his western Kentucky colleagues were driven by a more narrow, regional interest. All politics are local, as they say!"

"When you are in trouble, it seems that more trouble always comes around for a visit," Henry wrote. "It seems that most people could agree that Kentucky cities ought to have a right to contract with the TVA. To withhold the benefits of TVA power from them would be to block their opportunity to share in the progress that has come to other communities in the TVA area. A state administration which would refuse to make it possible for cities of the state to acquire these benefits would be going right smack against the best interest of the people it is supposed to represent. But there are selfish interests which look after themselves first, and unfortunately, the selfish interests often times have great influence in political circles because they know how to get control of those in power. I am expecting a hard fight to secure the enactment of fair legislation at the 1942 session to enable the cities to get TVA power. Contrary to what private utility executives may say, the private utilities will be in here fighting with everything they have against the passage of this legislation. Governor Johnson holds the answer to the question in his hands. The majority of the legislators will not be interested particularly, since the majority of the counties represented in the legislature have no immediate prospect of benefitting from TVA power."

He sought guidance from TVA officials on how to structure the bill in advance of the session of 1942, and a cascade of events at home and abroad worked in his favor.

After Germany attacked Britain in September of 1940, President Roosevelt expressed his sympathy to Prime Minister Winston Churchill, but that was all he could do. Too many Americans, nearly 20 years later, still grieved their losses from the first World War and the U.S. remained neutral in the conflict.

Roosevelt pursued a second option—equipping Britain material to defend itself. In the spring of 1941, Congress passed the Lend Lease Act, authorizing the manufacture and shipment of war material to aid Britain. The agreement created an urgent need for increased U.S. electrical generating capacity to honor those defense contracts.

TVA pivoted from teaching farmers how to rotate crops and switch to contour plowing, to powering up the factories that produced the aluminum, copper, rubber and steel that helped save Europe.

In the winter of 1941, Reynolds Metals Company, based in Louisville, won a $15 million dollar defense contract to supply Britain with aluminum. Paducah officials hoped to persuade Reynolds to build the new plant in McCracken County. But the plant required a minimum electrical capacity of 22,000 watts to operate. Robert Watt determined it would take Kentucky Utilities at least 11 months to increase capacity to supply Reynolds. Reynolds built its new facility in Alabama, a state that had already accepted TVA power.

More bad news arrived when the Kentucky Court of Appeals ruled that until the state constitution was amended or a new law passed, the constitution prevented the state from purchasing power from a federal dam located on its own soil. The ruling barred TVA from selling electricity directly to Middlesboro or any other city in Kentucky.

In January 1942, Henry and forty other advocates from west Kentucky met with Governor Johnson to secure his support for TVA. During the meeting, local officials noted "...that Representative Ward has been and is the leader at Frankfort in carrying on the campaign for proper enabling legislation [and] the group agreed to urge Representatives and Senators from their various counties to support him in his efforts."

TVA advocates assumed that the bombing of Pearl Harbor, Roosevelt's declaration of war on Japan, and the loss of the aluminum plant would soften the utility industry's stance against an enabling bill, but they were wrong. Executives and attorneys doubled down on efforts to influence public opinion against it, and persuade legislators to vote "no." One writer characterized their resistance as a "copperhead type of opposition against the bill in whatever form it might take."

As Americans remained glued to newspaper and radio reports from Europe, Kentucky newspaper editors were suprised to receive a letter from *Sentinel-Echo* newspaper publisher Russell Dyche urging opposition to the bill. His letter made front pages across the state, headlined "Publisher Charges TVA Wants to Wreck Utility."

Dyche accused "little men with large ambitions...for destroying human freedom...Government in competition with private business has no rightful place in Kentucky, nor in these United States." The reference to "little men" aimed at Henry, members of the Kentucky press believed Dyche's letter crossed a line of professional ethics.

But Dyche made a serious miscalculation. He viewed Henry primarily as a newspaper editor who worked part time as a legislator. After the Speaker of the House, Joe Robinson became ill, Governor Johnson appointed Henry to serve as interim Speaker. Ward's promotion boosted his morale and supplied extra leverage to move the hearings along.

No surprise then, that Ward ordered Dyche's letter be entered into the record as "opposition testimony," because it unfairly aroused the "prejudices and emotion of Kentucky newspaper publishers, and that there is no real foundation for [his] charge."

Hearings on the bill opened in January, 1942, and the first witness, Robert Watt, condemned the legislation, calling it unfair and socialistic. If it passed, he warned, "We shall say goodbye to all privately owned, tax paying utilities."

On February 3, a packed gallery listened to the testimony of William Fitts, Jr., chief counsel for TVA. Fitts denied that TVA was promoting a market in Kentucky, because power from the Gilbertsville Dam, he said, could be sold to better advantage elsewhere. It was up to the General Assembly to decide whether Kentucky would receive the power. 'If you don't want TVA, it is not my business to sell it to you,' he said. '[But] in selling power to the city at wholesale, we must make contracts with certain agreements as to rates, revenue and accounting methods.'"

Opponent S.L. Blakely, an attorney for Union Power, registered his objections to the bill. As Henry questioned him about certain points in his testimony, both men quickly lost their tempers. "And now, Mr. Ward, I have finished my speech. You may ask me what I think of TVA," said Blakely.

"You have shown by your untrue accusations what you think of it," Henry replied. "I resent your stupid insolence, Mr. Ward," the speaker retorted. "What I said was not untrue."

Blakely then approached the committee table, "...and the two men shook with anger as they faced each other across the narrow desk top." "Look here, sir," Ward said, "I represent the people of Kentucky. You are up here representing a private utility." "You mean I can't talk?" Blakey demanded. The committee chair, Charles Montgomery, ended the confrontation: "Your time is up, Mr. Blakely, Sit down."

As Chairman Montgomery moved to end the day's testimony, John Kirtley, a former Speaker of the House, asked to be heard. Kirtley was infuriated by a recent column of Henry's that charged "I can testify that the head of another private utility company in Kentucky told me, in the presence of a high state official, that he had declined to contribute to a 'jackpot' being raised to defeat the TVA enabling act."

Just ten years earlier, Henry scoffed at threats from the bootleggers and gamblers he taunted in his newspaper column. In the winter of 1942, he confronted the chair of the Public Service Commission, who, backed by powerful industry executives, played a high stakes game of influence. Yet this time, Henry's authority as Speaker and the rules of the chamber were on his side, forcing Kirtley to play by the rules.

"Did you want to appear for the bill or against the bill?" Ward asked. "Neither," Kirtley snapped. "I presumed I was to be called upon for what little information I could give on the subject." Ward replied he could appear at any time and say anything he wanted to. Kirtley stormed out of the chamber. Yet Henry simply had to have the last word.

Kirtley turned and stomped out the side door as Ward shouted, "I am sure you can't come here in opposition to this bill without registering as an opposition speaker!"

Ward was not grandstanding—he was angry. That week, Henry learned the PSC accepted a version of an enabling bill prepared by Kentucky Utilities attorneys, but Kirtley instructed the Legislative Council to submit it under the Commission's name. Ward served three terms in the House with Kirtley, and during many discussions, Ward remembered "He has fought public ownership at every turn. He once told me he is just constitutionally opposed to public ownership."

Kirtley returned the next day and testified for almost two hours. He argued the bill interfered with states' rights, and exempted TVA from paying taxes. Exempting TVA from the jurisdiction of the PSC gave TVA an unfair advantage over the competition.

Ward listened closely, and when the objections appeared reasonable, he amended the bill. Revisions included structuring in lieu tax payments to recover an estimated 50% loss in local revenues resulting from TVA's nonprofit status; required a voter referendum for construction of new plants and revenue bonds authorized to pay for their construction; and the elimination of competition between the REA and TVA.

The provision requiring annual tax payments marked another state and national "first" for TVA and Kentucky. These negotiations were tedious, detailed and complex—the kind of challenge that energized Henry. Under the guidance of TVA officials, he revised a complex and technical piece of legislation that sorted out jurisdiction, exemptions, rules for territories and distribution systems.

At the midnight hour, negotiation stalled over taxes, and he inserted a provision that required TVA to replace the amount of state, county and municipal taxes lost under the distribution contracts. It solved the problem, and Kentucky became the first state to require TVA to compensate a state for lost taxes.

As Henry raced to finalize the bill for a Senate floor vote, the news Kirtley submitted Kentucky Utilities' version of the bill to the Council ended Governor Johnson's silence, and he struck out at Kirtley "with cold, cutting fury."

He agreed with Kirtley's statement during his testimony that it "...should not be taken by anyone as representing the views and position of the governor of the Commonwealth of Kentucky. Mr. Kirtley is absolutely correct in that statement," said Johnson. "I don't have to take insults from anybody," Kirtley snapped, and he resigned from the Commission.

Johnson arrived at his decision to support the bill after careful consideration. In the House, the bill passed by a vote of 85 to 10, but Johnson focused on another number. The deaths of 38 Kentuckians at Pearl Harbor, barely two months before, were fresh in his mind. The nation now at war, the Kentucky Dam would increase U.S. generating capacity crucial to an Allied victory.

In a speech broadcast statewide over the radio, Johnson addressed the Senate in chambers prior to debate. "I implore you in the name of the inarticulate masses of Kentucky who will be benefited in years to come to enact this legislation into law," declared Johnson.

The choice to accept TVA power rested with the voters, he said, and he batted away the industry's argument TVA be placed under state jurisdiction: "By what strange logic do these critics justify the argument that municipal plants, using TVA current, should be under the Public Service Commission?"

Despite claims to the contrary, he reiterated TVA must pay local taxes, and that both consumers and manufacturers would benefit from lower rates. Cost estimates projected a residential savings of $3 million per year on light bills, and "The savings to industrial and commercial users of electricity would be approximately $4 million a year. That sum is a million and a half dollars more than the total state income tax collected last year from corporations who are the industrial and commercial consumers of electricity."

Johnson tapped out a staccato rhythm to his plea:

...It is *shortsighted* to stand in the way of progress. It is *stupid* to stand in the way of labor-saving inventions. You cannot hold back the dawn. It is impossible to keep the sun from rising. It is just as impossible to expect to be able by legislative action to build a wall along the Kentucky-Tennessee line so high that it will exclude cheap TVA power from Kentucky forever...
*I have never had a stronger conviction on any question of public policy.* No public issue has ever appeared clearer to me than this... It is a momentous question. If you solve it correctly, it will hasten the dawn of a new day, with new opportunities in which Kentucky will go forward to a richer fulfillment of her destiny.

The Senate opened debate and the Governor stayed to watch. Republican D.C. Jones, from Harlan, drew laughter as he declared "The straps are around my ankles, and around my wrists. My head is shaved, I am ready for TVA juice, I move the previous question."

His motion failed. Senator Earle Clements moved the bill be amended to require that any municipal utility referendum be decided by a vote of 2/3 of the eligible voters, instead of a simple majority. Senator Jones proposed an amendment to bar cities from establishing plants (potentially seeking to buy cheaper TVA power), in direct competition with any privately owned utility in their territory.

Democrat E.O. Moore, the Senate Majority Leader, angrily protested that if senators voted for Clements' amendment, "...TVA will never see the light of day in Kentucky." Both amendments failed, and the Senate approved the bill by a vote 32-6.

Governor Johnson signed House Bill 142 into law, and in April, Henry's friends in Paducah organized a testimonial dinner honoring his 10-year anniversary in public service. Held at the Hotel Ritz in Paducah, the ballroom held 250 people. 260 were seated, but one hundred more were turned away.

Governor Johnson presented Henry with a "handsomely decorated scroll" citing his continuous devotion to unselfish causes. The *Courier Journal* praised him for leading the charge as "the Bull Moose of the opposition." Ward, a genuinely modest person, was moved by the tributes.

That show of support convinced him it was time to run for state wide office, and he filed to run for Lieutenant Governor.

Ward ran for state wide office twice. Each time his campaign was negatively impacted by timing and history. In 1942, Kentucky's election cycle took a backseat to the second world war.

For the past 10 years, Henry spent most of his time "taking a crack" at doing all the things he believed would help the people of his state. To win a statewide election, his time should have been spent building a loyal network of county contacts, many of whom traded their support for state jobs.

Kentucky voters accustomed to Senator Barkley's rambling folk tales and bursts of song from Happy Chandler could not relate to the gruff, no nonsense newspaperman warning them the business of government did not belong in the hands of "back slappers" or "glamour boys." Henry fought for the way government *should work*—but it's not the way government and politics *did work*—a line Henry refused to cross.

## 11 First Rate Candidate—Third Place Finish

> "And because Keen encouraged me, I ran for Lieutenant Governor in...'43. There were three of us in the race. I was doing pretty well, although I was such a novice and thought, hell, I don't know anything about state politics, didn't have any money, didn't have the organization. I was relying on Keen because he said that he was going to endorse me."

In the summer of 1940, Henry's column gradually shifted from state politics and news that Paducah's No. 2 hook and ladder truck, its clutch worn out, would be towed to fires, to U.S. protests over European censorship of American mail, and France and Britain's attempts to blockade Germany.

During that decade, a steady stream of radio broadcasts and newspaper headlines about the war dominated daily American life. As people listened to their radios, read newspapers and watched newsreels, casualties and death, rationing, shortages, and punishing work schedules tested our national character. A mix of guarded optimism, tenacity and personal resolve carried the Allies to victory in 1945.

The Third Congressional Session was "...the longest in American history, which sat nearly every day between January 3, 1940, and January 3, 1941, [and put] issues concerning the war front and center. The Compulsory Military Training

Bill alone consumed 302 pages of debate in the Congressional Record in the House, and 665 in the Senate."

Public opinion lagged behind Congressional support for the Allies. In historian Ira Katznelson's study of the New Deal, *Fear Itself,* he cites a *Forbes Magazine* public opinion survey that reported 54% of Americans opposed fighting the war. Congressional members from the southern states played a key role in changing public opinion, he observed, and their attitude "...made all the difference. Ever since World War I, a curiously provincial internationalism—motivated by local concerns but looking assertively forward—had emerged in the region."

They acknowledged the isolationist views of their colleagues were understandable, and reflected their sensitivity to the "...fears of many of their German, Italian, and Dutch constituents, whose memories of World War I still remained. ..." Yet the delegation from the south controlled "...the key foreign relations and military affairs committees, [and] their nearly unanimous support for activist overseas policies made it possible" for President Roosevelt to justify aid to Europe.

Henry's newspaper column is a "life and times" perspective into how the coming war impacted his family, friends, neighbors and community. He often shared research about national trends and public opinion. A *Fortune Magazine* survey of 15,000 businessmen expressed continued dissatisfaction with Roosevelt's economic policies: 77% still opposed the New Deal recovery programs. No surprise, then that in the upcoming presidential election for 1940, 91% of the respondents supported Republican Wendell Willkie.

Just 2.6% of the respondents opposed trade with a "...Hitlerized economic bloc in post-war Europe." If Hitler won the war, close to half (48.3%) believed U.S. business should accept trading with a totalitarian regime.

Sixty-eight percent supported limitations for companies profiting from future American defense contracts. Most agreed a shortage of skilled labor existed, that extending the work week beyond 48 hours, if the shortage continued, would not harm productivity and that strikes be declared illegal during a national emergency.

The survey revealed many American businessmen believed capitalism could survive a world war, but Henry shared a story from Alsace, France, that underscored the brutality of Hitler's regime.

Members of the Hitler Youth army marched into the village armed with axes, and destroyed a tree planted as a World War I memorial to the town's dead. Henry believed resisting that fanaticism and violence to protect democracy and human rights outweighed economic fears.

In 1942, as the front page of the *Democrat* reported that "Forces Drive Japs Back in Batan (*sic*) Fight" and "Enemy Suffers Heavy Losses on the Peninsula,"

Paducah residents collected scrap metal and sewed blackout curtains. Doing something, *anything*, helped to ease the anxiety of waiting for news about family or friends fighting thousands of miles away. Personal comfort and convenience took a back seat to the war effort. A sales freeze on rubber boots and shoes went into effect, but the Office of Price Administration permitted the sale of industrial footwear, for workers deemed essential to the war effort.

A new page one feature in the *Sun-Democrat,* *"It's The War,"* reported that a Paducah war plant checked references for an applicant by contacting a girl who worked in an office in the applicant's neighborhood. "She answered the telephone and after a little uncertain stammering gave the applicant the rosiest recommendation possible. In her estimation the plant could find no better man. He was tops. The applicant was her father. The plant, in its haste, hadn't bothered to check the girl's name against the applicant's signature. IT'S THE WAR!"

Few complained about rationing, curfews, or blackout drills. "City's First Blackout is Excellent," confirmed the *Sun-Democrat,* and "...the general public performed so satisfactorily in Monday night's first city-wide blackout practice that they let themselves in for something a good deal tougher"—next time, no advance notice would be given.

"I have watched many practice blackouts in Kentucky," Major Williams told the protection division chiefs in Paducah's secret control room. "The practices are given one of four ratings...and I am going to report yours as excellent." Paducah proudly joined three other cities awarded that rating statewide.

Kathleen Rowlett sent Henry a letter donating two large cannonballs on either side of her father's monument in Oak Grove Cemetery for the local scrap drive. "They are loaded and the years have about covered them. My father would want this. These came from Shiloh."

Her letter inspired him to inventory his own basement and attic, which yielded a discarded hot water heater, an old automobile radio and his daughter's first tricycle.

Yet too soon, reports of casualties and deaths heightened sorrow and anxiety for families. In nearby Lone Oak, Mr. and Mrs. Malcus Moore waited for their son, Earl, a sergeant stationed in Panama City, Florida, to return home with the body of his brother—Lieutenant Martin Moore, killed when his pursuit plane crashed on a practice formation flight at Perry Air Base in Florida.

Patricia Paxton Brockenborough worked at the paper for five years, and remembered that "during the war, our pages were filled almost daily, it seemed, with pictures of servicemen who were wounded, killed, or missing in action. My father decided we needed more balance, something to lighten the paper up during those terrible years. So, he hired a socially prominent woman, Peggy Trimble, to write a social column. It was written in the form of a letter to her friend Nanny Steinhauer, who had moved away and it was very popular. A column like that would be ridiculous in a daily paper of our size today, but it did fill a need, I think, for frivolity during those awful times."

In 1942, Henry attended another legislative session, sent a daily column home, re-drafted the TVA bill, and agreed to replace Joe Robinson, the ailing Speaker of the House.

Aside from Henry's cranky comment that as acting Speaker, he refused to play the "stooge" for anyone, he settled in immediately. "Ward's force as a speaker does not rest on political oratory," commented *Courier-Journal* columnist Allen Trout. "He always speaks in a conversational tone. What he says, rather than how he says it, is his strength on the floor."

Eventually, with the governor's help, the TVA bill passed. Although the dam came online too late to help with the war effort, it expanded generating capacity to attract new manufacturing, and lowered electricity rates for west Kentuckians.

In April, Henry's friends and supporters organized a testimonial dinner for him, celebrating his tenth year in the legislature. That show of support nudged him into running for Lieutenant Governor. After he filed his declaration, he announced "For 10 years as a member of the state legislature I have tried to represent the people honestly. If they have any appreciation of that type of representation, I will be elected. If, on the other hand, they want one of the old-fashioned politicians who specializes in soft-soaping them, I will be defeated...I've had to work hard and to battle all my life for anything I got, and I know this race is no exception. I'm used to working and to battling."

His opposition included John Whittaker, a farmer and Logan County attorney endorsed by Tom Rhea, and state Agriculture Commissioner William May. Henry's legislative and newspaper background worked for and against him. A vocal critic of trading state jobs for votes, his opponents, Whitaker and May, controlled a sizeable block of votes from state employees.

A cascade of circumstances worked against him. By late 1940, nearly 6,000 men in Paducah registered for the draft or enlisted, a number that would rise dramatically. It impacted turnout, and Kentuckians working round the clock shifts in war plants had little time, energy or enthusiasm for a state election. Tied to his job in the increasingly short-staffed city room, gas and rubber rationing limited his travel around the state.

His reputation as an honest and independent legislator played well with the newspaper crowd, but the average voter related to a candidate on a more personal level. Historically, Kentucky politicians set a high bar for entertaining crowds with colorful stump speeches.

At best, Henry presented himself as a sincere, clean cut policy wonk who preferred writing a 10-part series analyzing municipal tax rates to bounding onto a stage to deliver a barnstorming campaign speech.

Still counting on Keen Johnson's help, Henry anticipated a boost from an endorsement from Alben Barkley. Yet, during his oral history interview, Henry's voice falters and grows very quiet as he recalls their conversation.

"But after Rhea's boy (Whitaker) got in the race, Barkley told me, 'Tom Rhea's come to me and said 'Now look, you owe me a lot, you know what we've done for you, and I know you're close to Henry Ward, but the least you can do is stay out of the race.' And he said 'I'll just have to stay out of it.' I said I could understand that. So he stayed out of it."

But his strong-willed wife, Gladys, who'd known Barkley longer than Henry, did not. She never forgot or forgave Barkley for sitting out that campaign. During Barkley's occasional visits to their home afterward, she refused to greet him and stayed in another part of the house.

In July, he delivered a major radio speech in Louisville. He reminded listeners that as House Speaker in 1942, "I aided in bringing about the passage of more than a dozen bills of vital importance to Louisville and Jefferson County. ... Government today is a big business. Its direction ought to be placed in the hands of capable men—men qualified by knowledge and experience. This is not a time to elect men just because they are glamor boys or back-slapping political stooges."

The tough-guy crack was aimed at William May—for drawing his state salary as commissioner while campaigning in a brand-new department station wagon paid for by Kentucky taxpayers.

Early in his campaign, Henry reported that "...for weeks [they] have been riding over the state with their political henchmen, seeking to perfect campaign machines. I have not been able to do that thus far, for it happens that I have to work for a living."

Decades before the U.S. Supreme Court ruling upended restrictions on corporate campaign financing, and the advent of television and digital campaigns, the tried-and-true methods of persuasion included shaking hands, cradling infants, rallies on the courthouse steps, endless breakfasts, lunches and dinners, and quietly arranging state patronage deals.

Ward lacked any strong organizational support outside Paducah, so he took a leave of absence from the newspaper to travel around the state and visit people in shops, courthouses, cafes and local radio stations. He often received a warm welcome, and in Carrollton, a man introduced himself, commenting one of his friends urged him to vote for Henry. He telephoned Ward's friend and he came straight to the courthouse to visit; they had been classmates at Tilghman High. Yet this was not a high school student council election, and Henry invested too much trust and hope that the praise he received at his testimonial dinner translated into votes.

Days before the August primary, in Jefferson County, *Courier Journal* headlines read "Vote for Ward or We'll Bolt, Unions Say." 30 business agents from the American Federation of Labor dropped by Mayor Wilson Wyatt's office demanding Wyatt and County Judge Mark Beauchamp "put over" Ward, or else.

If the city failed to turn out for Ward, they threatened to hand the labor vote to the Republican nominee. There were more than 400,000 votes at stake in Jefferson County, but Wyatt, who supported Henry, was blocked by rival factions who swung the votes over to May.

Two Trigg County kingmakers, brothers Smith and Clarence Broadbent, split the vote in west Kentucky. Smith backed Ben Kilgore, while his brother backed Donaldson. Smith offered to swing votes to Donaldson and Ward if Donaldson would agree to let the brothers control their patronage and organization, but Donaldson, then Kentucky's Highway Commissioner, refused.

In Paducah, a tireless and enthusiastic "Win with Ward" crowd planned a parade, live music and speeches downtown the night before the primary, and the *Sun -Democrat* published a steady stream of front-page endorsements from around the state.

Still, McCracken County's popular crusader could not close the gap, and the Governor's race of 1943 took a back seat to the war.

John Whitaker won the election by 20,000 votes. Henry finished third, behind William May. Discouraged and disappointed, he did not foresee the most productive decade of his career was just ahead.

## 12 Following in Their Footsteps

"Ward was brash enough to think he could sell a new philosophy of park administration to practical minded legislators. Heretofore parks had been established primarily because legislators felt it their duty to preserve natural wonders. ...But Ward believed that in a modern society, with its greatly increased leisure time, the emphasis should be shifted to recreation. Perhaps the time had come when the state had a duty to provide recreation, even as it provided free education."

FALCON O. BAKER, "Kentucky Strikes it Rich"

After the election, Henry was free to focus on the vast new recreational area created by the Kentucky Dam, right in the heart of his district. As the tiny village of Birmingham was slowly submerged under the reservoir, Henry joined other west Kentucky park advocates to discuss how to add Kentucky Dam to the state park system.

Henry recalled that in 1938, "...after the Barkley election, I took Gladys and Pat [to visit the parks]. I had been out in the state enough that I'd seen the light. And particularly on parks because I had already become interested in the possibility of doing something when they built it [the TVA dam] and turning it into a park. So we went and made a trip each [year]...all of the parks at the time—there weren't very many. Cumberland Falls was the only one that had any development of any kind and it was very crude and we stayed there. ..." One stop included Natural Bridge: "Yeah, we stayed there, of course at the time it was a wreck," said Ward.

John Ed Pearce asked Henry "Do you think of yourself as a conservation man, a highway man or both?" Ward replied, "Primarily conservation...That was my first love and one which I had the deepest personal interest."

In 1947, Congressman Earle Clements resigned from his Congressional seat to run for governor, and he pledged to upgrade Kentucky's park system and increase road funding. Under his administration, both investments were critical to attract new industry and create jobs as Kentucky adjusted to a post-war economy.

Clements appointed Henry to lead an expensive overhaul of a patchwork collection of parks, monuments and historic sites neglected for years. Earle, a powerful state and national Democratic party kingmaker—once described by *The New York Times* as a "colorless" yet effective "vote conjuror," and Henry, sponsor of half a dozen conservation bills, delivered on that promise.

A combination of factors led to Kentucky's chance to shine in the 1955 *Saturday Evening Post* article titled "Kentucky Strikes it Rich". It credited Earle's foresight and Henry's "get it done now" management style for creating a nationally acclaimed park system in under four years.

Before undertaking any sweeping changes, Ward visited the parks. My Old Kentucky Home drew visitors from around the world, and Cumberland Falls State Park featured one of the only "lunar rainbows" in the western hemisphere. Kentuckians bragged about their horses, bourbon, bluegrass and Stephen Foster's famous song, but many of the sites were run down. Concessions controlled by local residents often charged high prices for tacky souvenirs, poor quality food and primitive lodging.

My Old Kentucky Home, now in need of a total upgrade, was saved in a statewide campaign to restore it in the 1920s, a success story reflecting an exceptional era in park history driven by grass roots activists dedicated to protecting historic, scientific and scenic attractions from private development.

In 1948, Ward, the "man who made Kentucky modern" and praised as the "father of Kentucky parks" declared "old fashioned parks wouldn't do for postwar America." He was correct that a dramatic shift from preservation to leisure time recreation was underway, but he stood upon the shoulders of the conservationists who fought battles to protect these scenic landmarks. They included the "wilderness men" who discovered shooting flames and geysers in Yellowstone, and fearless touring car drivers bouncing along rutted cow paths that passed for roads. "John of the Mountains"—John Muir—honored as the father of the national parks, and Stephen Mather, the national parks' first superintendent, played significant roles in the evolution of the national and state park systems.

The conflict between conservationists and developers peaked in the late 1800s. Congress's new policy setting aside these landmarks for public use came just in time; in 1890, the U.S. Census Bureau officially confirmed the boundary between settled and wild territory in the U.S. had disappeared.

In 1926, the battle to save Cumberland Falls from a utility tycoon renewed the public's national support for the preservation of America's scenic treasures. Industrialist Coleman DuPont offered to buy and donate Cumberland Falls to the state as a public park, and eventually, Kentucky's magical "Moonbow" was saved from destruction.

The rapid expansion in the western U.S. and its transition from isolated frontier to a growing number of settlements, served as the catalyst for a vibrant national and state park movement. Congress passed the "Organic Act" in 1916. It established the National Park Service, and approved funding for parks and a national highway road fund, to improve the condition and safety of roads in the states.

America's first national parks superintendent, Stephen Mather, evaluated new sites, developed park policies, and promoted uniform hospitality standards. At the same time, "good road" advocates, eager to lift their states "out of the mud," celebrated the new Highway Act. Road construction accelerated, and an exceptional network of state parks followed. Enthusiastic tourists mapped out new adventures via roads and routes now accessible year-round, and the states happily collected their tourist dollars.

In 1920, in Bardstown, the last surviving heir of the Rowan family persuaded the Governor to lead a campaign to save her family home, long linked to the famous Stephen Foster song, "My Old Kentucky Home", from ruin. In Louisville, a tough, reform minded newspaperman launched a national crusade to save the moonbow at Cumberland Falls from a utility tycoon intent on building a power dam there.

The American state park system owes its existence to our national park system. Kentucky's modern transformation, led by Henry in 1948, and the impact of his leadership, is best understood within the context of our national park history, which begins with the "champion liars," surveyors, explorers and prospectors who returned from treks through Yellowstone, amazed by the "... molten brimstone, bubbling hot pools and a river that flows so fast it gets hot on the bottom."

John Colter, a legendary American explorer, and a member of the Lewis and Clark Expedition, trekked alone through the wilderness in 1808, and encountered shooting flames on the valley floor in Yellowstone. Skeptics suggested he was ill or hallucinating. Fur traders later passing by nicknamed the spot "Colter's Hell" in his honor, yet no one believed them, either.

From 1810 through the 1860s, rumors spread about a "canyon so deep that a man could shout into it at night and be awakened by his echo the next morning." Gold prospectors tried to sell their written accounts describing geysers, hot springs and super-natural rock formations, but "...editors in the East refused to publish what they deemed to be a work of fiction."

"The period of speculation began as the gold seekers made inroads into the region via the Yellowstone River. And occasionally, some deposits were unearthed. Yet more often strikes consisted of spectacular scenery and natural phenomena," observed Alfred Runte in his book, *National Parks: The American Experience*.

In 1869, William H. Jackson, one of the finest scenic photographers in the west, accompanied Ferdinand Hayden, the chief of the U.S. Geological Service, on a fact-finding trip funded by the U.S. Congress to survey the territory near Yellowstone, a "region rich with scenic effects and interest."

Hayden, his staff and Jackson were joined by a young painter named Thomas Moran. Moran cheerfully helped Jackson haul his bulky, heavy equipment over the rutted trails. During the survey, Moran sketched out a scene he turned into a 14 x 8-foot canvas masterpiece titled *The Grand Canyon of Yellowstone* that conveyed both the majesty and stillness of one of the world's most beautiful landscapes.

Hayden's report included Jackson's glass plate negatives and Moran's sketches, which revealed "these grand, panoramic paintings and photos[that] ultimately convinced the public and our government these lands were worth preserving," noted Cincinnati art historian and curator Dr. Julie Aronson. "Those American landscapes were instrumental in not only documenting the beauties of the West, but they showed our importance as a country, too," Aronson said.

Historians credit these inspiring images for persuading Congress and President Ulysses Grant to establish Yellowstone as the first national park in 1872. Congress set aside 2.2 million acres for public use and enjoyment, protected from development by timber companies, mining operators, ranchers or gold prospectors.

Yellowstone emerged as a tourist destination in time to rescue the railroad industry from an economic downturn in the 1860s and 70s. They launched a marketing campaign urging gilded age millionaires, bored with trips to Europe, to "See America First." Those trips revived rail travel, and hotels prospered as they catered to wealthy tourists.

*433 Hot Springs on Gardiner's River, Upper Basins*

In regions east of the Mississippi River and Rocky Mountains, the evolution of the state park movement is tied to the rise and fall of the era of fine resorts for patrons seeking relief from the heat or chronic illness.

Politicians, industrialists, and wealthy families escaped the stifling summer humidity by enduring a bone-jarring five-hour carriage ride up a steep trail to the Catskill Mountain House, rewarded by its gorgeous view of the Hudson River Valley. Opened in 1824, the classically designed wooden hotel, perched on a steep bluff, offered comfortable rooms, an elegant atmosphere, music and fine dining.

In Arkansas and French Lick, Indiana, patrons flocked to mineral springs seeking relief from a list of physical ailments running nearly a full page long.

In 1886, visitors boarded Kentucky Central rail cars or hired a horse and coach service to for trips to the Arlington Hotel at Blue Lick Springs, Kentucky. Patrons suffering from "disorders of the Blood; rheumatism, Gout, Scrofula, Syphilis, together with a variety of chronics..." paid $12.50 per week to bathe in the water and amused themselves playing billiards, bowling or formal dances in its ballroom.

Kentucky was home to two spectacular wonders—Cumberland Falls, a seven-story tall, 125-foot-wide curtain of water famous for its moonbow, and The Mammoth Cave, the longest cave in the world, spread over 52,000 acres. It was once the site, two miles down, of the wedding of 16-year-old Kentucky bride Mattie Barr to P.P. Huffman. Held in an opening 50 x 12 feet wide, they exchanged vows underneath the cool, damp ceiling supported by stalagmitic and stalactite columns.

Yet over a span of just 30 years, the dominance of the railroad weakened as a fresh generation of inventors and investors tinkered with electric and gas-powered automobiles. As automobile production and ownership increased, drivers demanded better roads.

In 1903 a dozen Ford Motor Co. investors burned through their initial $28,000 investment as the first Model A car rolled off the line in July. By October of that year, they made a $37,000 profit.

Since the late 1890's, bicycles were the most popular form of transportation and recreation—a "nationwide craze"—despite the fact cyclists complained that the roads were "Wholly unclassable, almost impassable, scarcely jackassaable!" and Americans traveling on horses, in buggies and wagons agreed.

In 1904, Martin Dodge, an official with the Office of Public Road Inquiries, released the first inventory of rural road mileage in the U.S. "Of 3,462,522 km (2,252,570 mi) of rural public roads, only 247,288 km (153,662 mi) had any kind of surfacing."

In many states, unpaved roads were limited to seasonal use. "…It was not until after World War I and its accompanying lessons of the military importance of mobility that any significant progress began to be made in the creation of such a road system," explains author Griffeth Borgeson in *The Golden Age of the American Racing Car.*"

"Except for urban centers the United States was devoid of roads that motor vehicles could use in any reasonable, practical sense. …Decent roads ceased to exist about fifty miles west of New York although it was possible, if terribly arduous, to drive to Chicago in the warm months of the year. In the winter the trip was outright impossible. And west of Chicago road conditions got worse. Whenever or where rain fell or snow melted there was the terror of being trapped in seas of mud."

In 1912, W.O. Westgard, "the official pathfinder for the National Organization of Automobilists," traveled through Kentucky and Tennessee in a Flanders electric car, mapping out a safe route for drivers competing in an automobile touring contest. The transition from "wagon boxes"—carts made of nailed planks and canvas hauled by horses or mules, to 6-cylinder passenger cars, some of which weighed nearly 4,000 pounds, proved both liberating and dangerous.

These hardy drivers, nicknamed the "ditch finders" by skeptics appalled by the rickety death traps they drove, traveled at the mercy of unpredictable weather, carried extra water to refill radiators, and gambled on the chance a broken axle did not necessarily lead to a broken bone.

From 1904-1913, Boston millionaire Charles Glidden sponsored a long-distance competition called the Glidden Tour, designed to test the reliability of various models of cars over long-distance routes. Prior to one contest, Westgard noted "Mammoth Cave Kentucky is to be on the route of this year's tour, sufficient hotel accommodations having been found for the tourists. This will break up the 124-mile trip from Nashville to Louisville, which in 1910 brought disaster to many cars."

As the popularity of street cars and automobiles increased, mule and horse ownership declined. In 1912, Kentucky's last stagecoach line closed and the Kentucky General Assembly created a Bureau of Public Roads.

Still, mules saved the day in 1913, as Westgard "blazed the way for the all-Southern transcontinental motor highway between Los Angeles and New York," an adventure that required the physical stamina and mental toughness of any modern-day Navy SEAL.

He informed *New York Times* reporters that at one point, he and his companions, "a motion picture man and Lord Branston of England," drank water from the car's radiator after it stalled in the desert.

Those adventures and mishaps gave the League of American Wheelmen, newly formed American Association of State Highway Officials, the American Road Builders and the American Highway Association more ammunition as they pestered Congress for funding for a paved national system of roads.

Congress took action and passed the Federal Aid Road Act. It authorized a 50–50 matching fund to assist the states in building up to 6% of their roads over a five-year period. As Stephen Mather settled into his new job as national parks superintendent, from the very beginning he envisioned a secondary system of state parks.

Irrepressible and energetic, Mather began his career at the Pacific Borax Company, where he launched the world famous "twenty mule team borax" ad campaign. The cross-country tour featured colorful Death Valley Desert mule drivers, rough and craggy characters, who over a period of six years hauled borax out of the desert on wagons hitched to a twenty-mule team. The mule skinners and swampers, "both sensationally uncombed," traveled from city to city advertising the soap.

Mather became wealthy after investing in a borax mine. A Bull Moose progressive and friend of Theodore Roosevelt, Mather organized camping expeditions through the Kern Canyon and Sequoia Park. His social circle included a network of influential and wealthy conservationists, and they lobbied members of Congress to protect the nation's scenic treasures.

He volunteered as Special Assistant in the Department of Interior, and was good friends with the Assistant Secretary of the Interior and the Chief Geographer of the U.S. Geological Service, relationships that likely influenced his selection as superintendent.

It was an inspired choice. Although Mather suffered periodically from debilitating episodes of "nerves" and was institutionalized for depression off and on throughout his life, one of his closest associates, Horace Albright, recalled "His was a lightning-fast brain with an electric nervous energy to go with it." As Mather maintained a punishing schedule and set national parks policy, automobile manufacturers raced to keep up with the demand for automobiles.

*Stephen Mather, Washington, D.C. (Circa 1920)*

The average wholesale cost of a Ford Model T car was $750.00, and as the number of "Sunday drivers" increased, so did automobile injuries and fatalities. Nationally, U.S. automobile fatalities jumped from 6,779 in 1915 to 12,155 in 1920, an increase of 55%. *The Spectator*, a New York trade publication for the insurance industry, reported that Covington, Kentucky's fatality rate climbed from zero to 70.

Kentucky railroads offered new excursion lines that were popular with tourists. Destinations included the Civil War era Moonbow Inn, perched at the ledge of Cumberland Falls, or Mammoth Cave and Natural Bridge.

In 1917, half a million Americans died from the flu, and the U.S. declared war on Germany. On 5th Avenue in New York, fifteen thousand Blacks staged a silent protest for civil rights, and in California, a 100-inch mirror telescope was installed at Mt. Wilson Observatory.

Historian Rebecca Conard documents one of the earliest milestones in state park development. Her journal article, filled with a wealth of detail, describes the 1921 gathering of 200 men and women at the Fort Des Moines Hotel for the first meeting of the National Conference on Parks, and her scholarship highlights an era distinguished by civic pride and self-determination.

Bird club and wildflower society members mingled with officials from the Federal Highway Council, U.S. Bureau of Biological Survey and National Park to Park Highway Association. A roll call of numerous civic groups, it included landscape architects, and Sierra Club members, members of the American Scenic and Historic Preservation Society, and the General Federation of Women's Clubs and Garden Club of America.

They "grappled with a host of issues that came up in the designation of 'state parks,'" writes Conard, and at the second annual meeting, guest speaker Stephen Mather urged the development of a "state park every hundred miles."

Before 1916, his suggestion would have been laughable, given the lack of paved roads. But the Dixie Highway Association, a group of individuals, businesses, and state and local officials acted on Mather's vision. Completed in 1925, the Dixie Highway ran from Sault Saint Marie, Michigan, to Florida, a much celebrated and famous 1,989-mile route that linked numerous cities and towns.

*The New York Times* noted the Dixie's impact in Kentucky, reporting the state "...has ceased to be the 'detour state.' Roads so bad a few months ago that the State maintained mule teams and drivers to haul motorists out of the mud, when they failed to heed the warning of the American Automobile Association which sent 189,000 motor tourists southward last year by way of Washington and the Eastern highways, have been replaced by hard surfaced thoroughfares. The last link of the famous Dixie Highway has been completed."

A special delegation traveling the Dixie from Michigan to Florida stopped for receptions and dinners organized by the Governors of Ohio and Kentucky, Nicholas Longworth, Speaker of the U.S. House of Representatives, and the Mayors of Cincinnati and Tennessee. The motorcade stayed in Lexington, then traveled through Knoxville, Chattanooga, and Stone Mountain Georgia, heading to a triumphant finish in Miami.

Although Kentucky lagged in state park development during the early 1920s, the state accepted a generous gift of forest land in Harlan County in 1919. In Nicholas County, a volunteer collector, history buff and curator nicknamed "Uncle

Willie" Curtis, used his own money to purchase and curate a significant collection of pioneer and Native American artifacts in and around Blue Lick Springs.

In McCreary County, local residents grew tired of people asking, "How can we get to Cumberland Falls?". A beautiful yet isolated attraction, Obie Sams, an L & N railroad superintendent, volunteered to lead a work crew of Kiwanis Club members and volunteers in constructing a wooden bridge (a rickety pine trestle), "260 feet long and 25 feet high" over a spot called "the Narrows."

In September of 1927, over 200 volunteers, men and women, completed the Kiwanis Trail from Corbin to the Falls—a nine-week ordeal every bit as daunting as the plot from the film *Bridge Over the River Kwai*.

In Bardstown, two curious businessmen cautiously poked through weeds and brush, inspecting the crumbling foundation and rotting window sills of a brick mansion called Federal Hill. In downtown Louisville, newspaper editor Tom Wallace "thundered like jove" to block a federal permit for construction of a hydroelectric power dam at Cumberland Falls.

Imagine a panoramic mural of American rivers, canyons, mountains, historic battlefields and monuments. The artist gives prominent placement to the figures of Muir, Roosevelt and Mather.

As your eye follows along, a colorful patchwork of state monuments and parks follows, and Kentucky is represented by a melancholy songwriter from Pittsburgh, whose song immortalized an image of the Old South caught between sunshine and shadow, slavery and secession in a sentimental ballad called "My Old Kentucky Home."

Soon after the dedication of Federal Hill, the Kentucky General Assembly passed a bill creating a state park commission in 1924. Two years later, a highly publicized battle raged over control of another natural wonder and scenic attraction—the Moonbow at Cumberland Falls.

In 1928, Henry Ward graduated from high school, survived his two-week newspaper probation and prayed his typing speed would improve. Although he enjoyed frequent outings to Kentucky and Indiana parks and monuments, he never imagined that by 1948, he would lead the park system's most significant modernization in its history.

24 years earlier, a staunch conservationist and tough Kentucky newspaperman, Tom Wallace, won his crusade against a corrupt utility millionaire to save the lunar Moonbow at Cumberland Falls from construction of a dam.

Fast forward to 1948, and Henry fought a similar battle, but the construction of a hydroelectric utility dam served as the catalyst for the largest increase in park funding in the state's history.

The sentimental, dramatic and suspenseful origin stories of My Old Kentucky Home and Cumberland Falls divides the era of state park history in two. Beginning in 1920, grass roots activists fought to preserve historic and scenic sites from profit. In 1948, Earle Clements and Henry Ward promoted park development to appeal to a new generation of post-World War II park goers seeking affordable recreation and entertainment.

One story features a Governor and the schoolchildren who collected pennies to save My Old Kentucky Home. Soon after, a dying millionaire Senator from Delaware and a crusading newspaperman saved Kentucky's Moonbow from dimming forever. You cannot finish Henry's story without revisiting theirs.

# 13 The Beautiful Old House & The Moonbow

"You also are privileged and invited to join with the sons and daughters of Kentucky in a contribution to this fund, which shall be used alone to preserve the home of the song that is your song and our song. You have stood with uncovered head and tear-dimmed eyes as the old song tugged at your heart strings. Now let it tug at your purse strings."

GOVERNOR EDWIN MORROW, announcing a subscription fund to restore My Old Kentucky Home.

Governor Morrow's appeal to save the old Kentucky home, the former Rowan estate, was an overwhelming success. Rowan, a judge and U.S. Senator, built Federal Hill in 1795, and it was dedicated as a historic shrine in 1923.

In an article to encourage donations, Willard Jillson, a geologist and the Kentucky Park Commission's first chair, praised Judge Rowan as someone who represented the "advanced ideals and inspirations for his time." A fine Kentucky gentleman, he also earned a reputation as "...one of the surest shots in this part of the country. In those days of dueling, he played his part, and fought one of the deadliest personal conflicts in Kentucky." During an argument over a card game in a tavern, Dr. James Chambers challenged Rowan to a duel, and Chambers died from his wound.

Brushing past the scandal, Jillson switched from homicide to hospitality, noting that the Judge's "spacious country home" at Federal Hill served as a "... hospitable stopping place for travelers of distinction."

Yet by 1921, Rowan's last descendent, Marge Frost, could not afford to maintain it. She was willing to sell the dilapidated mansion for $65,000, and Catherine Connor, who ascended through the Kentucky's Democratic party ranks to join Franklin Roosevelt's administration, recalled how the home was saved her in memoir.

Will Stiles, a friend of her father's, invited him to look the property over as a potential tourist attraction. "We drove out to Federal Hill and found it a complete wreck," she remembered. "The shutters and windowpanes were broken, and the overgrown grass, weeds and brush covering the front steps to the main part of the house sheltered snakes and wasps' nests."

"Looking around, Papa said, 'This is what happens when the money runs out.'" Frost's asking price in 1921 dollars was steep. "If Stephen Foster had not visited there and received his inspiration to write 'My Old Kentucky Home', the property would have been worth about $10,000, if that much," Connor wrote.

They met with Governor Morrow to suggest the state purchase it, but there was no extra money in the state budget for that purpose. Instead, he agreed to launch a state wide fund raising campaign to restore it as a historic shrine.

In April, Morrow appealed "To Every Expatriate From Kentucky in All the World" and all the "Loving Sons and Daughters of Kentucky" to join him in raising $100,000 to save the Old Kentucky Home.

In Nelson County, the locals just shook their heads. Despite the family's claim that Stephen Foster composed his famous ballad at Federal Hill, they doubted the story, as did several of Foster's biographers.

John Chamberlain concluded Foster "knew very little first-hand of the real South. But he worked in Cincinnati, and his sister, Charlotte, at least knew something of Kentucky life. Charlotte refused to marry John Rowan Jr. of Federal Hill whose ante-bellum mansion became known as the 'old Kentucky home' of Stephen's song. But there is no proof that Stephen ever saw Federal Hill. ...He might have easily have visited there, however and he would have learned something of Kentucky life simply by working in the Ohio Valley."

Kentucky newspaperman Young Allison believed Foster wrote the song in Pittsburgh. On outings to the riverfront where the Monongahela and Ohio Rivers join, Foster witnessed:

> "... the great spectacle of African slavery at 'close ups'... from the roustabouts to the cabin waiters, the 'house servants', the maids of young mistresses, the 'body

servants' of arrogant and fiery old and young masters—more significant than all, with the cargoes of the unfortunate or 'intractable' slaves that were being carried from preferred homes in Kentucky and Virginia to cotton and sugar plantations 'down South', sold or to be sold, as the result of the breaking up of the fortunes of their masters. ... He had seen beings who, whether they had souls or just human bodies, had been lost at stakes over the gambling table and were transferred to new and unknown destinies by two lines on a scrap of paper."

Their sorrow left a deep impression on Foster, reflected in his song's lyrics: "The head must bow and the back will have to bend, wherever the darky may go; A few more days and the trouble all will end. In the field where the sugarcanes grow. A few more days to tote the weary load, no matter, 'twill never be light, A few more days till we totter on the road, Then my old Kentucky Home, good night!"

As Connor and her friend Amy Guthrie solicited donations, some people scoffed the story and song were a sentimental fraud. They visited Mrs. Frost again and "She insisted that Foster had written his plaintive and sentimental melody at a particular desk. She pointed it out, still sitting in the hallway."

In Louisville, Mrs. Millard Cox suggested asking Kentucky schoolchildren to donate just a penny to their cause. "We thought it was a fine idea, and Mrs. Cox offered to have cardboard replicas made of the house at Federal Hill with a hole in the chimney through which pennies could be dropped. Mrs. Guthrie and I drove miles and miles visiting schoolrooms all over Kentucky."

Four and a half million pennies later, the children raised $45,000. Newspaper publisher Judge Robert Bingham pledged another $5,000, and Mrs. Frost agreed to sell for $50,000.

In the spring of 1922, the General Assembly passed a bill accepting the money, appointing a Commission to manage the site, and budgeting annual appropriations for maintenance and improvements. On July 4, 1923, officials from Pittsburgh, Foster's birthplace, joined Governor Morrow and his party in Louisville and boarded a train to Bardstown. Hundreds of motorists gathered at the "Foster Shrine," and *The New York Times* reported the celebration symbolized "in tangible form the sentiment of Kentuckians for their native state. ..."

Officially changing Federal Hill's name to My Old Kentucky Home, Morrow declared, "This song has touched the hearts of the world. It comes from the pennies of childhood. It comes from the poor in purse but rich in heart."

In 1924, as young Henry Ward, Kentucky's future state Conservation Commissioner, pedaled his bicycle around Paducah, state legislators took note of the crowd of 20,000, and the steady stream of tourists who visited. Now seemed a good time to capitalize on that good will, so they passed a bill creating a state park commission staffed by three unpaid appointees.

The established parks at that time included Federal Hill, the Old Capitol and Grounds in Frankfort, and 3,400 acres in Pine Mountain. The Commission recommended acquiring Carter Caves, Cumberland Falls, Cumberland Gap, Natural Bridge, the Breaks of Sandy, the lands "In Between the Rivers," the Ohio Lowland and Reelfoot Lake, and the Red River Gorge.

In the absence of a state park system, tourists purchased food, gas and souvenirs from private operators and owners. Automobile tourism on the increase, during warm weather, over flowing crowds visited Kentucky parks, monuments, rivers and lakes, and the Commission anticipated that "A State Park with adequate up-to-date hotel accommodations surrounded by suitable temporary camping sites would be a success beyond any reason of a doubt."

In his Presidential Address to the Kentucky Academy of Science in Lexington in 1924, Jillson declared that these sites should be acquired immediately, or else "industrial and commercial interests will creep in and make such acquisitions impossible for all time...In the case of Mammoth Cave and Cumberland Falls, such permanent losses are a certainty unless these areas be acquired by the state within the next year or two."

His lecture coincided with a battle over control of Cumberland Falls that lasted from 1924 to 1930. In March of 1926, the Brunson family signed an option to sell the Moonbow Inn and surrounding land at the Falls to the Cumberland River Power Company (CRPC). Prior to that transaction, the wealthy industrialist T. Coleman DuPont, who worked for a coal operator near the Falls in his youth, offered to buy the Inn and the land (200 acres), along with an adjoining tract of 2,000 acres and gift it to Kentucky as a state park.

His offer ignited a controversy that pitted the heirs of the DuPont "gun powder trust" against utility tycoon Samuel Insull's "power trust" for ownership of the Falls. If the Federal Power Commission approved the permit, construction for the dam would begin upstream from the wide porch of the Moonbow Inn, perched on a crescent shaped ledge overlooking the Falls.

The Inn was named after the waterfall there. At 125 feet wide and 65 feet high, during various phases of the moon's cycle, its orientation produced the only lunar rainbow found in the western hemisphere.

The Brunson family also owned the Cumberland Falls Hotel, and for more than 30 years operated it as a summer resort. With 40 rooms and an expansive view of the Falls, ads described it as a "...beautiful resort in the heart of the Kentucky mountains [that] has several fine mineral springs and hay fever is relieved at one. No extra charge for bathing, fishing, dancing, bowling and music. ...Poker was also a popular activity, although not as highly publicized as the rest. As the story goes, it was not too uncommon for $50,000 to cross the table in a single night."

But in those early days, the trip to "this enchanted wilderness" resembled a stagecoach ride on the old frontier. There were no paved roads, and sawmill owner P.P. Walker operated a Cumberland Falls Station at a stop on the Cincinnati & Southern Railroad, loading passengers and their baggage into "jolt wagons" pulled by mules. The 12-mile trip east took four hours, and eventually Walker switched to Model T Fords.

Yet Harlean James, president of the American Civic Association, assured readers the trip was worth the trouble. "The waters fall like a finely woven medieval lace net set with jewels, the selvage edge as plainly marked as though the marvelous fabric were being reeled relentlessly from a giant loom... [and are] eminently suited for a State Park that would achieve fame far beyond the borders of the state."

While waiting for a hearing on the permit, the CRPC hired publicists to travel across the state extolling the new jobs and affordable electricity the dam would bring.

A press agent stopped at the *Louisville Times* office, and during a meeting with editor Tom Wallace, called the resort a "sewer for mining camps." The lie infuriated the editor, who in his youth joined friends on a flatbottom boat trip to Florida, in search of an "authentic" and rugged outdoor experience. A nature lover and staunch conservationist, and with the full support of his publisher, Robert Bingham, Wallace embarked on an editorial crusade to save "America's second-ranking scenic wonder" from development for the people of Kentucky to enjoy.

After the Commission tabled the CRPC's application in 1926, Wallace used the delay to organize a letter writing campaign to Congress, and to alert retired National Parks Director Stephen Mather, forester Gifford Pinchot, and the current national parks superintendent Horace Albright, that it was possible the Moonbow would be destroyed, forever.

By 1927, the controversy consumed all of Wallace's time, and he wrote a fellow editor that "... I am almost detached from my regular job ... and I am working night and day to keep the project going and at the same time keep my editorial work in shape."

Yet in Corbin, local residents just as determined to showcase the Falls tackled a different problem. Local residents and Kiwanis Club members grew frustrated by hundreds of pleas from visitors and tourists eagerly asking, "How can we get to Cumberland Falls?"

Three adventurous club members answered that question by driving a modified Model T Ford on a tortuous journey to the Inn, a trip that lasted eight hours. They proved you *could* get there from here, and even faster if only someone would clear the way, pave the route and add a bridge to shorten the distance.

In August of 1927, Obie Sams, a Louisville & Nashville railroad bridge superintendent, designed the bridge. Local volunteers, using hammers, nails and brute strength, constructed the "Ole Pole Bridge," which Sams confidently calculated could support the weight of a ten-ton truck. Yet most people, doubtful about the safety of what now resembled a giant, spindly tinker toy, parked at one end of the bridge, and walked on foot to view the Falls.

The road came next, and 200 men and women labored over the Kiwanis Trail. On September 22, 1927, Governor William Fields dedicated the trail, driving the last spike, made of gold, into the trestle. Soon more than 2,000 cars made the two-hour trip from Corbin to the Falls, bolstering Wallace's argument the site was best suited for a state park.

In 1928, Kentuckians elected Republican Flem Sampson Governor. An unabashed booster of all things Kentucky, he created the Kentucky Progress Commission, which produced a lavish, full-color magazine designed to "advertise Kentucky to the World."

"Flim-Flam-Flem" Sampson's flamboyant style appealed to voters, but the General Assembly was controlled by the Democrats, who, frustrated by Sampson's inept management and offended by rumors of his incessant womanizing, stripped him of nearly all his executive power. Initially Sampson opposed Insull's permit, but Wallace reported that the Sampson administration was controlled by the utility lobby.

Solid proof the allegation was true came as another hearing date approached, and Sampson triumphantly (but unsuccessfully) announced he brokered a better deal. The utility offered to donate $250,000 to the state for new roads, a bridge and a state park downstream of the dam, in exchange for Sampson's support for the permit.

Samuel Insull's power and influence over lawmakers in Illinois and members of Congress peaked in the mid-1920s, but eventually, his arrogant behavior turned the tide of both Congressional and public opinion against him.

In 1926, Arkansas Democrat Thaddeus H. Caraway accused Insull of buying a U.S. Senate seat for Frank Smith, then chair of the Illinois public utility commission. Smith received $400,000 in campaign contributions, $125,000 of which came from Insull - a blatant conflict of interest.

Illinois Republicans urged Smith to withdraw, but he refused. In December, Illinois Senator William McKinley died, and Republican Governor Len Small appointed Smith to fill McKinley's vacant seat.

In the aftermath of the Teapot Dome scandal during the Harding administration, Congress stepped up efforts to police itself against conduct they deemed to be "undignified" or "unseemly." The Illinois governor's appointment met the criteria for both, and they summoned Insull to Washington to meet with the Committee investigating Frank Smith's campaign. Insull refused to testify, and Nebraska's Senator Norris condemned the Illinois election as "...but one more example of a 'battle royal of the millionaires.'" In 1928, Norris introduced a successful resolution to deny Smith his seat.

Conditions were just as corrupt in Kentucky—in 1928 Wallace reported that two dozen lobbyists had been indicted for ethics violations during the legislative session, many of whom worked for Insull. The drumbeat of state and national utility industry investigations drew Senate scrutiny, and the Federal Trade Commission launched an investigation into the gas and electric utility industries, their holding structure and practices.

The twists and turns for control of the Falls continued. After the death of one of the federal energy commissioners, President Coolidge appointed Roy O. West, an ardent pro-business, anti-regulation appointee, to fill out his term. West served as legal counsel to utilities owned by Insull. No need to guess which way West would vote—and the fight to save the Falls seemed hopeless.

Another permit hearing was set in December of 1928. A ruling in favor of the CRPC seemed imminent, after the Commission circulated a proposal recommending the company restrict the water flow to the Falls instead of stopping it, which in theory, would minimize the dam's impact and pave the way for granting the permit.

No practical way to enforce that provision, it was a false compromise, and Wallace refused to give up. The witnesses opposing the permit included Stephen Mather and members of the Cumberland Falls Preservation Association. Herbert Hoover, then Secretary of Commerce, opposed it, as well. Other advocates on standby included Acting Park Service Director Arno Camerer, former Kentucky governor William Fields, representatives from the National Conference on State Parks and the American Civic League. The Commission allotted more time to the utility supporters than the conservationists, but they requested briefs and statements from both sides, then adjourned the hearing.

The testimony that day drew widespread interest and attention. Additional members of Congress voiced their opposition to the permit, and Kentucky's Congressional delegation (except for two Republicans), announced their support for a park.

Sampson's surprise announcement about a deal with the CRPC, coincided with the release of a U.S. Senate report that compared the costs of electricity in Canada to the United States. Utility regulation in Canada meant consumers paid 50% less for their power.

The benefits of a free market were not trickling down to ordinary Americans, and as Kentuckians and Laurel County residents waited for a decision, Insull's promise to deliver free flowing, cheap electricity seemed a self-serving lie.

As stock prices soared in 1929, in living rooms and at kitchen tables across the country, newspaper readers admired photos of Insull's salmon-colored, 31,000-square-foot Italian style villa in Chicago. For many Americans limping along during the recession following World War I, the photos stirred a twinge of envy and resentment over his staggering wealth and luxurious lifestyle.

In the autumn of 1929, the *Boston Globe* reported "Margin Account Dumping Brings Stock Crash," and a drumbeat of headlines chronicled the fall of wealthy investors. By the end of the year, the overvalued shares in Insull's holding companies plummeted, and by 1932, he was bankrupt. A headline grabbing lawsuit and trial painted him as "an example of the corruption and fraud which contributed to the Great Depression."

In January 1929, the Commission met again, but Commissioner West bowed to negative publicity and public pressure to recuse himself. There was a real possibility now that Insull would be denied his permit. The case was postponed until President-elect Hoover could name a new set of Commissioners in March, more receptive to Hoover's view that the Falls should be saved.

Public support for a park reached a peak after the hearing, the crash of the stock market, and the indictments of millionaires like Insull. As he waited for an official ruling from the Commission, Tom Wallace traveled across the country on a lecture tour featuring a color slide presentation highlighting the importance of protecting the Falls, and other scenic sites from lobbyists and developers exploiting them for profit.

In July 1929, a widely admired article in an influential national public policy magazine called the *Survey Graphic* published an article by Wallace titled "Caught in the Power Net," His hard hitting expose describing the threat to the Falls included a national call to action. "Under the necromantic name of 'development' the power net is closing, surely and not at all slowly, over every available power site in every state. Only quick work and hard work by a militant minority to educate the public as to the value of scene assets will save even the most priceless heritage to future generations." He described the Moonbow Inn as a magical place filled with "tumbling waters and pillars of bloom...Its clumps of holly, its seven or eight varieties of evergreens, including pine, cedar and hemlock, its wealth of ferns and flower recall Chateaubriand's description of the primeval forests of the South in Atala." Along with the fading Moonbow, the Inn would close, a unique destination by virtue of its proximity to the cliffs, "...its foundations registering, by perceptible vibrations, the impact of the water which thunders on the ledge on which they are laid."

From that idyllic setting, he drew readers into the world of arrogant and influential power lobbyists who controlled and corrupted state and national conservation policy in that moment. But more importantly, he forcefully argued that Kentucky lawmakers had a responsibility to preserve the state's scenic heritage for future generations. Cumberland Falls and the entire park system, still in its infancy, formed "a great revenue-producing heritage." As an example, he reported that New York paid $1,500,000 to acquire and operate Niagara Falls, an investment that returned $50,000,000 per year.

"Why should Kentucky, in an era of road-making, when the gasoline tax is building roads, be deprived of the income which would arise from Cumberland Falls and 2,000 acres of wilderness lying between two interstate roads connecting the North and the South?"

His publisher, Robert Bingham, valued the article for another reason—the battle over ownership of the Falls created a national opportunity to reinvigorate widespread support for progressive state and national conservation policy, and Bingham paid to distribute a copy of the *Survey Graphic* article to every member of Congress.

Over that summer and into the autumn, Coleman DuPont lay dying, but his family stood ready to honor his offer to donate the land. Long estranged from his wife and children, only his daughter Renee stayed close to him. As the months dragged on, he was unable to eat or swallow and in considerable pain. To communicate, he and Renee passed notes or read lips. At the end of one visit, "...she said, 'I wish there was something I could do for you, dad." ...and [Coleman] took up his pad and wrote on it: 'You can. Get a gun and shoot me.'" Du Pont died in November, and the Kentucky legislature voted to accept his gift soon after.

As Congress turned its attention to utility regulation, Franklin D. Roosevelt expanded access to public power on an unprecedented scale. The battle to block a hydroelectric dam to save a scenic wonder, was followed by the fight to amend Kentucky's constitution to permit TVA to sell hydro power generated by the Kentucky Dam. In this instance, the dam and lake would create a new park and massive recreation area. Like Wallace, Henry faced significant opposition from the private utility industry over his enabling bill, and like Wallace, their intimidation hardened his resolve to succeed.

As Kentucky's attorney general James Cammack finalized the legal transfer of the Falls to the state, the Depression deepened, and Kentucky parks expansion coasted to a temporary stop.

Yet, thanks to the Civilian Conservation Corp., the parks were soon filled with laborers clearing trails, building shelters, benches, and natural stone and wood beam park lodges.

Throughout that decade, Henry praised the program, but he warned that eventually, the federal funding would end. For over a decade, legislators refused to accept responsibility for maintaining the park system, and Henry's push for more funding and the acquisition of Kentucky Lake drew resistance. "Many rural legislators especially did not appreciate the expenditure of large sums on parks. They simply 'took the beautiful woods, hollows, hills rivers and streams for granted,'" wrote historian Thomas Syvertsen.

What they viewed as a waste Henry viewed as an opportunity. He began his term as Conservation Commissioner with $450 thousand dollars to invest. By 1955, the state was earning over $500 million dollars in revenue from its parks.

Henry Ward capitalized on the old Southern hospitality tradition born from the popularity of "My Old Kentucky Home" and the spectacular beauty of the Moonbow, to create a modern and affordable vacation paradise, popular with tourists flocking to new golf courses, marinas, beaches, lodges and cottages.

# 14 Roosevelt's "Tree Army"

> "Although we now look back upon the depression years of the 1930s as one of the great catastrophes of our time, the federal assistance provided through the programs initiated during this era laid the groundwork for the great system of parks we have in Kentucky today.
>
> HENRY WARD, Spindletop research report on Kentucky Parks.

In 1970, Spindletop Research Corporation hired Henry to complete a state park history for the Kentucky Park Department. Organized into 36 drafts, Ward praised the Works Progress Administration and Civilian Conservation Corps for establishing the "groundwork for the great system of parks we have today. ...at its peak, there were 2,635 CCC camps operating on projects in the United States, 561 of which were assigned to national, state and local parks."

Prior to the arrival of the CCC in Kentucky, park appropriations totaled thirty thousand dollars per year. In the State Park Commissioner's 1925 annual report, they quoted extensively from a *Saturday Evening Post* article titled "Scenery a Cash Cow", emphasizing Kentucky's unwillingness to invest in its parks was a lost opportunity.

Colorado and Minnesota collected fees for attractions, parks, restaurants, camping and lodging that totaled $49 million and $90 million. Michigan operated 53 parks earning $200 million while Florida and California drew in $500 million and $200 million respectively.

In 1926, Natural Bridge reported annual attendance of 52,000—most of it originating from train excursions booked by the Northern Kentucky Sunday School Association. By comparison, in Vermont, a smaller state, a popular park called The Notch attracted 60,000 automobiles and 270,000 visitors.

Yet Kentucky received a significant boost after Mammoth Cave was designated as a national park site by Congress in 1926. In 1928, the General Assembly approved a request by the Kentucky Progress Commission to launch a new marketing tool, the *Kentucky Progress Magazine*. Designed to attract visitors and new industry and jobs, the magazine drew out-of-state praise for its high-quality design, photography and feature articles.

"I want to complement the commission on the makeup of the book...which was so ably presented to the visitors on the occasion of the Legion convention," wrote Commander Jesse L. Jones, from the Illinois Council of The American Legion. "It contained information which thousands of boys wished to know, where to find Mammoth Cave, Shakertown, The Old Kentucky Home and other places of interest, and I want to assure you that your magazine was the greatest guide to the visitors that we saw there."

N. Buckner, from North Carolina, picked up a copy in Asheville, and then, "on a recent visit through Kentucky I visited Frankfort and secured a complete file of this quite unusual magazine. Leisurely and carefully looking over the ten numbers, my estimate of its value as a vehicle carrying information about the resources and opportunities of Kentucky along with its brilliant part in the history of the Nation is one hundred per cent plus. It may be easily classed as a magazine of high literary merit, making all the more value to Kentucky in telling the world of its vast resources and opportunities."

Some issues are as colorful as circus posters, and the publicity team could not resist touting *The Glamour of Kentucky—Scenery, Shrines, Sentiment, All Combine to Make the Atmosphere of the 'Old Kentucky Home' Intriguing, Incomparable and Irresistible—State Has Seven Alluring Domains.*"

A nostalgic glimpse into Kentucky's past, the issues are still lively and engaging. Articles profiled pioneers and statesmen Henry Clay, George Rogers Clark, Abraham Lincoln and William Whitley, the Revolutionary War veteran. Daniel Boone's gravesite drew a steady stream of visitors. In Mayfield, sightseers crowded inside Colonel Henry G. Wooldrige's family cemetery to view a granite procession that never moves. Eighteen life-sized statues memorialized his brothers, sister, three sweethearts, nieces, two dogs, a deer and a fox.

The Progress Commission paid for an 11-reel film praising Kentucky's "Beauty, Agriculture, Good Roads, Educational Plants and General Progress." Ads appeared in the *American Motorist,* and 600,000 pamphlets (*"Why Not Move to Kentucky?"*) were distributed at national and state conventions. Radio advertising praised Kentucky as "the Workshop and Playground of the Nation."

In 1932, the state operated seven parks and two memorials totaling 4,781 acres valued at $881,000. In 1936, Governor Chandler kept his campaign promise to improve the roads. The legislature approved $2 million to ditch and resurface 6,000 miles, add 2,000 miles of new roads and build 65 new bridges.

The Emergency Conservation program of the National Park Service operated in seven state parks. In Mammoth Cave and at Cumberland Falls, historic markers identify improvements added by the CCC. Crews quarried stone to build a museum and teahouse at John James Audubon Park, built lakes and amphitheaters, cleared roads and trails, and built cottages. One of the finest examples of workmanship is the rustic Du Pont stone and beam lodge at Cumberland Falls, completed in 1937 at a cost of $63,000.

Despite that much progress in just a short time, Henry warned the CCC funding was temporary, and that the General Assembly needed to invest more in the parks. During a 1935 trip to Columbus-Belmont Park, Henry and his wife, Gladys, grew frustrated searching for the park's main attraction—a massive iron anchor and chain Confederate General Leonidas Polk ordered troops to stretch across the river's bluff in Hickman County in 1861.

A crude homemade sign pointed them along a trail ... "To anchor and chain. We are called to scale the cliff, and jump along its side. What a way to treat a visitor. ...We puff along, and after walking for miles and miles, arrived back where we started. Is this a system? Where is that anchor and chain?"

Along the way, they asked a local woman for directions. "'Don't follow the regular path, or you may get lost,' she gently chided them. Hah, she is telling me! Little one, I know all about getting lost." Following her directions, they finally found it.

"It is an inspiring sight, this view of the river and the surrounding countryside. ...I can visualize the roar of cannon from the opposite shore and the answering crash from the Confederate fortifications--the glory and splendor of the battle which this park commemorates. But I might suggest that the park custodians save other visitors all the trouble. A few more signs of direction and information would serve well. I believe in advertising, and that is what Columbus-Belmont Battlefield Park needs, in Columbus as well as elsewhere."

Fees were another sore point with Henry, who complained that "...when the [federal] money of the taxpayers is used to develop a public park, and then the taxpayers are forced to pay to obtain admission to the park, it is high time that a lot of squawking be done. ...Now despite the fact that it has cost the state little to create the park, the state charges each person who enters an admission fee of 10 cents. It isn't the dime that matters; it's the principle of the thing. ...While on the subject of Columbus-Belmont, the state highway department, or someone, ought to do something to improve the roads leading to the park. However, as long as they drive [people] away with admission charges, they need not worry about decent roads. ..."

In the summer of 1940, Paducah hosted the 71st annual meeting of the Kentucky Press Association. The keynote speakers included former U.S. Senator James Pope, the current Director of TVA, and Robert Kincaid, Executive Vice President of Lincoln Memorial University in Tennessee. Although the Kentucky Dam, the largest project in that chain of dams and locks was under construction, Henry reported the site itself was a a popular attraction. "Thousands of motorists drive through the village each week; gazing at the homes and all they see with concentrated interest. As one of the residents put it, 'You'd almost think we were a bunch of monkeys--the way people look at us,'" Henry reported in his column.

Yet in west Kentucky, residents still carried vivid images of the death and destruction of the "flood of the century" in 1937. For many survivors, the flash of lightning or threat of heavy rains triggered new anxiety, despite the federal government's $118 million engineering promise to control that danger. TVA's long-term impact, in addition to flood control, was primarily recreational, adding a multi-state chain of lakes and thirteen new parks—three in Kentucky, seven in Tennessee, two in Alabama and one in Mississippi.

Pope predicted Kentucky Lake would attract "... thousands of tourists annually to this state through the promotion of its park system and the recreational facilities that will be made available by completion of the TVA's Kentucky project."

In turn, Mr. Kincaid warned that based on current conditions in the state parks, Kentucky was woefully unprepared for the arrival of tourists planning to rent boats, fish and swim in the lake, and enjoy picnic lunches in new shelters. Clearly, the annual parks budget, frozen at $30,000 for years, was inadequate to cover the additional expense of building docks and marinas, and maintain the beach, hiking trails and picnic areas.

The second challenge ahead was to implement an effective state wide publicity program, said Kincaid. It was true the Audubon Park and Museum in Henderson housed the nation's premier collection of Audubon paintings, but, he asked the crowd, who knew about it?

A recent park survey revealed that "...only 2.7 percent of out of state visitors stopped at the park. Kentucky cars did little better ... with only 8.2 percent of the state tourists visiting the park." By comparison, Old Fort Harrod State Park recorded 25,000 visitors; in contrast, Mammoth Cave, a national park, drew 113,389 tourists.

"But even these aren't drawing up to par ... when compared with the annual gate of the Great Smokies National Park in North Carolina -750,000 persons per year," he noted. To date, Kentucky had acquired 12,191 new acres of park land, as compared to 61,464 in Tennessee, 933,209 in Michigan, 1,637,556 in Pennsylvania, and 2,327,612 in New York.

Kincaid encouraged editors and publishers to do more to "sell Kentucky through its parks," and the press enthusiastically responded for decades. Yet, the same year, Conservation Commissioner Bailey Wootton released his annual report, highlighting one of the lowest points in Kentucky park history. "The Division of Parks has had to scrimp, beg, borrow and swap to obtain enough to get by. This should not be. Such penury is not in keeping with the wealth and dignity (not to mention pride) of the great state of Kentucky."

An annual appropriation of $30 thousand dollars, for a far-flung collection of monuments and parks he scolded, was "wholly inadequate." Admission receipts increased the total to $99,000, then operation and maintenance costs drained it back down to $6,490.

The problem was compounded by "...a number of so-called state parks (that) should never have been accepted ... as such but since we have them the only thing we can do now is to maintain them. ... Another outstanding addition to the park system ... is the Audubon Memorial Museum and tearoom erected by the joint efforts of the State of Kentucky and the WPA at a cost of $150,000. There is housed in the museum the finest collection of Auduboniana in the world, valued at $400,000, displayed in dustproof steel cases and protected by guards serving twenty-four hours a day."

A tone of frustration shades his report, and it is easy to imagine that when Wootton tried to sleep at night, a flood of details blinked off and on in his mind like an annoying neon sign: more coverlets! more blankets! new road signs! power lines at Butler Memorial Park! a custodian's lodge, sewage and water systems! a water grist mill and a loom house! "...and the doing away with wood railings, steps, towers built of unseasoned logs cut at the wrong time of year and replacing these with stones."

Henry's defeat for state office created a more significant opportunity. There was a lot of talk about the parks, but Henry grew impatient about all the complaining and started planning. Con Traig, the Paducah businessman who encouraged Henry to run for the legislature in 1933, remembered that after the 1943 election, "...Henry has been giving more time and thought to the development of our park system than he has to his own job at the *Sun-Democrat*."

"I had adopted promotion of an effective state park program as a project in the early 1940s. Kentucky had a few state parks then, and had done little with them. ... In trips over the state I had been impressed with the possibility of doing something with them. ..."

He admitted he tended to "fret about things not going the way I think they should." During his first ten years in the legislature, Kentucky's industrial payroll ranked second to last, and per capita income ranked nearly 60 percent below average. 63 percent of Kentucky schoolchildren finished eighth grade, as opposed to 95 percent nationwide. Two thirds of Kentucky schools had unsafe drinking water, 14,000 cases of tuberculosis were reported, and the state ranked fifth in typhoid mortality. Some legislators pointed to these issues as a priority over parks funding, and legislators uninterested in park improvements outside their districts criticized any increase as a waste of money needed somewhere else.

Henry worked to persuade skeptics that parks funding also included conservation. Conservation included stewardship of Kentucky's forests, its coal and mineral deposits and water quality, and the protection of natural and geological resources.

"Yeah, I had been interested in conservation. It was somewhat a coincidence, after I became [Parks] Commissioner, to find out how many, how much legislation had been enacted that I sponsored, administered, with the Department of Conservation. I had been very much interested in parks and worked like hell to get a big increase in appropriations for parks. I don't know why—I'd always been interested in agriculture. I had worked as a newspaperman fairly closely with the farm bureau in Paducah. I had—was very close to Bill Johnstone, who was then county agent in Paducah, and we, with the newspapers sponsored the first soil conservation district in Kentucky in McCracken County, got it there. And we got it established and a watershed which served, you know, the hometown. So I was very much interested in following the soil conservation program from its very inception. I became interested in—in water, as a resource. I sponsored the act under which Kentucky agreed to be a member of the Ohio River Valley Water Sanitation District, a compact with the states. ... I sponsored the bill which provides for the operation, creation of soil conservation districts in Kentucky, which would wind up in the Department of Conservation, forest, soil conservation, water pollution control. Was a member of the Ohio Valley Commission for eight years, was chairman for one year, very, very interested, very active in the program. I mentioned strip mining, water pollution control, and I was a member of the state water commission—I wrote the act for the water—Kentucky state water pollution control commission and it's in the Department of Conservation. I've been extremely interested in the whole broad subject of water, and the water is Kentucky's most valuable resource—it's only really renewable resource, that and forestry. I sponsored some legislation related to water rights—there was no statute of any kind in Kentucky regarding water rights and—in other words, anybody could go out and build a dam on a stream and block it up and take all the water and there was nothing in the law to keep you from doing it. This act provided that he could not deny downstream owners from their rightful share of water, so that my legislative background and my own interest as a newspaperman, as an individual, in conservation just sort of naturally fitted together, in addition to the park thing. And of course, at that time on the big vision of conservation was publicity, so that fitted in, too."

During this decade, Kentucky park highlights fit neatly into a two-page brochure. The illustrations included antebellum homes, statues and monuments commemorating battles dating from the Revolutionary and Civil Wars, and World War I.

Illustrations featured coonskin caps, flintlock rifles, mint juleps, galloping thoroughbreds, real bluegrass, and giant yellow tobacco leaves, along with the dreamy faces of dozens of girls dressed in white lace frocks and pearls yearning to be crowned Queen of the Mountain Laurel Festival.

From 1924 through World War II, the gracious charm embodied by My Old Kentucky Home dominated the state's image for genteel southern hospitality. Life's troubles vanished while sipping a refreshing mint julep on a broad veranda, accompanied by the sound of lilting bluegrass music played on dulcimers or fiddles.

World War II and the Kentucky Dam brought that era and image abruptly to an end. Twenty miles upstream from Paducah, a new lake 184 miles long, stretched across two states. As the war dominated the daily lives of Americans, in west Kentucky, about 500 families, or about 12 percent of Marshall County's population, did their part for the war effort by moving—pushed off land that stood in the path of the dam. One tenth of the rich, fertile bottomland overlooking the Ohio and Tennessee Rivers was removed from production. Previously, the villagers made their living farming, shell digging and fishing, as carpenters or running ferry operations; the region's median annual income was less than $600 per year.

2,609 families were relocated and 3,390 graves removed. 365 miles of new roads and 65 new bridges were built. When the reservoir began to fill, the tiny village of Birmingham disappeared forever.

Several years before, Henry criticized Robert Watt when he complained that every time the federal government gave someone something, it took something away from someone else.

As TVA construction crews blasted, scraped, dug and bulldozed the trees and land, something *was* being taken away—residents' land, farms and livelihoods. "We felt that something needed to be done to help the economy of western Kentucky recover from the loss of agricultural production in the rich lands along the Tennessee River flooded by the building of the Kentucky Dam. Stimulation of a tourist industry offered possibilities," said Henry, and his commitment to improving the parks, and park planning intensified.

During the 1940s, Henry admitted he felt there were never enough hours in a day for him to accomplish all the things he wanted to. He worked long hours at the newspaper to compensate for war time staff shortages, and drove to Frankfort to lobby against repeal of the TVA bill. His efforts, interest and effectiveness as a legislator drew admiration and gratitude—the Junior Chamber of Commerce honored him as "Outstanding Young Man of Kentucky" in 1942.

Near the end of 1945, Americans found the adjustment to post-war life as challenging as fighting the war. Inflation and shortages of rubber, tires, meat, sugar and butter continued. Construction materials were scarce and expensive, and a housing shortage persisted. American women reluctantly gave up their factory jobs and steady wages, and Black veterans returned to menial jobs, their sacrifice quickly forgotten.

In 1947, Kentucky, park attendance jumped by 71 percent as people enjoyed picnics, hiking and fishing. During a trip to Natural Bridge State Park, Henry and Gladys discovered the dam collapsed, and the cabins built by the CCC were in ruins. On one trip, they stayed at the old Hemlock Lodge at Natural Bridge, (which later burned to the ground.) He recalled that although the scenery was gorgeous, "...the lodge was a wreck!" It motivated him to "work like hell" to increase park funding.

Ward characterized the 1940s as a time when he had very little influence. Yet some of his most significant achievements were straight ahead. But he did not do it alone. Another prominent Kentucky politician, with a distinguished and progressive record of national and state public service, was key to Henry's success.

Henry and Earle C. Clements, who was elected Governor in 1947, acted immediately to invest in the parks. It took Indiana fifteen years to earn recognition as one of the nation's top three park systems. But Henry, backed by Clements, led Kentucky to national prominence in less than four.

# 15 Ready, Set, Go...

In 1946, the General Assembly passed Henry's $800,000 capitol appropriations bill for the parks. Governor Willis signed it, but he vetoed half the amount, and "...we couldn't get the money spent," said Henry. The money was just sitting there, because Commissioner Dyche refused to release it, but "...we kept on working."

In 1943, Republican Simeon Willis scored an upset victory for Governor, and stunned Democrats responded by fighting over who to blame for the loss.

Willis's pledge to repeal the state income tax proved popular, and his silver hair and distinguished demeanor appealed to voters he later described as "...simply fed up in the high-handed operations of the State House band of politicians which had been running the state for many years." With World War II at the forefront of daily life, state politics faded into the background. Henry's patience grew thin listening to conservative state legislators complain the TVA bill threatened states' rights, especially after TVA's Board of Directors, "...concerned about future load growth, approved five generating units at Kentucky, instead of four, and directed that "...the date for the start of reservoir impoundment [be] advanced from the summer of 1945 to the summer of 1944."

As factories in the U.S. converted to war production, every additional kilowatt hour of electricity built the planes, tanks and ammunition needed to save Britain from destruction and reinforce the Allies' defensive line spread across Europe.

Yet much to Henry's frustration, nothing—not even a desperate battle over the fate of Europe—could stop Republican floor leader Ray Moss from attempting to repeal the TVA bill. Moss detested "King Franklin," and he was clearly a "stooge," growled Henry, for Robert Watt and Kentucky Utilities. Moss made four more tries to kill the bill through 1948.

Henry recalled the "...1943 election convinced me, I thought, that I was ready to forget the legislature and politics. I had run for the legislature in the first place because of my interest in specific legislative reforms, and they had been achieved."

The condition of the parks captured his attention, and he spent much of his time researching ways to increase funding, promotion and expansion of the parks.

"We knew the state legislature could not provide funds for state park development in one area, even with Kentucky Lake—the largest of the TVA system and one of the largest man-made lakes in the world. So [in 1944] we organized a Kentucky Lake Association and invited participation by groups all over the state interested in specific parks. Eugene Stuart, of the Louisville Automobile Club, who had been a leader of the establishment of Mammoth Cave as a national park, was elected president of the association because he was a Republican and it was being formed just as a Republican was becoming governor. I was selected secretary-treasurer. The association had no money, but we tried to make a lot of noise."

Just as Henry backed away from politics, Earle Clements, a Tom Rhea protégé from Union County, assumed leadership of the Kentucky Senate. Clements, a burly ex-high school football coach, regarded as "...one of University of Kentucky's gridiron greats," drew deep satisfaction from coaching, mentoring and encouraging self-improvement.

His physically imposing demeanor was offset by his affable, (often described as "bland") personality. His coaching experience influenced his political style, and that playbook emphasized building strong local relationships. He judged people by their actions and character, and he built a loyal, statewide political base—one of Kentucky's infamous political "factions" -designed to win elections and control the statehouse.

"He was a bare-knuckle politician," said former Republican Governor Louie B. Nunn, adding that he and Clements were "political adversaries and warm friends. ...He wasn't a powder-puff fellow," Mr. Nunn said. "He could dish it out, but he could take it, too."

One of Clements' former Senate assistants, Catherine Hampson, remembered his energy and vitality, and she observed "...he's fearless, you know. By that I mean he is not afraid to try something. ... procrastination just drove him, you know, wild."

Those qualities helped him offset the damage caused by the intra-party feuding between the Johnson and Donaldson factions. His job was not easy. In 1944, he guided the Democratically controlled House and Senate through contentious budget negotiations with the Republican administration that earned bi-partisan support.

In a series of small but thoughtful gestures, Clements retained some veteran Republican legislators as chairmen of key committees, signaling he valued their input. His timing was shrewd, due to the increased friction between Willis and members of his own party, who doubted Kentucky could avoid increasing taxes during and after the war.

Willis grudgingly agreed to sign the budget bill, and at the close of that session, according to Clements' biographer, Thomas Syvertsen, Earle "... emerged far more powerful than he had ever been, while [Governor] Willis was significantly weakened."

Capitalizing on that success and his popularity, Clements challenged Beverly Vincent for his seat in the U.S. House of representatives and won.

Progressive and detail oriented, he remained popular in Kentucky, but today Clements' voting record on civil rights, labor issues, and to disband the House Un-American Activities Committee, would be considered left of center. He grew close to Alben Barkley and together, they "...pushed the state party much closer to the mainstream of national Democratic thought."

Henry continued to juggle his newspaper duties and volunteer with the Kentucky Lake Association. 23 state parks, monuments and memorials operated year-round. The total Civilian Conservation Corp, Works Progress Administration, National Youth Administration and federal grants spent on Kentucky parks totaled just under $3 million, with the state contributing $335,889 on materials.

"But I had become interested in the parks and realized if Kentucky was ever going to do anything, it had to do something about them. And also realized we weren't going to get anywhere getting any park in western Kentucky unless interest developed more state-wide. ... I had been working with TVA and I was very close to TVA from the very beginning. ... I had been working with them on what was going to be the future of Kentucky Dam Village when they were through with it—get through with it. And they were anxious to have somebody take and do something with it. They didn't have a lot of use for a lot of those buildings. And worth too much to just be thrown away or given away. We even explored the possibility of the Kentucky Lake Association taking it over and running it ... but we couldn't because it was too big a project for us to think about."

Nationally, state park investment and expansion slowed during the war. Rubber and gasoline now strictly rationed; domestic automobile production did not resume until 1945. The war caused extended hardship, yet Kentuckians who landed defense jobs enjoyed new stability and prosperity.

On the home front, historians noted that "The notion of World War II as the 'Good War' owes as much to the full employment, new opportunities, unprecedented prosperity, and rising living standards on the home front as it does to the defeat of the Axis abroad. The voices of home front Americans make that clear. A Kentucky woman who found employment in a shell-loading plant said that the income "was just an absolute miracle. ... We had money and we had food on the table and the rent was paid. Which had never happened to us before."

*In Kentucky* magazine issues shifted to highlighting Kentucky's wartime contributions on the home front. "Parks are popular with troops as War Halts Expansion," the magazine reported. Facilities were offered to the War Department for use as camps for soldiers, and despite gas rationing, correspondent Paul Brannon noted that "...patronage of the 23 parks and shrines embraced in the system far exceeded expectations and, in some cases, surpassed former records for attendance in the face of impending curtailment of traffic."

In the winter of 1944, Governor Willis shared his optimistic outlook with magazine readers: "Even in the midst of the world's most catastrophic war Kentucky is not unmindful of her great heritage as a land of scenic enchantment; and is glad again to proclaim to her sister states and to all the world that she is looking forward to happier days when peace shall return and she may again throw wide her doors to give hearty welcome to visitors."

It was easy to see why Willis, so staunchly opposed to tax increases was so enthusiastic—Congress appropriated road money for aid to the states, sending Kentucky $72 million in funds for a federal highway program. Allocated in an 80 percent—20 percent split, Kentucky's investment was around $14.4 million.

Kentucky's reliance on federal park funding continued from 1941 to 1946, but the money was distributed to two of the state's national parks—Mammoth Cave and Cumberland Gap.

On a sunny day in October 1945, standing on a wood platform crowded with public officials, President Truman dedicated Kentucky's $118 million public power dam.

As spectators watched and listened to the roar of the water pouring through the concrete spillway, Truman declared this engineering achievement symbolized a "...new high point in modern pioneering in America."

The last of the nine dams built in the valley, it came on line late in the war, but the President emphasized key benefits that would last for generations: protection from the destructive floodwaters of the Mississippi, Ohio and Tennessee Rivers, and the "water wheels" that now electrified more homes, farms and industry. It created a deep-water channel 183 miles long that flowed all the way to Nashville, 650 miles away. This improved inland waterway, he explained, would benefit river communities from St. Paul to New Orleans, and St. Louis to Kentucky.

Senator Barkley and Congressman Noble Gregory were gratified by the size and turnout of the crowd that day. Following the ceremony, Truman chatted with reporters, noting that Barkley whispered Kentuckians always turn out "'...like this for them when they come home...if the people keep treating him like this, there is no possible way for him to retire from public life.'"

Truman made no apology for his unsophisticated Midwestern values and emphasis on "common sense," and he praised the dam as a symbol of America's dynamic energy, buoyed by the optimism of Americans eager to rebuild their lives after the war.

Truman issued a call to action that day. "We created the greatest production machine in the history of the world. We made that machine operate to the disaster of the dictators. Now, then, we want to keep that machine operating...The greatest age in history is upon us. We must assume that responsibility. We are going to assume it, and every one of you and all of us are going to get to work for the welfare of the world in peace just as we worked for the welfare of the world in war...Now let's all go home and go to work. Cut out the foolishness and make this country what it ought to be—the greatest nation the sun has ever shone upon."

Since 1924, the sun shined steadily on My Old Kentucky Home, one of the state's major attractions, but the Kentucky Dam's official opening marked a new era in tourism. In a region often viewed as an isolated agricultural backwater, Kentucky Lake would draw thousands of visitors within a 500-mile radius—a day's drive—to fish, boat and swim in one of the largest man-made lakes in the country.

As Henry listened to Truman's speech, he knew TVA was in a hurry to get rid of its surplus land and buildings and that any lease or sale required authorization by the state legislature at terms acceptable to TVA.

According to Henry, good luck put him in the right place at the right time to make that happen. In 1946, he reported to the legislature again, this time as State Senator for the Second District. He prepared two bills—one to increase capital improvements for the parks and the second to authorize the transfer of TVA's surplus land and buildings to the state.

Three years earlier, Strother Melton, who served for 18 years as the district's senator, dropped by the *Sun Democrat* office to let Henry know he planned to retire in 1945. A fixture in west Kentucky politics, Melton chaired the McCracken County Democratic Executive Committee from 1936 until 1968.

"I'm not going to run for re-election in '45, and you ought to be in Frankfort. Your interest is there. If you will agree to run, I will not say I'm going to run for re-election. You go and file. There's a good possibility, then, you'll be without opposition."

Despite Melton's close ties to Happy Chandler, he respected Henry's experience and qualifications. Melton practically handed his seat over, and Henry chuckled it was the best way to win an election.

In Washington, Earle Clements stayed in close contact with state Democratic party officials throughout 1946. One of his close allies, Richard Maloney of Lexington, was elected majority floor leader, and Maloney later told Henry that Clements advised him to load Henry down with assignments to keep him too busy to "raise hell" in the Senate.

"I was not aligned with Clements, and his friends figured I would be a trouble-maker for them," Henry acknowledged. That tension stemmed from Clements' opposition to the TVA bill during the 1942 session. Henry wrote Earle off as a "KU man" after Clements introduced a last-ditch amendment to weaken what Earle judged to be an "excessively pro-public power bill."

Yet Henry acknowledged "His [Earle's] position was understandable. He was from Morganfield where the Kentucky Utilities Company, chief opponent of the TVA enabling act, had a district headquarters, and represented a district in the state senate which ... was anticipating receiving KU power. On the contrary, I (sponsor of the TVA Act and chief opponent of the Moss bills), was from Paducah, which wanted to ... obtain TVA power."

Maloney gave Henry a seat on the Appropriations and Rules Committee, where he kept close watch on him, along with *eight* other committee assignments. According to Henry, it all worked out all right. "I didn't come to the Senate just to make trouble," he later told Maloney. "I wanted to keep you birds from passing the Moss bill (Maloney supported it), and do some other constructive things. Being on the Appropriations Committee gave me that chance."

From the beginning, Maloney, Louis Cox and Henry worked so well together they formed a three-person subcommittee to draft the 1946-47 and '47-'48 budgets. Both passed and were signed by the Governor.

Although Henry rolled his eyes at Willis' foolish pledge to repeal the income tax, he cooperated with the administration on some issues, and he praised Willis as "...another fine old judge who found a place in the Governor's office. A very fine gentleman, I liked him very much, got along with him fine. ... I remember I was asked to sponsor a couple of administration bills and did. Ray Moss got real sore about it. He was the Republican leader of the Senate. 'They don't have any damn right asking a Democrat to sponsor a bill.'"

After Henry returned to the Senate, just nine days later, he lobbed an $800,000 parks appropriation bill earmarked for capital improvements, the largest in the state's history, onto the floor.

The bill allocated $500,000 for capital outlay, $100,000 to the Division of Forestry, $35,000 to the Conservation Department to increase publicity and marketing and $100,000 for Cumberland Gap National Park. Governor Willis signed it, but he vetoed half the appropriation. Willis' Conservation Commissioner, newspaper publisher Russell Dyche, (whose bitter public feud with Henry over TVA made headlines) informed Henry that because post-war construction costs "were too high right now," the administration would only release half. "So, we kept on working," said Henry.

In Washington, D.C., Earle Clements evaluated his next career move. His first term, he served on the Agriculture Committee. In 1946, he was appointed to a Select Committee to investigate what was rapidly becoming a serious nationwide post-war food shortage. Meat, butter and cooking oils still scarce, the Committee succeeded in lowering prices and reducing bottlenecks in the food supply chain.

After President Roosevelt's death and the war ended, Republicans dominated the Congressional agenda. "[T]he old Southern bulls"—Tom Connelly, James Eastman, Harry Byrd and Richard Russell, formed a solid block of opposition to bills banning lynching and the poll tax.

Clements never wavered from his staunch support for civil rights. That commitment to equality was cemented by the bonds of friendship he formed with families and students in the Black community in Morganfield. In an interview with Thomas Syvertsen, he recalled being pressured by Washington segregationists to cancel his speech at the Kentucky Club, which recently welcomed Black members, but he refused.

Staying in Washington appealed to him even less after Happy Chandler, now Baseball Commissioner, procrastinated resigning from his Senate seat. The delay bolstered support for Republican John Sherman Cooper, who defeated Democratic candidate John Y. Brown. The Democrats were losing ground to the Republican Party, nationally and in Kentucky.

As Earle considered his future in Congress (some urged him to run for the Senate), he believed he could make a stronger impact back home, and he decided to run for Governor in 1947.

Author Thomas Syvertsen sets the stage with historian James T. Patterson's description of Kentucky as a backward state that suffered from "an outdated constitution which obstructed the financing of new services; a legislature 'full of ill-prepared, ill-experienced, and poorly paid men;' districting which favored rural lawmakers amidst sharp urban-rural divisions; political bickering and factionalism which 'played a large role in blocking progressive state legislation' and governors who were 'nobodies.'"

After becoming Governor, Earle Clements decisively and boldly erased that perception. Later elected to the U.S. Senate, he and Lyndon B. Johnson made a formidable team. Johnson, the U.S. Senate majority leader, was an extraordinarily effective politician whose "hands in his pockets nonchalance" made the job look easy. It looked easy, but both Johnson and Clements exerted tight control over the party organization and all of the details required to keep the machinery of party politics running smoothly.

Clements served as interim Senate Majority leader after Johnson suffered a serious heart attack, and in 1958, he chaired the Democratic Senate campaign reelection committee, securing a record number of mid-term victories.

Harry McPherson, Jr., an influential lawyer and speechwriter for President Johnson, described Clements as a "pol's pol"—a "Back room man, an embracer and understander. ... I saw him as a George Bellows character in a room full of cigar haze and jousting laughter. He was aggressive and effective as Johnson's whip; not a modern politician with an orientation toward issues and PR, but a professional who understood the play of traditional labor forces—labor, farmers, and so on."

Deeply committed to his family, farm and community, his admiration for FDR and the New Deal, reinforced his belief that as an elected official, he use his power to improve lives and the daily living conditions in his state. Clements, the son and grandson of timbermen and farmers, identified strongly with his ties to labor and agriculture. Like Henry, he was convinced President Roosevelt was "...the greatest humanitarian this nation ever knew," and "...the greatest American of our time."

Drawing from personal interviews with Clements and a wealth of small details, Syvertsen circles back to how the crisis of the Depression forged Clements' political philosophy and style, leading him to implement a sweeping program of "foundation legislation" to modernize his state to ease hardships and foster progress.

After the war, federal funding for infrastructure increased. As Governor, he planned to implement programs building a modern post war economy attracting new manufacturers and creating jobs. Hardly a new or original idea, he made rapid and measurable progress by limiting his priorities instead of overpromising broad results he could not deliver.

While Clements campaigned, Henry tuned out Russell Dyche's negativity and prepared a bill to finalize a lease agreement between the TVA and the state to transfer the land and buildings to create a new state park.

He stayed in regular communication with officials at TVA and learned that only $60,000 of the approved $450,000 in parks money had been spent. Frustrated by the lack of action, Henry urged each gubernatorial candidate—Clements and Republican Eldon Dummit—to publicly commit to a rapid expansion of the state park program.

During the 1947 election primary, Henry supported his fellow newspaperman and public power advocate, Harry Lee Waterfield. Waterfield, like Henry, prided himself for being an "anti-administration" man, and he supported a parks expansion. He drew most of his political strength from a limited constituency—farmers—having served just a few terms in the Kentucky House of Representatives. Certainly a well-intentioned candidate, it was not enough to compete successfully against Clements.

After Clements won the primary, he called Henry to ask "... 'Can you get Mr. Paxton to meet with me?' And I did. Went over and had lunch with him. And he asked if the newspaper supported it. [parks expansion] And Mr. Paxton said 'Well. That's one thing we're very interested in. That's the development of the parks. We want another park over at Kentucky Lake.' And Earle said 'I'll commit myself to support the public park system.' So on the way back to the office, Mr. Paxton asked me what I thought and I said we ought to support him. He's going to win. And it'd be silly not to be on the winning side."

In the fall of that year, Highway Commissioner J. Stephen Watkins predicted: "The roads we build today will build the Kentucky of tomorrow." Better roads were key to drawing new tourists to the state. The pace of post war road construction accelerated, just in time to accompany the rapid pace of parks construction in 1948.

Tolls on 13 bridges were removed between 1943-1947, which brought more travelers, more traffic and increased gasoline tax revenues. Watkins was confident that "Better Park facilities, better highways, free bridges" were on the horizon, and that the Division of Parks, Publicity and Highways will bring "...thousands of new dollars into Kentucky."

Photos from the December 1947 inauguration of Kentucky's 47th governor feature men, women and children, dressed in their Sunday best, enthusiastically braving the cold as the governor's parade passes by. The coach—Earle Clements—and the crusader—Henry Ward, teamed up to erase Kentucky's image as a poor, illiterate state governed by "nobodies." Instead, they raced to build and promote a recreational paradise—a new Kentucky home committed to increased investment in education, infrastructure and industry.

# 16 Let's Make A Deal

In 1948, Henry arranged a dinner meeting with Governor Clements and west Kentucky legislators, where he announced: "I have been authorized by TVA to say that the facilities and 1,000 acres of land will be turned over to the state of Kentucky for park purposes. A fair appraisal of the value of the land is $2 million. TVA expects some compensation, of course, but has agreed that they will accept $35,000…Governor Clements commented: 'That sounds like a good deal,'" and suggested someone introduce a bill to grab it. Henry did the next day, recalling "With Clements' help, it passed easily, so Kentucky Dam Village State Park was born."

Earle Clements was inaugurated as Kentucky's 47th governor December 9, 1947. Cordial and courteous, he was still a man of few words, but on that day, he pledged that he would "not compromise with principle," and called for the renewal of unselfish service from every citizen. The scientific community would play an important role in his administration, he announced, by surveying "the resources we have and find new uses for them. We shall also search for new resources; each one found means added prosperity to our people."

As crowds lined the streets and grounds of the Capitol that day, the festivities included parades, music, songs, a day off and a day of pride for Kentuckians across the state. Men dressed formally in suits and heavy wool overcoats. Women wrapped in glossy fur coats and elegant hats enjoyed the music and spectacle of the inaugural parade. The procession featured 50 cars, numerous bands and drum and bugle corps. Elaborately decorated floats celebrated the Mercer County pioneers, the American Legion and Louisville's Mose Green Democratic Club. Two orchestras played at the inaugural ball, and "...guests danced on all three marble floors of the spacious state Capitol" into the early morning hours.

Legislators experienced some whiplash adjusting from the somber and plodding Willis administration to the fast paced management style ex-football coach Clements preferred. As John Ed Pearce recalled, "Clements was a man of terrific intellect and great personal power, a forceful personality. He would have made a great President."

Clements' priorities included modernizing the constitution, promoting tourism and recruiting new industry, and increasing education funding, reforms he believed could reverse Kentucky's decline.

The population recently decreased by 10%. Nationally, 95 out of 100 children finished eighth grade but in Kentucky, it was 63 out of 100. In 1944, Kentucky ranked 41$^{st}$ out of 48 states in education funding, and teacher turnover remained high due to low pay. In many counties, families lacked even basic telephone service, but the number of outhouses in rural areas remained steady.

Yet it was an era in politics and government driven by thriving civic engagement. Harry Schacter, an irrepressible Louisville department store president, organized a civic committee in the early 1940s to barnstorm the state, holding listening sessions to identify problems and issues holding the state back.

Schacter lamented the state's long fifty-year slide from the top to the bottom in educational, industrial and cultural progress. Once upon a time Kentucky was "a famed cultural and world-trade center. It was an important fashion center. Young brides-to-be came to Louisville for their trousseaus from as far away as New Orleans."

That sentence a throwback to scenes reminiscent of *Gone with the Wind* and the Rowan era of music and dancing at the old Kentucky home, the committee collected community feedback, and collaborated with professionals to submit reports on agriculture, health, education, housing, labor, natural resources, taxation and transportation. During the Clements administration, some of their recommendations were adopted by the General Assembly, and the committee summarized their findings in a book titled *Kentucky on the March*.

Governor Clements' files in the Margaret King Library at University of Kentucky are a testament to an era of citizen engagement evidenced by telegrams, letters and records of phone calls from Kentuckians from every walk of life. Inside the boxes and files, Clements' response, preserved on brittle, onionskin carbon copies, document a personal connection between citizen and politician.

The Izaak Walton League, Farm Bureau, conservation and wildlife clubs, church pastors, industry executives, disgruntled out of state visitors protesting speeding tickets and of course, state job seekers, all petitioned the Governor for help.

Those who knew him best, as Fred Paxton recalled, admired a master politician who knew how to get things done. Paxton, his father and brothers acknowledged that "if you wanted something done you better be right with Earle Clements or it wasn't going to get done."

In January of 1948, Clements addressed the General Assembly, anticipating legislators would carry out his agenda with a maximum of speed and minimum of fuss:

"80 counties in Kentucky are without industrial development of significance. ... The sound way to develop new income to defray the expenses of new and expanded governmental services are to develop new sources of income. A prime new source of new income will be the new industries which we will bring into Kentucky. An equally important source will be the development of the tourist trade through the expansion and construction of new facilities in our parks. No action on the part of the Legislature is required in connection with expanding the park and tourist program, but because the program will be of active and continuing interest throughout this administration, I mention it here and assure you that great effort will be made by those entrusted with this authority to bring the greatest development possible in the next four years."

That authority rested with the Conservation Commissioner. On the last day of the session, Earle offered Henry the job. Clements, a "KU Man," believed Henry was uniquely qualified to modernize the park system—a key component of his total economic development plan. For once, Henry was speechless. He voted against Earle in the primary, and everyone knew it. "You're kidding," Ward recalled having told the Governor. "Why, even your friends will cut out your heart for giving me the job."

Yet, Lester Cox, Richard Maloney and Lieutenant Governor Lawrence Wetherby all urged Clements to recruit Ward for the job—and Clements was in a hurry to start the job.

Prior to Henry's appointment, Clements and Ward each worked separately to advance park investment, but little communication passed between them. During his campaign, Clements met with TVA's chairman, Gordon R. Clapp, and requested TVA delay any transfer of surplus property until Earle was sworn in as Governor. Clearly irritated, Clapp replied Earle had not even been elected yet and lacked the authority to even ask, but "The Kentuckian boldly retorted 'Yes, but I am going to be!'"

Henry was also unaware that in December 1947, Clements asked Princeton builder and businessman Rumsey Taylor to undertake a confidential "... 'shotgun appraisal' of all the purchasable properties...[He] reported back that the TVA cottages alone were worth $18,000 to $20,000 apiece, that the land was worth $500 an acre, and that if Clements could buy everything for $250,000, he would have 'a steal!'"

Henry was preoccupied by two bills he prepared for the 1948 session. "I expected of course, that we'd make another effort [to block repeal of the TVA bill] in '48 because Clements had been very close to KU, particularly all of his life. When he was a member of the senate, he'd side with KU all the time, so that I assumed he would be for their bill. So I went up there prepared to have another fight about it."

He drafted a bill removing REA from the jurisdiction of the Public Service Commission. His strategy was to "give them something different to fight about," he remembered. It eliminated the requirement that the cooperatives obtain a certificate of necessity from the PSC—a tactic he hoped would force Republicans to abandon plans to advance the Moss bill and rally enough votes to kill the REA bill. To his surprise, the bill made it out of the Senate committee, and Henry got a call from the Governor to come see him. Earle informed Henry he would not sign the bill if it passed and explained why. After his inauguration, Clements let utility executives know he preferred they drop the Moss bill, telling them "that I would not do anything for the utilities, but that also I would not let anything be done to them. This bill would do something to the utilities—take them [REA] away from the power of the public service commission and I've got to oppose it."

Henry replied if had known Earle warned the utility companies off, he would not have introduced the bill. Explaining it was a "...defensive measure," the bill was now dead, but Henry respected Clements for taking the time to explain his position to him. Henry met with Earle three times during the session of 1948 before Earle offered him the job as Commissioner of Conservation.

"I had been working with the Tennessee Valley Authority to turn the village built by TVA at Gilbertsville during construction of Kentucky Dam into a tourist facility. It had numerous fine buildings, a modern water and sewage system, roads and other facilities. Dwellings which had been built to house construction officials and workers during building of the dam could be converted to tourist accommodations, especially since they were located in a park-like area that had been landscaped by TVA. The village even had a hospital, and a golf course. There was an auditorium and restaurant."

"TVA said if the state would take it, we'll agree to sell. Give the state twelve-fifteen hundred acres of land...And all those cottages, and all those buildings that are there, for what we considered the salvage value -thirty-eight thousand dollars."

I asked Governor Clements to attend a dinner meeting with legislators from western Kentucky. I explained the negotiations which and been carried out with TVA. I told the governor and the group: 'I have been authorized by TVA to say that the facilities and 1,000 acres of land at Kentucky Dam will be turned over to the state of Kentucky for park purposes. A fair appraisal of the value of the property is $2 million. TVA expects some compensation, of course, but has agreed that it will accept $35,000,'" (for a one-year lease.)

"Governor Clements commented: 'Well, all I can say is if I were a member of the legislature, I'd introduce a bill to take 'em up on it.' The next morning, I introduced the bill to take them up on it. So we got the original TVA for thirty eight thousand dollars. And later on, a whole lot of other stuff which was not included in the original deal. For a little over a hundred thousand dollars, we got a lot singled to be worth two to three million dollars. Now that was because that was the '48 session and I became the commissioner in April. The—I well remember from my prices. We had ten of those large—what we call deluxe cottages that were built for the supervisor of personnel. Well, they rivaled home, and there were more modest cabins scattered around there, and, well obviously we had to charge more for these deluxe places than the others. And I've forgotten the rates we figured out, but I was afraid at the time that God I—I was scared of the rates—and people just grabbed them up real fast because they were really damned nice places, but—that was the first major push. Well, that plus getting Kenlake started, building the hotel and new cabins and boating, and bathhouses and other facilities. Those two were the first two big pushes."

Henry's bill to purchase what was then called the Aurora Landing area, passed on March 9, 1948. The state paid $35,000 for 1,146 acres of land and facilities for use as a state park in Hardin, Kentucky near the city of Murray. The second development project was the lake and shoreline area of what was then, one of the largest man-made lakes in the nation. Henry remembered that with Clements' help, the bill passed easily, and "So Kentucky Dam Village State Park was born."

On the last night of the session, Clements asked Henry to stop by again. Clements reminded Henry that, "You and your friends worked to get me committed to supporting a good state park system, and I am ready to carry out that promise. But I cannot do it by myself, I need someone I know will take charge of this program and move it ahead. You are the man I want. I want you to accept appointment as commissioner of conservation."

"It came as a shock," Ward recalled. "While I had gained respect for Clements during the 1948 session, I had opposed him in the 1947 primary, giving very vigorous support to Harry Lee Waterfield. In addition to that, I did not want a job in government. I told Clements that I had a strong commitment to *The Sun-Democrat*, and I had already spent too much time away from my duties there as associate editor. I thanked him for his confidence, but declined to accept."

By the time Henry returned home, Clements had already telephoned Edwin Paxton, Sr., reminding Paxton that he and Henry had been promoting parks for years.

Henry explained to Paxton he was reluctant to leave the newspaper. "Mr. Paxton wasn't the type to try to persuade. However, he did point out that a lot of people had put time and effort into the move to get a state park program rolling, and perhaps I should not decide against it too hastily, since the governor seemed to be giving me the opportunity. ..."

A second worry held Henry back from accepting—he was proud of his reputation as an "anti-administration" man. As a longstanding and vocal critic of the state patronage system, he would not participate in a system that awarded state park jobs in exchange for political votes or favors.

This was one issue on which Henry and former conservation commissioner Russell Dyche agreed. In Dyche's 1945-46 annual report, he urged legislators to adopt a merit system for state employees. "It has proven suicidal to turn over the operation of a park to a concessioner," he wrote. Relying on private concessions "... reflected conditions sometimes closely resembling major political graft, and has not removed ineffectiveness of petty political influence."

Reporter Falcon Baker confirmed the strength of the political spoils system in his 1955 *Saturday Evening Post* article showcasing Kentucky's parks. When word got out Henry had been offered the job, "Everyone wanted a front seat on the patronage train," Ward remembered. Baker recounted one incident that convinced Henry it was hopeless:

"A county chairman who had produced an unexpected majority for Clements traveled halfway across the state to name the job he was willing to accept. Instead of discussing the kind of work he was qualified to do in the park system, he favored Ward with a half- hour lecture on his political prowess. Ward's patient smile began to fade.

"You're not really looking for a job," he said. "You're just looking for a monthly check from the state. Isn't that true?"

For a moment, the man looked hurt. Then he shrugged. "Well, the state has to have some way of paying us." Ward swept all the job hunters out of his living room …"

He met with Earle again, explained—"I'm not a patronage man, I don't believe in it. I'm not going to do anything improper. I'm going to have professional people. Not a bunch of damn political bums," he insisted.

Clements reassured him that "If you will take the job, I will put it this way: If you need me, call on me. If you don't need me, forget about me." "I was assured of his full cooperation and freedom to administer the program, including freedom from political pressures," Henry recalled. "To me, good government is good politics," replied Clements. "I believe you will do a good job."

Something else was on his mind, and Henry explained that since his campaign manager, Lucy Smith, had been appointed director of state parks, she would likely resent Henry taking over as commissioner, especially since he backed Earle's opponent in the primary.

"If I am given the job, I do not mind taking full responsibility, but I also have to have the authority," Henry told the governor. "I have already talked with Mrs. Smith," the governor replied. "She fully understands that you will be the boss, and that you will have my full confidence and support."

"So I agreed to become Commissioner of Conservation, with the idea that I would stay there two years, to get the program going. I stayed eight—being reappointed by Governor Lawrence Wetherby in 1952. And Mrs. Smith and I became good friends, and there was never any friction or disagreement. In fact, I think she was relieved, her background being in education, as a principal and county school superintendent with no exposure or interest in a state park program."

# 17 No More Pioneer Stuff

"For years I hooted at Frank's fishing trips,' she said. 'He'd offer to take me along-I guess he wanted a camp cook and pot washer- but I wasn't going to be roped into all that pioneer stuff. Not until the children were older, anyway. Then I heard about the park cottages here, and I agreed to a weekend trial.' Since that first trip, three years ago, they have spent a week at the park every summer. On their first day, Frank talked his wife into a try at fishing. Miraculously she caught a two-pound croppie on a cane pole. "Never have hooked another one that big,' she says, 'but I caught the fishing fever worse than Frank.'"

MRS. FRANK BURKES, vacationing at Kentucky Lake State Park, 1955.

Clements' announcement that he appointed Henry Commissioner received favorable statewide news coverage. "Some people might think this appointment is a bad one, politically," Clements commented. "But those who are genuinely interested in conservation will know it is a good one."

Ward confirmed the offer came as a complete surprise. "The Governor didn't even mention it to me until the last day of the legislature. He remarked he didn't want anyone to get the idea he was trying to influence me," Ward said, adding that during the last week of the session he opposed some of the administration's agenda.

The Conservation Department was divided into four divisions: Parks, Publicity, Forestry and Soil and Water Resources, and less than a month after Clements signed the bill adding Kentucky Dam Village State Park to the parks system, Henry hit the ground running.

"I had some credentials beyond my interest in state parks in conservation that made it a bit more appropriate that I take on the commissionership, particularly in the field of conservation legislation. At the 1942 session I sponsored the first bill in Kentucky relating to water pollution control. It was a bill to authorize Kentucky to join eight other states in the Ohio River Valley to combat water pollution in the valley through a compact commission. I sponsored a bill to permit landowners to establish soil and water conservation districts. I had promoted higher appropriations for the state forestry [division]. I had a background of 20 years in publicity, advertising and promotion. ... So, I found myself in the position of administering programs I had advocated as a legislator."

In his memoir, Henry remarked his interest in conservation never diminished. "I still think water is Kentucky's most important natural resource. I have seen with appreciation the growing concern about ecology, and remembered how little there was back in those early days when we were getting programs started. Back in those days, it was not considered good politics to be concerned with such things as water pollution and strip mining, and the general opinion was that the only pollution of the air came from political speeches."

The underfunded and long-neglected system included thirteen state parks and six historic shrines or monuments. At the end of 1947, $487,000 (approximately six million dollars today) was available for capital improvements.

As Henry and Gladys prepared to move to Frankfort, Henry asked Clements to trade the department's Jeep for a more comfortable car. "I am going to have to arrange for some form of motor transportation, for one part of the agreement I had to make with friend wife in order to persuade her that I should accept this job was that I would leave our car with her at Paducah. She is in charge of the Girl Scout camp on Kentucky Lake this year, and will use our car in that connection until late July," he explained.

He made it a priority to visit all the parks as quickly as he could to get a sense of the job ahead. In Falcon Baker's *Saturday Evening Post* profile, Henry described a visit to My Old Kentucky Home that guided his philosophy as Commissioner:

"All over the world they sing, 'The sun shines bright in the old Kentucky home' but I found the sun couldn't get in. The shutters were kept closed. In the dim light, visitors couldn't see the dilapidation. While Ward was discussing repairs with the curator, a woman visitor was trying to interest her two small boys in the antique furniture, and getting nowhere. When they began to play tag, she herded them toward the second floor. At the top of the stairs she yelled, 'John... Pete, stop!' Ward looked up to see the boys sliding down the rickety banister."

"This lack of reverence dismayed the curator, but it occurred to Ward that the boys had shown him the fault with Kentucky parks. Here was My Old Kentucky Home, a famous place. But what could you do with it? You couldn't ride it. You couldn't eat it. You couldn't even sleep in it. All you could do was look at it, and once you could say you'd been there, you didn't have to come back."

"That day convinced Ward that old fashioned parks wouldn't do for post-war Americans. They might pause at spots of scenic beauty. They might doff their hats at historic monuments. But then they would tramp on the accelerator and rush away in search of some place where the entire family could have fun doing something."

That was exactly what post-war Americans were doing, and hospitality professionals predicted revenue from automobile travel and tourism would increase from $6 billion to $10 billion in 1948.

From 1940-47, despite the war, Kentucky's annual park receipts grew from $63,860.01 to $172,558.80, a 37% increase. Russell Dyche hired consultant W.T. Ammerman, a landscape architect at the National Parks Service, to tour all of the parks and prepare a master plan for each. Dyche delayed spending the 1946 appropriations until Ammerman finished his report, but Dyche was no longer in charge.

In his oral history, Henry recalled his frustration over the delay. "And I raised hell but it didn't do any good. So, when I got over there, they had about seven hundred thousand of that eight hundred thousand still there, and I told Earle 'Now I told you about this thing. I said, 'Now I know one thing for sure, if you appoint me, I'm going to spend it before the first of July,' because if you didn't spend it by the first of July, it goes back to the general fund. He said 'Go ahead, go to it.' Well, I was appointed in April, April 15. The first part of May he called me over and said 'I've been checking around and I've discovered there's one hundred thousand dollars in construction funds available to the governor, which goes back to the general fund if it isn't under contract by first of July. You can have it if you can get it under contract—you can have it.'

"I said 'Oh, for God's sake, Earle. This is May, we have to have plans ... but ... O.K., we'll do it.' The biggest project of mine was a hotel at Kentucky Lake State Park. Got an architect, designed a hotel real fast. Goes out to the bids, expecting it's probably going to be at half a million dollars, came in at about three hundred sixty-five. We got a bunch of other projects ... did a bunch of other projects. So advertised for bids to come in before the first of July, and I talked to Earle. I said 'Not only we got enough bids, good bids to use your million, but I need two hundred fifty thousand more.' He said 'O.K.'"

"I never asked Earle Clements for a thing but what he gave me. I was reasonable. I'd been around the legislature myself and knew the responsibility, but I didn't try to gouge him. But he supported me one hundred percent all the way."

Governor Clements places the crown of laurel blossoms on the flowing tresses of Her Gracious Highness, Miss Lyde Gooding of Lexington, Queen of the 1948 Mountain Laurel Festival.
*Department of Highways Photograph*

*Governor Earle Clements crowns the Queen of the Mountain Laurel Festsival (1948)*

At the end of June, he accompanied Clements to Cincinnati to join the governors of seven states for a ceremony formalizing a multi-state compact to decrease pollution in the Ohio River and surrounding tributaries.

A significant public health reform, newspapers reported its impact would result in "Pure drinking water and better health protection for 20,000,000 persons in the United States...The compact, a reality after 13 years of negotiations, binds the states together to control sewage and industrial wastes through a joint authority. It affects 200,000 square miles and many streams which wind their way into the Ohio River."

The headlines were accompanied by photos of officials seated shoulder to shoulder at a long conference table, taking turns signing the compact. The same week, the White House announced President Truman signed the Barkley-Taft Anti-Stream Pollution bill.

During the ceremony, Governor Clements remarked the federal bill "is not as far-reaching as I would have desired," but that the compact was a good start. He pledged "the best efforts of his administration toward making the compact 'an effective success.'" The Governor paid tribute to Henry Ward, Paducah, new state commissioner of conservation, who, as state Senator, introduced the ratification bill in the Kentucky Legislature. 'Ward is a pioneer in sane conservation and I am happy that he is permitted to participate in the ceremonies today."

Henry had so much to do he may have resented the time away from his schedule that day. That summer the state magazine, *In Kentucky,* carried an informative article (likely written by Henry), titled "Kentucky On The March Toward Outstanding State Park System," that detailed multiple projects underway.

At Kentucky Dam, existing TVA village housing and cottages provided 100 available rooms, and more on the way because the agency planned to gradually relinquish all of its remaining facilities to the state by December 1949. TVA reported 111,000 people visited the dam in May 1948.

Major road projects included a bridge across the dam to handle increased car traffic and a second bridge to eliminate the need for a ferry on the Cumberland River. A new, 20-mile highway was under construction from Paducah to the lake as well.

During the Willis administration, a seawall and beach, trails, picnic facilities and a boat dock were completed and opened to the public. South of the Kentucky Dam, Henry authorized multiple construction projects at Kentucky Lake State Park that included a bath house, picnic shelters, concession stands and restrooms, an airport and fish cleaning facility. Because Kentucky Dam and Kentucky Lake were brand new, much of Henry's time and attention was directed to west Kentucky. But once underway, he and Lucy Smith supervised overdue improvements and maintenance at parks throughout the state.

At Cumberland Falls, he approved repairs at the DuPont Lodge and renovations in the Moonbow Inn. New cabins were added, and a new water system installed. The state reached a settlement with D.D. Stewart, the former owner of the Cumberland Falls Hotel, over damages from a fire that occurred three days after the state purchased it in November, 1947.

Tom Wallace assisted during the negotiations and the state retained ownership. That resolution was best, he explained, because the site "...literally speaking, overhangs Cumberland Falls State Park and which will be a menace to the park, no matter how owned or treated, until the state owns it."

Years earlier, during Henry's visit to Natural Bridge State Park, he described the Hemlock Lodge as a wreck, and a flood later washed out the dam and destroyed the lake. In the early 1900s, trainloads of visitors and sightseers disembarked there to enjoy music, concerts, dancing and picnics, events Henry hoped would resume after he awarded a contract for reconstruction of the lake and dam. The cabins at Butler Memorial State Park (now called General Butler Resort Park) in Carrollton were modernized. The Park's popularity was rising, despite the fact access via a modern highway—Interstate 71—would not be completed until 1966, under Highway Commissioner Ward.

Repairs, maintenance and improvements continued in east Kentucky at Pennyrile State Park, Levi Jackson Park in London, at My Old Kentucky Home, Pioneer Memorial in Harrodsburg, Carter Caves near Grayson and Pine Mountain in Pineville.

Sworn in as Commissioner in mid-April, Henry had little more than 90 days to commit all of the funding, and he succeeded, at a pace mirroring the urgent rollout of the relief programs launched by President Roosevelt in 1933.

The Roosevelt administration's speed and efficiency, aided by a Democratic majority in Congress, made a deep impression on Henry's approach to public administration. Still operating under a deadline mentality, once the newspaper editor corralled all the facts and research about a project or problem, he expected the staff to produce results.

State employees accustomed to a culture of low expectations and an indifferent attitude toward visitors now raced to keep up with "Hammerin' Hank." The Commissioner was not above grabbing a broom to tidy up a sidewalk near a lodge entryway, or to jump in and bus tables at a state park restaurant if he believed the lines of waiting diners were too long.

He guessed his leave from the newspaper would last two years, but he stayed seven. His on-the-job training earned the high school graduate the informal equivalent of a master's degree in public administration and construction management.

The *In Kentucky* article predicted that this program of progressive management would sweep away the "accumulated neglect of years," by building lodges and cabins to "care for the tide of visitors that want to come to Kentucky, to see the wonderful attractions this state has to offer, and to share in its famous hospitality. ... Kentucky is moving forward--at a fast clip."

The timing of his appointment marked a near perfect alignment of Henry's interests, skill and experience, culminating in a significant shift in state park management and policy. The speed of its modernization and the size of the parks' expansion and investment pushed Kentucky to the forefront in tourism and recreation.

*Ward and Governor Weatherby reviewing* The Saturday Evening Post *article (1955)*

He proposed two key conservation bills to acquire TVA's surplus land and buildings, and to boost the capital outlay for parks investment and expansion. As a former state legislator, he knew where the money was and how to get it released, and his knowledge netted the Conservation Department an extra $350,000 for construction. And once again, he claimed he was just "lucky" or in the right place at the right time, after Governor Clements offered to release an additional $600,000 from the Governor's Building Commission to keep going. In just a two-year period alone, Kentucky invested over $2,000,000 in the park system, (or the equivalent of 25 million dollars today), exceeding all of the money spent on parks from 1924 through 1949.

Kentucky Dam Village Park rapidly exceeded expectations, both for TVA and Kentucky. Administrators reported it "ranked second in tourism, exceeded only by the Fontana Dam parks complex of the Great Smoky Mountains."

In the modern recreational model Henry envisioned, the goal was to keep Mrs. Frank Burkes and her young family active and happy during their stay, and to keep them coming back. Professional park planners and managers were trained to deliver that experience. Henry's well-publicized plan to recruit and hire professionals to implement uniform hospitality standards triggered resistance among employees and concessioners who had been awarded, in many cases, long standing and lucrative leases. That threat to their livelihoods and those sweetheart deals (often approved by powerful county political party chairmen) stirred resentment that culminated in a massive fire of suspicious origin in 1949 that destroyed the famous Moonbow Inn.

## 18 A Firebugs' Playground

"Was negligence an unwitting ally of arson in the fire that destroyed historic Moonbow Inn at Cumberland Falls State Park Sunday night? An inquiry into that question would seem appropriate. ...Leaving so valuable a state property insufficiently guarded would have been imprudent and unbusinesslike in any circumstances. In this instance there was ample cause to be doubly alert by reason of the fact that two other hotels in the park area had burned in recent years. ...Mrs. Lucy L. Smith, state park director at Frankfort, has indicated there is no doubt in her mind that the Cumberland Falls Hotel fire, as well as that at Moonbow, was of incendiary origin, though no arrest was ever made."

*WHITLEY REPUBLICAN*, March 17, 1949

From April of 1948 through the date of that fire—March 13, 1949, it seemed everything crossing Henry's desk was urgent. They included several letters or, more accurately, ultimatums, from the nephew of "Uncle Willie" Curtis, asking the state to purchase Curtis' collection of Native American relics, antique firearms and prehistoric fossils he owned and curated for the Blue Licks State

Park Museum. Mr. Martin described his uncle as getting on in years, and not in the best of health.

At the young age of 14, William Curtis became fascinated with the history of the Battle of Blue Licks in Robertson County. In 1928, he led a fund drive to purchase and donate 32 acres of the historic battleground to the state. After serving as state representative for Robertson and Nicholas Counties in 1934, he was appointed superintendent of Blue Licks Park and retired in 1945.

Curtis spent a lifetime accumulating the park's exceptional collection of pioneer artifacts, some of which were linked to Daniel Boone. Unless the state paid his uncle a pension, Martin wrote, the family would sell the collection to the highest bidder. Uncle wanted to settle the matter and move to Florida, and Martin needed an answer now.

In June, Henry received an irate three-page letter from E. M. Gatliff, a prominent Democratic attorney from Williamsburg, complaining Mark Hardin resigned as manager at Cumberland Falls State Park. Hardin protested a request that he prepare a cabin for the New Assistant Director of Parks, H.E. Dahl, who was assigned to live there with his family.

Dahl immediately implemented "various rules and restrictions" that were "totally unnecessary," said Gatliff. He urged Hardin to reconsider, and assured him he would ask Commissioner Ward to obtain "some relief from the foolish and un-necessary orders that come from the Frankfort office."

Gatliff confirmed that "Governor Clements told me before and after the election to keep my eyes on matters in the Cumberland Falls State Park and assist him in every possible manner to remove the defects that had existed under the former administration," he wrote.

"Keeping his eye on things" included exerting unchecked political influence over state business in Whitley County. Heir to his father's coal business, Gatliff was also a former member of the state Democratic Party Executive Committee.

In 1936, Gatliff arranged for Hardin to win the contract to operate DuPont Lodge, the Moonbow Inn and 25 cabins at Cumberland Falls State Park. Citing Hardin's knowledge of the operation and clientele as an asset, Gatliff assured Henry that Hardin could "in many ways restore to the hotels the good name they once bore."

More than once, Henry took a combative and public stand against political patronage. Henry acknowledged state park jobs were given (or taken away), based on the whims of county "contact men" who controlled local politics and patronage, but Earle and Henry had a unique understanding, and Gatliff's complaint forced Henry to put his principles into practice as a political appointee in state government.

Gatliff asserted that Dahl's appointment upset the status quo: "The gentleman from Harvard is a total misfit and has about as much business trying to handle Cumberland Falls Park as some twelve -year-old child. Can you possibly tell me why we should be inflicted with all these northern republican Yankees in the State Park which could be easily be managed by a Kentuckian?"

Henry's response was to continue recruiting a permanent staff of state employees with professional hospitality and management credentials. He did not have the time or desire to smooth things over with Gatliff; he was too busy racing to get half a million dollars under contract for new construction and long overdue improvements.

Henry relied on facts and research to guide him, and so did Clements, although he obtained them through an informal network of close contacts across the state. A confidential report in Clements' files on the situation at Cumberland Falls, written by an unnamed investigator, confirmed what the Governor suspected—that the rumors about rampant bootlegging, shifty bookkeeping and indifferent service at Cumberland Falls State Park were all true.

Clements' informant stayed there as a guest, observing the daily activities of the key employees running operations at the park. The writer observed that Mark Hardin was "about fifty years old and appears very dissipated. When first observed, Mr. Hardin was wearing a green sport shirt which he wore for three days without changing. At that time he changed into a chamois skin jacket which he wore for two days and which was filthy. He then changed into a maroon sport shirt which he wore for three consecutive days. The purpose of the foregoing description is to show that Mr. Hardin puts forth no effort to appear as a business-like hotel manager, but that he enters the lobby and mixes with the guests of the lodge as though the guests were mountaineers."

Hardin and his wife under the influence of alcohol most of the time, "Mr. Hardin was very much worried about his wife, Elizabeth, as she was seeing 'pink elephants' coming in and out of the doors and windows and the walls. He called for a doctor to come to the lodge to give her a shot in the arm, in order to quiet her so that she would not disturb the guests in the hotel."

In September of 1948, Hardin's close friend, Walter Lanham, was indicted by federal authorities after they received a tip that Lanham was bootlegging inside the park. Hardin hired Lanham's wife as caretaker of Cabin Group #2 at the park. A convenient set up, after Lanham smuggled the moonshine and beer into the park, guests approved by Hardin were instructed to visit the Lanham's cabin, hand over some cash, and pick up their "refreshment."

After Hardin's resignation, his friends agreed to drive down the receipts so drastically that state officials would reconsider reinstating his lease agreement for the Inn, Lodge and cabins.

The detective's report often reads like a script for a soap opera. One night, during just one of the many loud and drunken parties in the Lanham cabin, an employee speculated that the loss of a ferry encased in ice and the Cumberland Falls Hotel fire were not accidents. "Mr. Hardin and Mr. Masters were very cagey about describing the loss of the hotel, and the loss of the ferry boat, as they winked at one another as if to say, 'better not say too much about it.' Mrs. Hardin started to sing a song so that her husband, Mr. Hardin, would get the hint and keep quiet."

The fire at Cumberland Falls Hotel in late 1947, located just across the river from the Moonbow Inn and DuPont Lodge, disrupted the state's plan to add additional lodging near the park. After the hotel burned, Harold Fisher and his wife were hired as superintendent and bookkeeper at the Falls, and it was no surprise their arrival stirred resentment and anger within Mark Hardin's tight-knit group of employees and caretakers.

Over that summer, Hardin's exit prompted his efforts, and that of Hardin loyalists, to disparage the Fishers' management of the lodge and Inn. Mrs. Fisher paid the bills and kept financial records, and Mr. Fisher announced all telephone calls now be centrally routed to his office. The couple's administrative efficiency was admirable, but they were unaware that departing guests were directed to stop by Walter Lanham's cabin, where he "had a little gift to give them to take with them, and this gift was a two-quart mason jar of 'Kentucky Moonshine.'"

The investigator also befriended Eve Sparrow, a hostess working at the Lodge. Vivacious and talkative, she declared she was happy to socialize with the guests and enjoyed playing cards or bridge "at the drop of a hat," but she also readily expressed her sympathy for Hardin's predicament.

Previously, Sparrow explained, Hardin leased the Inn and lodge in a way that paid him much more money than this new 1948 contract "under which he is forced to operate now." Their little group decided to deliberately curb profits, hoping to persuade state officials to return to a lease agreement with Hardin the next year.

Their tactics included booking to capacity, "but with single reservations when they should be doubles ... cabins which are suitable for two and three couples are being reserved [and charged] for one couple. If the revenue can't be controlled in this manner and the receipts for the month appear to be grossing too high, they have planned to increase the amount of the food served in the dining room and the quality of it making the food costs higher in the operation. Should further steps be necessary there will be abnormal breakage of dishes and an over purchase of supplies for the dining room. The remark was made that there were 130,000 place mats on hand but they would purchase 100,000 more to show increased expenditures. Also the plan is to purchase colored tablecloths and napkins for use at dinner time in the dining room at an approximate cost of $500.00."

As tension escalated at Cumberland Falls, enthusiastic crowds flocked to Kentucky Dam Village State Park and Kentucky Lake. TVA officials reported 42,000 people visited Kentucky Lake over the July 4 weekend. Henry was there, too, gratified by the sight of so many visitors enjoying the beach, lake and picnic areas. "We took over operation of the village July 1, and have our own personnel established in the restaurant and commissary," Henry reported to the Governor.

In September of 1948, W.T. Ammerman, a landscape architect with the National Park Service, submitted his completed survey to the Conservation Department. For two weeks in August, Ammerman and Hilbert Dahl visited 9 state parks. Ammerman was impressed by the scenery, noting their "excellent natural quality, the variety of scenic attractions is good, and the locations of state parks in the state is fairly well-balanced."

Yet, right next door in Indiana, "one-fourth of State Park hotels in the U.S. are located there," strengthening the justification for adding new hotels and cabins in seven parks: Cumberland Falls, Natural Bridge, Butler, Carter Caves, Kentucky Dam, Kentucky Lake and Pennyrile State Park.

Ammerman reinforced the need to remove politics (as much as possible) from the operation of the system: "The State of Kentucky, acting through its authorized representatives, and no one else, should retain complete control over all activities including planning, construction and development work and the management or operations of hotels or a system of hotels or other public concessions."

Those recommendations—to increase investment, build modern facilities and hire trained staff, were aligned closely with national park standards and guidelines, and Earle and Henry were determined to meet or exceed those benchmarks.

With all the previously budgeted capital funding now under contract, Clements and Ward considered a new option—revenue bonds, to continue the expansion. Annual parks appropriations jumped from $30 thousand dollars to a capital outlay of $840,000 thousand dollars in just two years; bond financing would continue that momentum.

Revenue bonds a new concept in park financing, Henry informed Clements he planned to move cautiously: "I explained to Mr. Graham and Mr. Cregor that this is a new administration and that it has the responsibility of carrying forward the program for improvement of the parks. Under the circumstances, I explained, this administration must assure itself that it is proceeding in the proper manner before taking final steps. I also explained that my recommendations regarding any contract between the state and the investment houses would have to be based on more information than is now available regarding exactly what the investment house would do in return for the payment they would receive."

To date, the rapid rollout of the parks program had been popular with the public, but the next six months tested Ward's patience as he scrambled to keep the Conservation Department from descending into chaos.

W.E. Martin fired off three more letters, demanding the state close a deal with Uncle Willie by purchasing his collection for $25,000. He mentioned three local judges willing to "lend their influence" during negotiations, because "everyone I talk with, volunteers to the effect that there would be no park without Uncle Willie's relics."

In late October, Martin asked Henry to increase his uncle's pension from $75 to $125 to pay for his medical care. Curtis' health was declining rapidly—he was now blind and confined to a nursing home. Henry wrote to Clements, explaining that "The Division of Parks does not have either $10,000 or $25,000 in its operating budget for the purchase of this collection." He agreed with Curtis' family that without the collection, the park held little attraction for the public, and suggested they treat it as a capital outlay expense.

Henry believed Uncle Willie's stewardship should be rewarded, and was sympathetic to his situation. "Mr. Curtis is entitled to consideration by the State, because he has devoted much of his life to the Park and to the collection, and the people of that area feel very kindly toward him. My personal desire is to do everything possible for him. I have explained that to him, but I added that as a state official, I had to keep in mind the best interest of the State, and I think he understands that."

Handing the decision off to Clements, Henry rushed down to Cumberland Falls in early October. The Whitley County grand jury indicted his new park manager A.J. Finlayson, on a charge of selling liquor in the park.

Henry met with Finlayson and the park employees who testified before the grand jury. He suspected Mark Hardin's friends were involved. Although Walter Lanham had been under surveillance by state and federal officials well before Finlayson arrived, Lanham's friends were furious and blamed Finlayson for his arrest.

The report in the Governor's files suggest this was true. One of the grand jury witnesses, Otis Masters, asked Finlayson to buy liquor for him. Masters owned the Jeep the FBI confiscated after Lanham's arrest, and he blamed Finlayson for his trouble. The investigator observed that Masters "...will do anything that Mr. Hardin asks him to do. There is a definite tie-up between the Masters and the Hardins, and it is the writer's opinion that Mr. Masters is in the clutches of Mr. Hardin...All of the time that Mrs. Hardin was under the influence of liquor, Mrs. Masters took care of her and stayed with her for days at a time, nursing her and watching over her so that she would not disturb the guests at the lodge, or make a scene in front of Mr. and Mrs. Fisher, so that the conditions existing in the lodge are not strained further than they are at the present time."

Henry sent a letter to Judge A.B. Johnson, summarizing his interviews with park employees. Finlayson explained that before he left for a trip to Lexington, several park employees gave him money and asked him to purchase whiskey and gin to bring back to the park.

"While this may be a technical violation of the local option law, and is certainly something that I do not approve, it is a common practice in Kentucky, and I can understand that the average person does not realize that it is a violation of the law," Henry wrote.

Finlayson had an "excellent record" as park manager, who "worked hard to eliminate some of the very bad conditions that exist there. We have had considerable trouble over the selling of moonshine whiskey to park employees and guests, and Mr. Finlayson has worked hard toward trying to stop that." Henry added that after Lanham was arrested, "there was talk around the Park that an effort would be made to 'get even' with Finlayson."

Ward arrived at the park prepared to fire him, but he discovered Finlayson did not intentionally break the law. He assured Johnson that he instructed Finlayson and the superintendent, Mr. Ballard, to keep liquor in any form out of the park, and to "discharge any employee suspected of handling liquor, or the illegal consumption of it. I am sincerely interested in clearing up this problem at Cumberland Falls, even if it requires a complete turn-over in personnel there."

Confident they "learned a lesson," Henry promised to conduct a "proper operation" at the park, and asked for a postponement to complete his investigation. Johnson dismissed the case in January of 1949, and Henry believed the worst was over, until the night of March 13.

Finlayson and three park employees passed by the Moonbow Inn on their regular rounds that night and noticed nothing unusual. The Inn was undergoing a $50,000 renovation, and all the furnishings had been removed.

The next day, bold, black newspaper headlines announced that the "Moonbow Inn at Cumberland Falls Park Burns to Ground in Spectacular Fire of Undetermined Origin Sunday Night."

# 19 Speeding Backward

> "The Chandler second administration was an undistinguished one. As usual, he forgot his promise about no more taxes. He let the state parks run down, and gave concessions in them to political cronies. The start that had been made under the Wetherby administration to control strip-mining dragged to a halt. Chandler was too busy running for president."
>
> Henry Ward, "Recollections of 45 Years in Government and Politics."

The Inn burned March 13, and the estimated cost to rebuild was $110,000. Previously, W.T. Ammerman recommended the state consider two options for the Inn: invest in a complete renovation or tear it down. Despite its colorful history, Ammerman wrote, its location at the edge of the Falls distracted from its beauty. Demolition would free valuable space best reserved for a viewing area and expanded visitor parking.

The fire forced Henry to change direction. He asked the State Building Commission to release the funds set aside for renovation (approximately $50,000) to construct 10 new duplex cabins, and add a larger trading post.

Some good news confirmed summer (peak) parks attendance continued to climb. Around this time, state employees nicknamed Henry "Hammerin'

Hank," as they adjusted to his hard driving management style and the rapid expansion of the parks.

Governor Clements promised to create one of the nation's best park systems, and he did—by investing one-million-dollars for capital improvements his first year in office, an amount equivalent to eleven million dollars today. In 1948, peak park attendance was 451,371 visitors; in 1949 it jumped to 1,408,631.

In 1949, Clements released the extra $50,000 he discovered in the state's emergency fund, and Henry purchased trucks for Carter Caves, curtains for My Old Kentucky Home, $15,000 to purchase Uncle Willie's relics, water pumps, electric repairs and new showers at Pennyrile Park.

He found ways to save money, too. Outside sales representatives solicited ads for the state's tourism magazine *In Kentucky*. In 1948, ad revenue totaled $2209, but the state paid agents a commission of $1104.00.

Henry delegated the job to his staff, and they increased ad revenue by $1400. Circulation grew by 10,000, and Henry gave them full credit for that success. "We are finding that, as advertisers learn that revenue is going into making a better magazine and an increased circulation, they are cooperating by giving us their support. It is my feeling that such State activities always will receive support when it is apparent that every effort is being made to do a good job for the benefit of Kentucky."

He traveled to Washington D.C., to coordinate Army Corps projects underway. Four federal flood control projects were completed at the Dale Hollow Reservoir, and in Middlesboro, Paducah and Taylorsville totaling $29,787,830.00. 12 additional local flood control projects were completed at a cost of $158,505,500.00.

An additional $30,427,000.00 was set aside for approved projects, while another 45 projects remained under consideration.

Kentucky's abundance of water was both blessing and curse, and along with flood control, Henry led the earliest efforts to improve water quality and control flooding.

Long before the Environmental Protection Agency was established, Kentucky's drinking water was unsafe, swimming in the rivers sickened people, and fish were unsafe to eat. Typhoid cases were common, and waterfowl and fish populations moved off or declined. If anything, what was once a beautiful river now resembled an open sewer.

In 1940, Ward introduced a bill permitting Kentucky to join seven other states in a compact to reduce pollution in the Ohio River basin. Organized formally in 1948 as the Ohio River Valley Water Sanitation Commission, their task was to agree on a uniform set of standards for water quality and sanitation. The same year, the General Assembly established a state wide water pollution control commission, and Henry was elected chair of both in 1950.

This led to approval for construction of 311 new sewage plants to reduce pollution from raw sewage and toxins. It was exactly the kind of community service Henry found so rewarding. The end result—cleaner, safer water, made an immediate and significant improvement in the daily lives of residents.

Still, the popularity of Kentucky's parks drew the most attention, proving one county politician's remark that the "greatest industry in Kentucky doesn't belong in a smokestack" was true. The state's annual revenue rankings listed tobacco production first, followed by tourism, then coal mining.

Kentucky's leadership in recreation widely praised and celebrated, the term "public park" was misleading, because Black Kentuckians were still excluded from both state and municipal parks.

Several letters in Governor Clements' files attest to the pain those daily injustices inflicted. In November 1949, Lincoln Hale, President of Evansville College in Indiana, wrote to Henry for permission to allow students from the Botany Department inside Audubon Resort Park for field work.

Henry replied he could not change existing law. "The State of Kentucky provides separate facilities for white and colored. Our own-colored citizens generally prefer this arrangement. It is our hope that we can avoid difficulties that have arisen in other places by an attempt to bring about the joint use of parks by both white and colored persons. I am certain that you can understand that this constitutes a most difficult problem and is one which must be considered from other than merely the point of view of principle."

Mortonsville Pastor J.E. Bowen described his congregation's humiliation at being denied entry into Natural Bridge for a church picnic. "Do you not think that since our boys faught [sic] hard in the last war and the better class of our folk are striving to make this world a better world in which to live, that we should not be mistreated because of our color? If you can do anything to better these conditions I will appreciate it very much."

In 1950, the Reverend J.E. Gillis, pastor of the First Baptist Church in Henderson, wrote to Governor Clements about the recent announcement that a $100,000 pool was being built in Audubon State Park. Although Gillis believed the Governor "to be fair minded and in possession of some facts...you know such a pool would like as not be available to Negro Participation. But Most Honored Governor, we do have a need. And I do mean need. There is no place in Henderson where the Negro Citizenry or their children may benefit by this wholesome and needed recreation under the proper supervision."

To date, the Black community raised more than two thousand dollars to build a pool, but the issue was equality under the law, not money: "That whereas the white citizenry have more than three pools or shall have...Can it not be that we who have contested the right to fight for this country and the freedoms which it entails have your aid in providing...a pool about which we may build a full time supervised recreation program...with an eye to the signs of times one who knows his field I believe it would be wisdom to invest ten thousand dollars ($10,000) in a Negro pool in Henderson, Ky."

Administrative Assistant Paul Combs replied on the Governor's behalf. Appropriations for Audubon's new pool came through the Building Commission for the Department of Parks, he explained, and were restricted to state owned property. Legally, the Governor had no authority to spend Building Commission funds elsewhere.

Across the state, Blacks watched Commissioner Ward's park expansion spree unfold right in front of them, but they were forced to settle for less or go without, even as their own tax dollars paid for parks they dared not enter.

According to a summary of Ward's record on civil rights released during the 1967 campaign, in 1936, he and another colleague prevented cuts in funding for the Western Kentucky Vocational School, a vocational school for Blacks. A reduction would have reclassified the school as a two-year college, rather than a four-year institution, and the General Assembly increased appropriations to $55,000.

In 1940, Black citizens asked Ward to sponsor a bill to establish two segregated park boards for cities of the second class. According to the summary, "In the context of 1940 this was a positive action to give Negro citizens in second class cities representation in municipal park programs where none previously existed whatsoever." In 1946 state Senator Ward voted "yes" to increase the per student state educational allocation for Blacks, and to admit Blacks to medical graduate school programs.

In *Landscapes of Exclusion, State Parks and Jim Crow in the American South,* historian William O'Brien traces the development of "separate but equal" accommodations in recreation, noting that trend peaked after World War II. The Willis administration approved construction of a segregated park for Blacks adjacent to Kentucky Lake, in the city of Aurora, but no park was built.

Henry explained what happened next. "There'd been a push, with the black population, particularly Hopkinsville and Paducah. And I had a meeting with a group of them, and I said 'Now, as far as I'm concerned, come on and use it, we don't have any quote 'policy' and Kenlake is open to you as well as anybody else.' And most of them said 'Well, frankly our people just wouldn't feel right. They wouldn't feel at home, it would be like there were going to—they wouldn't feel right.' And I said 'Would you rather do that, or would you rather we establish parks of your own?' And they said 'We'd rather have a place of our own.' I said 'O.K.' And that's when we established Cherokee," but Ward emphasized that "our policy—we never, never had any kind of suggestion blacks weren't permitted to go into the park." (Kenlake)

In 1951, he addressed a crowd of two thousand Blacks during the dedication of one of the nation's first segregated state parks—Cherokee State Park.

The *Courier-Journal* quoted Henry's remarks that day, as he acknowledged the problem of segregation: "I'm a person who speaks straight from the shoulder," Ward told the crowd. "The question of whether parks of this type should be built is one that is subject to continuing debate in the nation…Those of us charged with the responsibility of developing a park program for Kentucky do not claim that we have the final answer…there is one thing that is clear and that is that while the debate over segregation rages, the colored people of Kentucky are entitled to a park they can enjoy without confusion, conflicts or race riots…"

"The conservation commissioner said he holds to the belief that in a democracy every may[sic] stands equal before God. And some of these days the fight for segregation will be settled," he added. "But until it is, I feel it is the obligation of the State to provide equal recreation facilities for all of its people."

"Colored leaders of this area have indicated by their interest that they prefer a park of their own that their people can enjoy now than to wait until the segregation problem has been settled."

Cherokee, another addition to his bulging portfolio of construction projects, reflected the impact of the New Deal on Henry's philosophy of government. It measured economic and social progress by the numbers—releasing reports totaling the number of jobs, trees, refurbished parks, playgrounds and hospitals built or improved with emergency funds. Still, it remained a New Deal for some, not all. Unable to change the laws, Henry's response was to build something, and he did.

In 1954, the U.S. Supreme Court did settle the issue in *Brown vs. Board of Education of Topeka,* and Commissioner Ward "directed that all State Park facilities be opened to members of all races."

As Highway Commissioner, he abolished segregated maintenance crews, opened Engineering Scholarships to Blacks, and hired Blacks for accounting and drafting positions. He also hired the Department's first diversity coordinator in the Division of Personnel, to recruit and offer specialized training for Blacks to qualify for Highway Department employment.

Governor Clements made some incremental progress as well. He conducted a high-profile campaign to dismantle the entrenched system of politics and patronage in the state college system that threatened its national accreditation, and after an especially bitter confrontation with University of Kentucky trustees, opened Kentucky's professional graduate schools to Blacks.

Rural roads were improved, the park system was considered one of the nation's best, and Clements approved participation in a new topographic mapping program that later proved instrumental to the fast and furious expansion of Kentucky's highway system in the 1960s.

He succeeded in obtaining child labor reforms and improved workmen's compensation law. True to form, both as a U.S. Senator and Governor, Clements measured his administration's success by how well his cabinet and the General Assembly worked together to achieve their goals. By 1950, according to historian Thomas Syvertsen, "the Kentucky Democratic party was perhaps more unified than it had ever been in modern times."

But Clements moved on, again. In 1949, U. S. Senator Garett Withers, appointed to complete the unexpired term of Alben Barkley, now Vice-President, declined to run, and Clements resigned as Governor and won his seat in 1950.

During the coming decade, that quiet period of party unity was short lived, according to John Ed Pearce in his book, *Divide & Dissent: Kentucky Politics, 1930-1963,* and the 1955 governor's race set off more "Brawls in the House of Factions."

Pearce observed "It has been said, and with considerable truth, that Clements didn't care who was governor of Kentucky as long as he could run the state, while Chandler didn't care who ran Kentucky as long as he could be Governor."

Henry recalled that Emerson "Doc" Beauchamp, Kentucky's Lieutenant Governor, was "without a doubt, one of the most popular men in Democratic politics in Kentucky." In 1955, Beauchamp anticipated securing the nomination, but Clements, Wetherby and others were not as enthusiastic.

In his memoir Henry confirmed "I had my share of support for governor… But Beauchamp would not agree with that. If he couldn't run, no one else closely identified with the Wetherby administration could be the candidate, he argued."

Beauchamp, Clements and Wetherby eventually settled on Bert Combs, a Clay County judge serving on the Kentucky Court of Appeals. Henry described Combs as "…the worst candidate the state had seen, except Henry Ward in 1967. He seemed shy and timid. His mountain twang did not appeal to urban voters. But he insisted on being honest, and that was fatal." Early in his campaign, Combs announced the state needed more revenue, and as Governor, he would raise taxes to pay for those services.

To clear the way for Combs, Henry issued a press release confirming he would not run, because "…in asking the people for something for myself, I would lose the advantage of being able to speak out solely in the interest of programs which I consider to be important to the future of Kentucky."

"I have seen the good things that can come to the state through having a Governor who is dedicated to the advancement of the general good of the people, and the bad things that can come to Kentucky from having a Governor so engrossed in his own political ambitions that everything else is secondary….my deepest convictions in this campaign are not based on the past political record of Chandler."

"An example of the way Chandler operates is his position on the state parks issue. He has tried to be on both sides and straddle the fence all at the same time. He was against the state park development program until he found his stand was unpopular. Now he is trying to say he really has been for the parks all along. The only way he knows how to get himself out of a spot is to launch an attack on my personal integrity and honesty in the development and administration of the park system. It is a tragedy that the Chandler kind of politics refuses to recognize that anything good has been done for Kentucky during the administration of Earle C. Clements and Lawrence Wetherby. It is a shame that he denounces everything that has been done merely because he is now on the other side. That is politics at its worst. I do not claim that all is good on the side that is supporting Combs or all is evil on the Chandler side. Politics being what it is, there is going to be some of the bad mixed with the good that any administration can do. But I know that the programs in which I have been interested and on which I have worked as a state official for the past seven years have been good for Kentucky, and I prefer to spend my time this year fighting for them and their continuance."

Combs well intentioned, yet naïve blunder on taxes was gift to Chandler, who according to Henry, reverted to his successful playbook from 1936, promising "better government, more goodies, all without any new taxes."

The Clements faction struck back, alleging that as a U.S. Senator, Chandler used his influence to obtain an additional supply of whiskey, (then under tight government restriction during WWII), for a Lexington wholesaler. They accused Chandler and his law partner of pocketing $38,000 to broker the deal.

Chandler attacked the Wetherby administration, alleging Commissioner Ward granted some park goers exclusive access and special privileges through a "Gold Card" system.

"Chandler had been aiming some barbs against me and my conduct of my job as commissioner of conservation, so it was decided that I should reveal the liquor contract and checks, and go on a strong attack against Chandler. The plan worked. We got wonderful front-page publicity. Chandler was put on the defensive. He claimed the contract was for legal services...But the attack had a telling effect against him...The trouble was that the attack was started too early. It was felt necessary to launch it early in June, but that was too soon before the August primary. It was difficult to keep it alive as a viable issue. The public gets tired, and wanted something new."

Chandler ignored the National Distillers story. "Instead of an explanation he gave a glowing account of his heroics during the war and attacked Ward, whom he called 'nasty, ugly little hatchet-faced Henry,'" reported Pearce.

Chandler demanded personal loyalty; those who failed that test paid a price. During a campaign stop in Marshall County, Chandler anticipated an endorsement from Circuit Judge H.H. Lovett. A popular and respected figure, Lovett explained he was committed to Combs. Chandler warned him he would hand pick an opponent to defeat Lovett in the next local election, a threat that hardened Lovett's support for Combs. Chandler kept his promise, later causing what a local historian called "quite possibly one of the biggest upsets in the political history of Marshall County."

Happy claimed Wetherby installed a $20,000 rug in the Governor's office on the taxpayers' dime, (actual cost: $2700), and crowed that Democrats who refused to back him were controlled by the "Clementine" (Earle Clements) and "Wetherbine" (Lawrence Wetherby) political machine.

Combs' strengths included a distinguished record of service during World War II, and his experience as an Appeals Court Judge, but he spoke in a clipped, soft voice and was uncomfortable addressing large crowds.

He was no match for Chandler, who barnstormed the state, winning laughter and applause by winking "Do like your Pappy and Vote for Happy." Chandler won by a slim margin of victory—18,000 votes.

Henry resigned before Chandler's inauguration. Finished with state politics, he looked forward to returning to the newspaper, but Earle Clements persuaded him to move to Washington, D.C. to serve as his special assistant in the Senate.

The Wards moved to Washington in January. The previous summer, in July of 1955, Senate Majority Leader Lyndon Johnson suffered a near fatal heart attack, and missed the remainder of the Congressional session. Clements, as the Assistant Majority Leader, stepped in for him, and his crushing schedule on the Senate floor was part of the reason he offered Henry the job.

Johnson, just 46 at the time—the youngest Senator to serve as majority leader, and Clements enjoyed a productive working relationship during the Eisenhauer administration. *The New York Times* described the Texan as a "... 'team man'" not an individual star, not a great speaker. It is said of him that he can persuade the most improbable of people to move together in a cause. He has brought an extraordinary unity in action to the Senate Democrats."

Clements, ten years older, still possessed great energy and physical stamina. Johnson and Clements enjoyed a solid relationship of trust and respect, and Earle was the first person Johnson demanded his doctors allow in to see him during his hospitalization.

Initially, Henry was reluctant to move and start over again. "It really twisted my heart to give up the conservation and state parks program to which I had developed eight years in Frankfort, but I recognized the inevitability of this in politics. But it didn't take long to get embroiled in the Washington scene," he recalled.

He previously established positive working relationships with personnel at the U.S. Department of Forestry, and engineers with the U.S. Army Corps of Engineers in the Louisville, Huntington, Nashville and Memphis District Engineer's offices. After the state legislature approved creation of the Kentucky Office for Soil Conservation, he coordinated policy with contacts in the Washington, DC; Spartanburg, S.C. and Lexington, Kentucky offices in the U.S. Department of Agriculture.

With over 1,110 miles of waterways in Kentucky, flooding had been a long-standing problem and challenge, and an effective flood control program was a shared priority for Barkley, Clements and Ward. Henry expanded his knowledge when he joined a circle of Senate staffers deeply involved in federal flood control and highway transportation policy,

"It did not take me long to find that my Washington assignments in these fields were very rewarding, especially since Senator Barkley had asked me to represent him, too, in these endeavors. No other staff assistant was in a position of speaking for two Senators."

"But my primary reason for being in Washington was to help Clements in his campaign for re-election, and that included organizing and utilizing the resources available to a senator in Washington valuable for campaign purposes."

It was 1937 all over again as Henry took charge of campaign publicity across multiple formats—press releases, radio and television scripts, and a monthly newsletter distributed to Kentucky voters.

That outreach substituted for personal appearances, because Clements' workload made it impossible to return to Kentucky to campaign. "A 30-minute program was developed for television, taped in Washington, and shown in a statewide coverage of TV stations. I'm probably prejudiced, since I wrote and directed it, but I think it was one of the best things of the sort I have seen in politics. When Lyndon Johnson saw it later, he was very high in his praise. Coming from Johnson, that was something."

30 years later, (and decades before the invention of the world wide web, Facebook, Instagram and Twitter) Henry expressed delight at the ingenious way his workload was lightened by "...a whole battery of automatic typewriters that could grind out thousands of individual typed letters daily; and an automatic signature machine that could reproduce Clements' signature perfectly. And, of course, there was a large staff of employees very much interested in Clements' re-election, and a Senate re-election committee to lend assistance and financing."

Clements won the May primary, but the death of Senator Barkley in the spring of 1956 set up a chain of events that flipped Clements' senate seat to the Republicans. Joseph Leary was appointed to temporarily fill Barkley's seat, and Democratic party insiders assumed that Leary would become the party's nominee. But after the primary, Clements backed Lawrence Wetherby.

"Well, Lawrence talked to me about it and he said 'I don't want to run, I think it's a mistake.' And I said 'I think it's a mistake, too.' Well, they had a meeting over in Louisville in headquarters one night, oh it must have been a week after the primary. All these brain-trusters around, including Lenny, and Lawrence and some others. I was in the meeting. Ed Farris was there. And they preceded to get tight, most of them, and so, so certain that they had things going their way.

They'd win so big, determined that Clements just wanted his boy in the senate with him. So they'd agreed that Lawrence would run."

Traditionally, the Governor selected the nominee, but Clements was uncooperative and refused to defer to Chandler. Chandler, still a master at "the politics of destruction," rushed to Washington to persuade Republican John Sherman Cooper to run against Wetherby.

His timing proved effective for several reasons. It was a presidential election year, and the Republican nominee, popular General Dwight D. Eisenhower, faced the much weaker Democratic candidate, Adlai Stevenson, II. The press nicknamed the intellectual reformer "egghead," and Eisenhower won in a landslide. Cooper beat Wetherby by 40,000 votes, and Congressman Thruston Morton edged Clements out by 6,000 votes.

"Kentucky lost a great asset in Washington, for Clements was on his way to be a power in the nation's capital. He surely would have succeeded Lyndon Johnson as majority leader in the Senate, and would have [held] that position for many years," wrote Henry.

Because he and Gladys both enjoyed working and living in Washington, Henry accepted a new job in public relations for the National Association of Realtors.

"In less than a year I had changed my mind. In the first place, I had always been an active citizen, and in Washington the individual citizen doesn't count for anything. He doesn't even vote. The federal government dominated everything. And doing so called public relations in Washington is a lousy way to make a living. A measure of success of a public relations man seems to be his ability to drink martinis at luncheon. It's an easy life, though, if you don't have much self-respect. And there are thousands involved in the same racket—trying to influence Congress and federal bureaucrats and getting publicity about client interests."

Henry was relieved when the Louisville Chamber of Commerce offered him a job as Director of Area Development. "I accepted it because it meant I could go back to being an active part of my own community and spend my time working on what I consider the worthwhile projects. It also meant no active involvement in politics—which suited me perfectly."

Henry and his wife moved back in late 1957. He stayed out of politics, but not for long. In 1960, another Kentucky governor asked him to join his administration. Two men Henry respected and admired—Governor Combs and Highway Commissioner Earle Clements, faced scrutiny over an unusual lease purchase deal for some "run down dump trucks" parked in Alabama, and Combs turned to Henry for help.

## 20 Run Down Dump Trucks

" 'I am not a candidate, I am not an applicant, and I am not available, Ward said,' " after he and Governor Combs discussed the Highway Commissioner position following Combs' announcement that Earle Clements had resigned from the post.

*The Courier-Journal*, August 19, 1960

New Highway Commissioner Henry Ward confirmed that "the Department will serve the public and not the interest of private individuals...We must see that every dime of state money assigned to the Highway Department is spent properly."

*The Courier-Journal*, September 1, 1960.

Henry enjoyed working for the Chamber of Commerce, and was promoted to General Manager in December, 1959. He had zero interest in rejoining state government, especially Kentucky's notoriously political Highway Department.
Throughout his career, Henry insisted public officials be accountable for their actions, but the Highway Department failed that test within the first six months

of the brand new Combs administration, under the supervision of former U.S. Senator Earle Clements, now Kentucky Highway Commissioner.

A highway commissioner's power often exceeded the Governor's. 1960 was a presidential election year, and Clements was now well positioned to draw from the good will of his political organization to benefit the Kennedy-Johnson ticket.

On the job just eight months, his detached job performance contrasted sharply with his previous record. According to Henry, that anomaly spoke volumes about the how easily the power and prestige of the job clouded even the most experienced politician's judgment.

In April of 1960, Governor Combs blindsided Clements by cancelling what *The Courier-Journal* called the Highway Department's "malodorous" lease- purchase contract for some heavy-duty dump trucks. In August, the Associated Press reported Combs' Rural Highway Commissioner, Ted Marcum, looked the other way as county judge executives purchased road equipment without advertising for competitive bids, in violation of state law. Instead, he encouraged county officials to do business with one of a few companies apparently hand-picked by Marcum. Governor Combs sternly reassured the public, that going forward, competitive bidding procedures would be strictly enforced.

From April through August of 1960, Combs was forced to issue daily or weekly statements responding to reports of some kind of violation of Highway Department policy, or buying time until he could obtain an answer from Clements.

The tension between the two peaked after the press reported the federal Civil Service Commission opened an investigation to determine if Earle violated the Hatch Act in July. Passed shortly after the U.S. Senate race of 1938, it limits the political activities of certain federal or state employees. Clements drew their attention after attending the Democratic Party's National Convention as a delegate, while employed as Kentucky State Highway Commissioner.

Shortly after that news, Combs announced that Clements resigned to return to Washington, D.C. to assist with the Johnson-Kennedy campaign.

Seasoned veterans of Kentucky politics were not surprised by the turn of events. The state office tower, built in 1938, had 11 floors, yet only one floor was designed as a suite—the entire 10$^{th}$ floor of the building was set aside for the Highway Commissioner's office. From 1940 through the summer of 1960, 14 political appointees passed through that revolving door of patronage, and controlled and spent the largest slice of the state budget pie.

Calvin Grayson, an engineer-planner who rose through the ranks to become Secretary of Transportation in the 1970s (the title Highway Commissioner was dropped), recalled that the general public, along with the majority of the Department's employees, were oblivious to the amount of pressure the Commissioner faced from delegations demanding political favors.

Secretary Grayson recalled interviewing an engineer for a job, noting that the candidate seemed indifferent to the role the Department played for decisions that critically impacted the daily lives of residents. He seemed to shrug off the possibility he might encounter some ethical dilemma along the way. To make his point, Grayson remarked: "Did you know that one of the smartest politicians I ever knew in my lifetime got into trouble over here?"

In the interim between Clements' resignation and Ward's appointment, the *Courier-Journal* ran a series of editorials covering the history of the department, and explained what the role and responsibilities of the Commissioner are.

Clements' replacement would control a budget of $313 million over two years, and "he spends more money on building, year in and year out, than any other man in public or private life in Kentucky."

*Courier* editors focused on the Commissioner's power to determine road and highway routes, award contracts and hire staff. Columnist Allan Trout described a "vitally interested throng [that] includes state employees, contractors and their employees—the makers and sellers of equipment, parts, and fuel—and the makers, sellers and haulers of sand, gravel, cement, bituminous mixtures and reinforcing iron" who seek and demand the Commissioner's time and attention. "Because he cannot evade it, a Commissioner of Highways has no choice but to shoulder the power. It is his choice, however, as to how he applies it."

For Combs, under pressure to fulfill his campaign pledge to end "politics as usual," the timing of the story could not have been worse—Combs' top priority was to convince Kentucky voters to approve a sweeping multimillion dollar road and parks bond issue in November.

In the 1960s, *The Courier-Journal* and *Louisville Times* enjoyed a reputation as one of the nation's top ten regional newspapers. While some readers complained the paper was too liberal, Barry Bingham, Sr., its publisher, ignored the criticism. Instead, he encouraged a culture of public service reporting that earned the newspapers 10 Pulitzer Prizes.

It still retained the feel of a genteel southern newspaper—featuring decorating tips, food recipes, society news, civic club events and gardening columns popular with society matrons and homemakers, but breaking front page news captured the growing strength of Kentucky's civil rights movement, the violence and unrest during those protests, and damage to the land and public health caused by strip mining.

Both newspapers, then near their peak in subscribers and editorial influence, appeared skeptical the Combs administration could deliver an open and honest new era in state government. The *Courier's* editors concluded that "the presence of Old Pro Clements in the politically sensitive and powerful highway office gave the entire Administration an air of politics-as-usual, and led the public to suspect that the experienced Clements, rather than the inexperienced Combs, was the real master of the Administration."

That narrative swerved sharply in April, because Combs swiftly and decisively cancelled the lease. Throughout the controversy, Clements was difficult to locate, responding directly to questions just a handful of times. He once remarked that, "I never heard of anyone getting into trouble for talking too little to the press," and he followed that rule his entire career. That spring, as reporters peppered the Commissioner's office for details regarding the ownership and condition of the trucks, the burden of responding fell heavily and squarely on Combs' shoulders. If he was seething at Clements' disappearing act, he kept his feelings well hidden.

Call it graft, corruption, chiseling or waste, the trouble started after *Courier-Journal* reporter Kyle Vance reported the state agreed to pay $346,800 for 34 heavy-duty dump trucks located in Alabama. The trucks were formerly owned by Thurston Cooke, a wealthy and prominent Louisville Ford truck and automobile dealer, who served as the state Democratic party's campaign finance chair in 1959.

Vance noted that in the past, the state had not "found a practical use for trucks as heavy as those being rented," and "has not tried renting vehicles on a big scale before, choosing instead to make out right purchases."

For the next six days, new revelations backed the Governor into a corner. Police forced the trucks off the roads—they were too heavy to operate legally on Kentucky roads, and the low bidder for the deal—Louisville Equipment Rental Company—was a brand-new company, incorporated three weeks after Combs' inauguration.

Reporters checked into the rental company's ownership. Attorney Robert Grubbs and E.R. Van Meter were listed as officers, but the company's address was a vacant house leased to Thurston Cooke in Louisville.

The company submitted the lowest bid, but reporters noticed it contained specific details: "It called for exactly defined tires and tubes, wheels, and mirrors" unique to the particular fleet of trucks parked in Alabama. Was it just a coincidence, they reported, that a Louisville finance company held a lien in that exact dollar amount for that exact number of trucks? The mortgage, to Louisville Trust Co., was dated seven days after the opening of the bids, and the company was the winning bidder.

The Ford trucks were originally sold by Cooke to independent contractors who hauled rock, sand and dirt to construction sites. The next day, Governor Combs asked the Department for more information, but as reporters located new sources and details, they kept circling back to Cooke's Ford dealership. Several trucks arrived in Kentucky for an inspection by employees from the Highway Department, but for some reason, and under the direction of some unknown person, they were undergoing reconditioning in the garage at the Cooke dealership.

Combs protested the deal was not final, and no money had been spent, even as some of the trucks had already been painted yellow—the uniform color for Kentucky Highway Department equipment. Meanwhile, Commissioner Clements was out of his office and reportedly in Washington, D.C., but Kyle Vance kept digging, traveling to Opelika, Alabama to verify the trucks' registration history inside the Lee County Courthouse.

On April 17, the *Courier* reported the contract included a stipulation that after the lease period ended, it converted the lease to a purchase contract, at a price nearly $115,000 over the actual value of the trucks at the end of the two-year period. State employees submitted a physical inspection list that revealed only 13 of the 50 trucks from the Alabama fleet were in running condition, and that 25 of the 34 trucks needed new engines.

It was no surprise, then, that on April 19 Governor Combs announced he was personally cancelling the contract, citing the vagueness and secrecy surrounding the lease, no clear confirmation of who actually owned the trucks, serious doubts as to whether the company could even transfer a clean title to the state and, more obviously, their obsolete and broken-down condition.

Clements issued a single statement that he relied on the department's legal counsel's assurance the original contract was acceptable, pending verification of the trucks' condition. After reviewing the report, he prepared to cancel it, but the Governor acted first.

On May 22, *The Lexington Herald* reported that "Cooke Automobile Empire Collapses, Lawyers Announce." One of the lawyers quoted was Mr. Grubbs, officer of the Louisville Equipment Rental Company. Cooke, Governor Comb's former campaign finance chair, was indicted for fraud in the amount of $1,327,662.00, for forging notes, mortgages, conditional sales contracts and other finance documents without the proper collateral. Convicted of forgery and obtaining money under false pretenses, the 51-year-old automobile dealer was sentenced to four years in the LaGrange Reformatory.

Combs was relieved that scandal was behind him, but more disappointment followed. On August 4, an AP story reported that "A number of counties are spending hundreds of thousands of dollars, without taking competitive bids, on road-building equipment under a new plan promoted by the Rural Highway Department."

T.R. Marcum, the current Rural Highway Commissioner (and cousin) of Governor Combs, dismissed the article as much ado about nothing, declaring "We can't afford to meddle in the affairs of fiscal courts...I'm confident none of the equipment companies are jacking prices up. They can't because it's a very competitive business," declared Marcum.

On August 8, Governor Combs overruled Marcum, announcing that the Division of Rural Highways would enforce the rules restricting equipment rental reimbursement to those counties following "the spirit and letter of the law," which required advertising for sealed bids.

On August 18, Combs announced the resignation of Earle Clements, effective September 1. who accepted an offer to return to Washington, D.C., to assist in the national campaign headquarters for John F. Kennedy and Lyndon Johnson.

The search was on for a new Highway Commissioner, and, once again, Henry Ward was in the right place at the right time. He returned to Kentucky in the autumn of 1957 as area development director of the Louisville Chamber of Commerce, where he focused on two major goals: to encourage cooperation between Jefferson County city and county officials; and coordinate communication between local and federal officials.

Working with Lieutenant Governor Harry Lee Waterfield, they asked the Legislative Research Commission to study problems in local governments in urban areas. Ward served as chair of the group and prepared a report in 1959. A key proposal included the organization of special districts to perform countywide functions, and copies were distributed to the legislature in 1960. But according to Henry, "That was the last anyone heard of it. There was not then, or now, any real enthusiasm among most local officials and members of the legislature."

He was more successful gaining traction on the highway issue. As early as 1956, the Eisenhower administration and Congress approved a $41 billion allocation for a federal interstate highway program to fund 41,000 miles for a "superhighway" system stretching nationwide.

A public works project rivaling many of the New Deal programs, the sticking point was establishing the routes, and here Henry predicted trouble. "In Louisville, everyone was an expert, and the air was full of arguments, particularly as to where two Interstate bridges to be built over the Ohio River between Louisville and Indiana should be placed. I got a meeting of the local 'power structure'—a group of 15 community leaders who get almost anything done then if they were in agreement. I said something like this to them:

'You asked me to come down from Washington because I am supposed to know how to get things done in government. Well, one sure way to get nothing done is to give strong evidence that there is a lot of disagreement here as to what should be done. Washington and Frankfort are not in a hurry to push the program. They can now say that since there seems to be so much local disagreement, they will delay action until they study all sides of all the arguments. Local people are not going to settle such things as the location of a bridge across the Ohio River. That is an engineering matter. What we ought to do is to agree on the principles involved, point out the needs, and present a united front favoring early action.'"

They agreed, and the metro civic groups signed a pledge to accept the recommended priority schedules for both new interstates or any other related projects.

Henry believed collaboration sped progress, and that it was important to include Governor Chandler. The bitterness between the two intensified during the Governor's race in 1955, (including allegations by Chandler that "hatchet faced Henry" dodged the draft in WWII), yet it did not stop Henry from updating Chandler on the interstate planning.

"So I went to Frankfort to see him, and said: 'Happy, I'm out of politics and glad of it. I want to bury the hatchet, and not in your skull. I need to work with your highway commissioner. I know you can order him to tell me to go to hell, and I wouldn't blame you. What I would like to do is to forget the past and work on the present and the future.' We had a pleasant visit, and agreed to forget the past. I had a good relation with him and his highway department for the rest of his administration."

After Clements' resignation, Lieutenant Governor Wilson Wyatt and Earle talked with Henry about the vacancy. "In fact he called me—Clements called me before Bert did. And he said 'He'll appoint you if you'll take it.'"

During their conversation, Clements explained what happened. Cooke recommended Clements take a look at a fleet of bigger trucks located in Alabama to do hauling for the Department. Up to the point where Clements learned of their true condition, he believed leasing heavier, larger trucks was more cost effective and efficient. After he reviewed the inspection report, he contacted the Finance Department to cancel it, but learned Governor Combs just publicly announced he terminated the deal.

Combs informed Clements he had to protect his administration and get the credit for cancelling the contract, and Clements replied "Hell, I'm working on cancelling it." In Henry's opinion, "... that's what stuck in Clements' craw; he felt that Combs threw him to the wolves to protect himself." The tension and bitterness dissolved the Combs-Clements faction of the state Democratic party. After he returned to Washington, Clements' influence in Kentucky politics declined significantly.

Combs planned to announce Clements' replacement in two weeks. Several potential candidates were mentioned, including Henry, but he had recently been promoted, and was settled happily into the job, and a pleasant family and social routine.

The next few days' press coverage of the Governor's search for a replacement confirm what Ward's daughter, Pat Willis, meant when she called her father the *Courier-Journal's* "fair-haired boy." Henry received the Kentucky Press Association's Man of the Year Award in 1954 and remained popular with his colleagues. He was also held in extremely high regard, as Governor Ned Breathitt discovered in late 1966, by *Courier-Journal* publishers Barry and Mary Bingham.

While Combs privately fumed over the *Courier's* relentless coverage, and Earle stayed silent, the *Courier-Journal* promoted Ward for the job. His appointment could restore confidence that the Department was functioning lawfully and cost effectively, and his reputation for integrity could boost public support for the upcoming $100 million parks and road bond.

In the meantime, Wilson Wyatt lobbied the Chamber's Board of Directors to approve a leave of absence for Henry to assist Governor Combs. The Board confirmed, reluctantly, they would if the Governor needed him, and Henry met with Combs to set some conditions for accepting the job.

"Bert, you're in trouble—your administration's in trouble over purchasing. And I've got my reputation to maintain. Because I expect to go back over to the Chamber of Commerce, and I'm not going to come over here and *ruin my reputation* about participating in any kind of deal regarding purchasing. And if you name me a Commissioner of Highways, *by God, it's going to be wide open to competitive bidding. Everything we buy!* He (Combs) said, 'That's all right. I want you to protect your reputation, because if you protect your reputation, you'll protect mine, too.'"

"So I think Bert was in complete agreement with what I was doing. He just had to concede that these people that were so disappointed that—yeah—he'd committed to them, but this fellow Ward over there, he was just a hard-headed nut—that I can't do these things."

A few days later, after listening carefully to his wife Gladys' list of sensible reasons to just skip it, he took the job at a $3,000 a year pay cut.

The culture and climate in the Highway Department changed drastically after Henry's arrival. Calvin Grayson observed that Ward's identity as a newspaperman was so deeply rooted that it protected him from even a hint of scandal as Highway Commissioner.

As a 20-year-old cub reporter, Henry was proud of his byline, but it came with some risk: your personal and professional reputation and credibility were on the line each time your name appeared under a story. His entire career he sought to build an honest reputation and protect it, and he relied on gathering and analyzing facts to do a job, no matter what it was. The scandal in the Highway Department required Henry to keep a tight reign over operations and policy for six long and exhausting years.

Combs and Ward enjoyed a productive relationship despite Combs' occasional complaints that Henry routinely, and sometimes gleefully, infuriated people seeking "favors." In addition to a long list of firsts in road building achieved during Ward's tenure, many point to the fact he managed to stay the longest—six years—as his greatest contribution. That continuity of leadership permitted planning and construction to move forward at a rapid pace, unaffected by factional rivalries or politics.

When asked by reporters why he left a job he loved for another state government post, he replied, "There was a feeling expressed by a lot of people that taking this highway job was a public service that needed to be done. That feeling even came from the people I work for. On that basis and only on that basis was I willing to do it." As to the pay cut, he said "Well, money doesn't mean that much to me. I never have thought much of money when a question of public service was involved."

But the public was unaware of how fiercely he resisted a culture of corruption on their behalf. His daughter remembered him telling her those first days and weeks on the job, he announced that any highway employee caught delivering free gravel or blacktopping driveways without prior authorization would be fired. *"From now on, by God!"* he warned employees, *"no one buys a pencil around here unless I approve the requisition."*

Calvin Grayson and John Witt recounted how, initially, the entire staff was afraid of him. The new Commissioner was worried about "that 5%" of employees who, he told reporters, violated rules or policies, and he promised rule breakers would be disciplined or fired.

After "Hammerin' Hank" moved into his $10^{th}$ floor office, he launched the Department into the go-go years of highway and road building without a single incident of fraud, abuse or corruption.

# 21 Stranger in the Kingdom

> "Ward said this his experience taught him that 95 per cent of all workers are conscientious and want to do a good job. "The trouble is with the other 5 per cent. I'll have trouble with those 5 per cent, but it doesn't bother me. I've had that trouble before and I know how to take care of it."

A common thread runs throughout the Ward oral history projects—people uniformly and affectionately observed he was "one of a kind," a character who deserved a higher profile in Kentucky history. His tenure in the Highway Department is the strongest example of why Hammerin' Hank deserves that recognition, and a newsletter later published by Kentuckians for Better Transportation singled him out for a number of firsts.

*Highway Department Commissioner Ward*

Under Ward's leadership, the Department completed five major parkways and established the routes for and constructed major segments of Interstates 64, 65 and 75. He ended the policy diverting road money into the General Fund, and calculated a formula for allocating rural road funds that became state law.

"I'll take care of the politics—you take care of the engineering and planning," he told the staff, and the formula is still followed today. Previously, the Governor and Rural Highway Commissioner controlled how and where that money was spent. It is no surprise that nearly all of it was spent in their home counties. Henry designed it as an end run past Governors who promised new roads in exchange for votes, and to discourage those who demanded them—and it succeeded in doing just that.

He reorganized the department into twelve districts and built new district headquarter offices and garages, obtained federal funding for rest areas (with toilets!—a battle he fought and won), restricted the location of billboards or junkyards within a sightline of a highway, and promoted the integration of natural stone and landscaping into the design of Kentucky roadways.

In 1965, the department coordinated planning for 414 miles of new roads in east Kentucky, through the Appalachian Development Act, with funds to be split on a 70-30 percent basis. Kentucky ranked second nationally behind Texas in miles of roads under construction. Just a short list of highlights in that transportation newsletter, after Henry read it, he joked it was "a damned fine obituary."

In September of 1960, Henry discovered the pressure to perform political favors, award contracts, or blacktop a county political chairman's driveway was intense. His toughest assignment- he bucked a decades old tradition of patronage inside one of the largest and most powerful departments in state government. According to Highway Department employees, the former crusading reporter who "busted up rackets" and shamed political "stooges," stood up to anybody obstructing official highway business.

The oral history of John Witt, his principal engineering assistant, provides a firsthand account of that environment. He remembered Ward's emphasis on engineering and planning gave them the freedom to concentrate on building interstates and parkways at a breakneck pace—to complete as much as possible before the next election cycle disrupted their momentum. Witt, reserved and conscientious, possessed a remarkable memory for detail and a fierce loyalty to Henry Ward.

Witt shows how the two sides of the Commissioner's job—its power and impact on ordinary Kentuckians' lives -- existed in tension at all times. Yet, Ward managed to achieve a balance so that, "Aside from the outside appearance of him being a rough fella, there wasn't a kinder man alive. He was so honest he would not have spent a penny of taxpayer money under any conditions, no way would he have misappropriated a penny of the state's money. You know, the Highway Commissioner in those days was king—all you had to do to build a road was write an official order and start doing it. I don't have enough adjectives to describe what a great man he was." Witt believed if Ward had been elected governor, "He wouldn't have pleased everybody but he would have been right."

Witt also insisted that although decades passed and the public memory is short, "The public doesn't know how much he did to protect their interests," and Witt was often in the room when Ward defied the Army Corps of Engineers or officials with the Bureau of Public Roads, or even the governors who appointed him.

Witt's perspective is valuable because he was involved with so many of the early "firsts" in Kentucky parkway and interstate construction. A graduate of University of Kentucky's engineering program, he served in the Korean War, then returned home to begin work as a right-of-way engineer with the Highway Department. Assigned to the office in Bowling Green in 1956, he remembered, "I had the privilege of acquiring the rights of way for the first 14 miles of interstate in the state of Kentucky, and probably one of the first ones in the country, from Elizabethtown to Upton. It's the straightest piece of road in Kentucky—not a curve or angle in it."

At that time, Witt remembered planning had already begun for the Mountain Parkway, a proposal pushed by Bert Combs and his supporters before Combs was elected.

After it was approved, it took Witt 15 months to hire appraisers, negotiate purchase prices with sellers and coordinate the location of utilities. Before the parkway was built, he remembered the route from Salyersville in east Kentucky to Winchester, near the edge of the Bluegrass region, followed a rough, crooked road. Forty-three miles long, the parkway was the first "1st class" highway ever built into east Kentucky. Many of the property owners affected by it were violently opposed and "threatened me," Witt remembered.

The district office he worked in was a house that was in poor condition. "It wasn't a nice place for someone to come in and talk to me about a problem. People didn't even know where to go to talk to [the Highway Department]. Each time a new governor came in, the structure of the department and the office changed. We moved continually—every four years you moved, and usually the office was a rental property owned by someone who had influence with the governor."

Henry consolidated functions in the field to align with the central office. He organized twelve district offices and approved construction of modern office buildings, garages and maintenance shops. "Out in the districts, they...oh, hell, they were housed in old garage buildings, and messy places, and they didn't ... their reputation was not very good because of considerable pure politics. And I set out in trying to better that," Ward told Pearce. Witt remembered how that step alone improved morale and stabilized the department.

In 1962, Witt worked as the principal district engineer acquiring the rights of way for the West Kentucky parkway. He modestly remembered that because he had "the best people working for me," they secured all the rights in just nine months. The parkway ran 127 miles and later extended to Interstate 24.

Not long after, he received a phone call from Ward on a Friday, asking him to come to Frankfort late that afternoon for a meeting. Witt replied he was not sure he could drive all that way and arrive on time. Ward replied, "O.K., then we'll send a plane down for you," but Witt begged off and agreed to leave immediately.

During their meeting, Henry offered him a job as his principal engineering assistant, and Witt moved his family to Frankfort. During John's oral history, he paused, and then remarked that once you gained Henry Ward's trust, it was total. Not long after Witt started, Ward signed an order that authorized John to sign off on any road-related document, from inception, planning and design to construction, maintenance or abandonment. "Believe me, I felt the pressure of that. The day I left, he rescinded the order, something I believed to be a high compliment."

Witt also emphasized that Ward "would stand up to anybody" if he believed they were wrong about the design, location or layout of roads, routes or facilities. The Bureau of Public Roads (now the U.S. Department of Transportation) disbursed a proportional percentage of federal highway funds for state projects that complied with mandatory federal requirements. Early on, Ward tangled with Kentucky's Bureau representative, J.C. Cobb, over toilets, sinks and water for interstate rest areas.

In the late 1950s, the Bureau agreed to fund five acres of grass and exit and entry lanes for vehicles to pull off the freeway for rest or breaks. No water, sinks or restrooms were built to avoid competition with local businesses. The owners bitterly complained the new interstates meant potential customers sped right past them and turned their communities into ghost towns.

Ward felt strongly that the choice of where to exit belonged to the drivers, and if they preferred to use a rest area, at minimum, they be provided access to bathrooms and water. During two or three meetings with Cobb, Henry asked the Bureau to pay for toilets, sinks and water fountains. Witt remembered the Bureau was "dead set against it," and Cobb reiterated the Bureau would pay for the acreage and turn around, and nothing more.

During the third meeting, Ward replied "I don't give a damn if you do or not, I'm going to do it anyway. We'll build it with 100 percent state money, and by the way, since you said you were from Georgetown (Kentucky), you'll be interested to know that's going to be the first rest area in the state."

It was the first rest area in the state -- off I-75 with water and bathrooms -- and shortly after the Bureau changed its policy to include restrooms and water.

Witt listed other key milestones. Ward was the first Commissioner to host information meetings– "don't call them public hearings," Henry often reminded the staff, to obtain feedback about the location of new highway corridors.

Employees listened carefully, Witt recalled, to the point of adjusting the location of the Mammoth Cave corridor off of I-65, and during several other projects. Calvin Grayson, a new employee in the advanced planning division remembered: "He said we—the engineers—never informed the public well enough. He was approachable. He always divorced himself from the engineers and did it so well the public trusted him, and it made the public say he's on my side."

Before the Mammoth Cave meeting, Henry instructed the staff to just listen—"I'm just going to see what the people want." He often opened the meetings encouraging the audience to 'Talk to me, don't talk to those engineers.'" Plans were shown for four proposed corridors, but Ward encouraged the audience to "tell us which one you like best."

The meeting turned into a bit of a free for all, but Ward patiently listened, then suggested the group "...go to UK or any other state university and ask for an economic impact study on all the corridors. Bring it back to me and we'll listen, because we want to listen to you...and so that's what they did." The Mammoth Cave corridor was adjusted based on the impact study they obtained.

From Grayson's perspective, public input was critical to guiding the highway planners through those "long, difficult, soul-searching decisions" about where to locate the corridors for the parkways and interstates. But what stayed with him far longer was the role modern roads played in improving the daily lives of Kentuckians. Residents cut off and isolated for decades by poor or non-existent roads struggled with their safety, health and a low standard of living. New or improved roads ended that isolation. For some communities, those improvements triggered growth that positively impacted their schools, local businesses and the public health.

Governor Combs supported public outreach as well, and introduced a new program called "taking government to the people." Employees from different departments visited every county to assist residents with problems or issues. After attending his first session for the Highway Department, Grayson told Ward he would not do it again. "I don't want to go back again—I'll tell you what." "Why?" the Commissioner demanded. "I cried," Grayson explained. "When a big strapping man walks up to your desk and said 'I just want a road that I can use twelve months a year so that I don't have to carry my children or my wife out on my back to get to the hospital'... It tore me up, still does to even talk about it. And almost all of them saying, 'I just want a road I can use twelve months a year, or a bridge, it would tear your heart out," said Grayson.

John Witt cited another example of Ward's commitment to thinking a problem through from the public's standpoint, that caused a significant revision to the Army Corps of Engineers policy on road access near flood control projects. "It came to his attention that school kids had to walk through woods in Leslie County because the Corps of Engineers had built Buckhorn Lake Reservoir, and in times of floods or high water, they had taken sufficient land up to what is called a 'yellow line' that can be flooded, and sometimes during extraordinary rains, the roads would be inundated.

"And the kids were having to walk around or above the water in the woods to get to Hyden or some other place to get to school. And he found out about it. Naturally, the people told him about it, and he was very sensitive to that. He didn't think kids should be mistreated that a way and then he got to work solving that problem, but at the same time, a new, much bigger project was taking place in West Kentucky.

"And it was called Barkley Lake. And they were going to inundate a lot of state highways down there, and he said 'not a thing a doin'—you're not going to inundate those highways, they are state highways, and I just refuse to let you do it.'"

"And he went to Washington, D.C. and had a debate with generals and anybody it took but at any rate he won again. He went to Washington, Louisville and had them here. It was a matter of negotiations, but he had it his way. There was not going to be anybody cut off by lakes. If they were going to be cut off, then they had to buy them out, was his position. 'If you are going to take a person's road and leave them with a 100-acre farm that they couldn't get out of anytime they needed to, well then, you're not going to do it. I won't permit it.'"

"So, anyway, the Corp of Engineers, as a result of Mr. Ward, they changed their whole strategy on building reservoirs which needed to be built. He wasn't arguing the point they need to be built for flood control and power generation; his position was that you are not going to inundate these [state] roads. That was a big accomplishment," Witt remembered.

Ward also prioritized long-range planning. Recalling his early impression of the department, Henry exclaimed to Pearce, "Planning?—we had no planning

... completely reorganized it, put entire brand-new young personnel in there and brought the thing along."

Calvin Grayson's introduction to the Ward school of public administration came by way of that need for planning. Henry contacted Calvin and explained "We need urban planning and we need a young grad to get a masters in urban planning." He asked Grayson to research a state he believed had an excellent master's program in urban planning. If Calvin agreed to go, the department would pay his salary and tuition and guarantee him a job after graduation in the advanced planning division.

Grayson remembered that when he complained to his wife he was tired of going to school, she just shook her head in disagreement. Ward called soon after to follow up on his offer. She answered the phone and said, "He'll go." He returned from North Carolina with a master's degree, to begin what would become a distinguished career guiding Kentucky highway and transportation policy for the next thirty years.

When Grayson reported to the tenth floor, he recalled, "I was scared of Ward, by the way, he had everybody in the department scared of him." He joined a group of recent college graduates Henry recruited to bring new energy and skills into the department.

Ward, who long nursed a deep insecurity about his lack of a college degree, valued professional development programs. He encouraged state workers to attend and learn, even if it meant it qualified them to leave the Highway Department to achieve at a higher level.

While Witt's memory centered around the Commissioner's battles with federal authorities, what Calvin Grayson valued most was Ward's philosophy that the Department existed to serve the taxpayer, a radical departure from its former reputation.

During those early weeks and months, breaking the rules became nearly impossible because every purchase order crossed his desk first. A powerful message sent and received, he delegated some compliance authority to trusted employees like Witt, Grayson and others, but his daughter remembered him telling her that he never let his guard down over purchasing. What exhausted him most was maintaining strict oversight over every penny spent by the department.

When John Ed Pearce asked him to describe that time, there was a long pause, and Ward blew out a heavy sigh. "I was convinced that I had to get on top of purchasing because this was where the scandals had arisen. So I issued an order that there'd be no more purchasing without my personal approval." In Henry's memoir he recalled "There were protests that this hampered the department, that they couldn't even buy a pencil. That was exactly the purpose of the order—to make everyone aware of the importance I placed on the purchasing function. So I issued an order that there'd be no more purchasing without my personal approval."

He also warned that employees caught paving private driveways with gravel or blacktop as a favor to a family member or friend (or as a reward for their vote), would be fired on the spot. After a trial period, he relaxed the requirements on some items for approval, but all requests for trucks and heavy equipment required his final signature.

It was a long-standing tradition in Kentucky politics for a governor to honor the "commitments" made to loyal voters and supporters, and Governor Combs was no exception. "This produced the biggest difficulty I had as commissioner of highways," Henry confirmed.

"A custom for many years had been for the county chairman of a successful governor's campaign to be the administration's 'contact man' in that county after the election. In most counties that meant that the administration would look to him for recommendation of what employees of the old administration should be fired and their replacements. I found that in many counties the practice had been for the county contact man to do the actual firing and hiring. No resident of their county could be hired by the administration anywhere in the state without the contact man's approval. And in many instances, they made the decisions about what projects the highway department would carry out in the county...I let the contact men know that my understanding with the governor was that I would be the highway commissioner, and this meant that I would do the hiring and firing and decide how the highway funds were to be spent. To say that there were many unhappy contact men is putting it mildly. They ran screaming to Governor Combs. He backed me up. But many of them also got their revenge in 1967."

It was as if Henry entered a ramshackle house and decided to take it down to the studs—and he did, rebuilding the department one crisis at a time. The contact men, now powerless, furiously settled back to wait for the next election, and Henry moved on to reforming the bidding process for construction contracts and equipment manufacturers.

According to Ward, bid rigging on heavy equipment, trucks, automobiles and "everything else," was widespread. "... particularly in connection with the purchase of scrapers. "At that time the highway department bought a lot of 'em because they were maintaining the hell out of a lot of gravel roads, around the state, particularly rural roads, which required graders. And they're expensive, they cost four to six thousand dollars apiece. I found out very soon ... that it had been the tradition for the highway department to have a deal where a certain manufacturer, [contacted] a designated agent in the state, to represent him in putting in bids on scrapers."

The governor hand-picked those agents, and Ward discovered the agent's commission ran as high as forty percent. "I was determined to bust this up. And we developed specifications, because what they would do, hide specifications— was something in there that only that particular grader would be. And we had to develop specifications that were wide enough and broad enough that any of the reputable manufacturers would be. And we did. And we bought graders for half what the state had been paying for them. Of course, I got tremendous kickback that this was unfair—that uh, the promise had been made that they'd have these commissions—and uh, but I said, 'Well, we're not going to do that anymore.'... This was merely a continuation of a practice that'd been in effect I don't know how many years. But they had the same kind of arrangement on buying automobile truck tires, batteries, oil, all those, under the commitment. [T]hey would in advertising for it, they'd rig the bid in such a way that only that particular brand was going to compete." Pearce interrupted to ask if Combs or Clements instructed Ward to honor those commitments, but Ward was very firm—"No. Not Earle. Not Bert."

In 1948, Henry persuaded Earle Clements to give him the complete authority to run the Conservation Department free from political interference. In August of 1960, Governor Combs, besieged by reporters and negative public reaction to the truck scandal, readily agreed to the same deal—too much was on the line for his brand-new administration.

"So I think Bert was in complete agreement with what I was doing. ... So as a result of these policies we bought at prices, at say, half what they'd been paying. ...We also developed some real close supervision over bidding by a contractor. And that one was the toughest thing in the world to keep the highway contractors from agreement among themselves to divide up bids. The hardest thing in the world to catch. Hardest thing to prevent," and Henry was not satisfied until everything was "wide open for competitive bidding."

The culture did not change overnight, but eventually, the anxiety employees experienced after receiving terse notes from Ward to "See me" faded, replaced by their respect and affection for "Hammerin' Hank." He still threw his glasses on his desk when he grew impatient, and John Witt remembered he insisted "You have to be sure of the facts. Don't open your mouth unless you are sure of the facts!" an admonition the newspaperman used often.

In the spring of 1962, Senator Burt Kiser of Olive Hill, a former Chandler appointee, (linked to a scandal that involved paving driveways or roads for individuals on private land), demanded Henry appear before the Senate to answer charges the department was insolvent and barely functioning.

Henry confirmed it was not, then set Kiser straight. "I took the job as commissioner of highways not because I sought it, which I did not, but because I felt it my duty as a citizen to assist in developing and carrying forward a program to give Kentucky a system of highways essential to its needs. ... For too long the people have been lied to about their highway program. For too long the facts have been misrepresented. As a citizen I am resentful of the kind of politics that has hung like a dead weight around the road program. It was that kind of political system that kept Kentucky from having one decent highway from one border to another. I am proud that I am part of a program that is carrying Kentucky in the other direction. I am proud of the progress that is being made during my tenure as commissioner of highways."

*Ward at Groundbreaking of Kentucky Route 15 (1965)*

In 1964, the General Assembly approved Senate Bill 156, the bill establishing the rural secondary road formula. Henry studied the problem—a patronage lovers' dream—then recommended a proportional method to divide funding fairly. To their credit, the General Assembly adopted it as law.

"Finally, Ward broke up the old political practice by which secondary road projects, financed by 2 cents of the gasoline tax, were subjected to two grave abuses. First: The home counties of influential politicians got a lion's share. Second: Projects were squirreled back for concentrated awards in the heat of political campaigns," a Courier Journal editorial explained.

Henry divided the money as follows: one-fifth divided equally among all 120 counties; one-fifth based on the ratio of rural mileage in a particular county as a ratio of the total 120 counties; one-fifth allocated to each of the 120 counties based on population, and two-fifths among the 120 counties based on the percentage of rural area.

The rapid roll out of the interstate program could be traced to Ward's experience in Washington as a special assistant. Those assignments familiarized him with how the federal highway program worked, who to contact when there were issues, delays or problems, and how to speed the process along.

He implemented a streamlined process for auditing and billing that "qualified Kentucky as the second State in the nation for drastically quicker payments of federal aid by the U.S. Department of Public Roads," reported The Courier-Journal.

He ended another long-standing practice that diverted funds from the Highway Department to other departments. State government departments routinely billed the Highway Department for "services rendered." Previously, beginning in 1952, the diversion of highway money to other departments soared from $3,658,446 to $7,739,000 in 1960. When Henry arrived, he rejected any billing that exceeded the two-year figure budgeted for that purpose.

In 1964, Democrat Edward "Ned" Breathitt narrowly defeated Glasgow Republican Louie B. Nunn,. Nunn presented himself as a populist defending the values of rural Kentuckians, and he vowed to repeal Governor Combs' executive order desegregating state licensed businesses.

Breathitt asked Ward to stay, but he replied "... I won't stay if you put Bert's cousin, Ted Marcum in there for rural highway commissioner." Breathitt confirmed he was committed to Marcum, and Henry replied "O.K., get yourself a highway commissioner, because I'm not going to put up with him for another four years. I've had that with him now—and I'm not going to do it cause he's a son of a bitch if there ever was one. ... He just was a typical mountaineer politician who wanted to have everything. ..."

Marcum spent $600,000 of road money in Clay County, Bert Combs' home county, during the first six months of Combs' administration. After Henry took over he informed Combs "Now it's not going to work this way," and he sent the rural road formula over to the General Assembly.

"I just completely bypassed Marcum, and of course he was mad and tried to cut me every opportunity and snipe at me and I just wasn't going to go over there again and go through that all again. So Ned gave him a job as an assistant over in his office. ... It didn't make any difference in our relationship. ... I had a lot of respect for Ned and he had a lot of respect for me. And a completely free hand."

That continuity in the Highway Department—another four years under the same Commissioner, assured an uninterrupted highway and road construction schedule.

A final controversy near the end of Ward's tenure affirmed his commitment to natural landscaping design, and his determination to have the last word on the subject.

A disagreement between Louisville Mayor William Cowger and Ward dragged on over the Highway Department's proposal to build a tunnel to carry Interstate 64 beneath Cochran Hill. The plan included the acquisition of land adjacent to Seneca Park to provide "park-like" landscaping. The Bureau of Roads refused to approve a tunnel citing the expense, and recommended cutting the interstate straight through the hill.

"They wouldn't give me any money for planning and I wouldn't plan anything except a tunnel," said Ward. "That was when (Lyndon B.) Johnson was president. Well, one day I saw that Lady Bird was planting pansies next to a highway... beautifying it. "So I called up the highway commissioner in Washington and said, 'I see that Lady Bird is out beautifying highways…Well, if you don't give us that tunnel…I'm gonna sic Lady Bird on you…We got the tunnel."

In 1966, Calvin Grayson remembered Henry made an odd comment that seemed out of character. The department recently adopted a state primary road classification system consisting of four categories—federal, primary, secondary, urban or rural, and that designation determined the corresponding responsibility for funding and maintenance to the appropriate authority—federal, state or local. Before the new policy went into effect, the state maintained 3,500 miles of county roads at state expense. The new policy specified the conditions under which the state could return that mileage back to the counties.

New maps were drawn to reflect those classifications, and Grayson informed Ward they were ready to be signed, but Ward put it off: "'I don't want to make 120 county judges mad.' But he came back two days later and said 'Get the maps out,' and he had to sign 120 of them, one for each county." Grayson speculated Henry had already quietly decided to run for Governor, and that signing the maps risked his chance for success.

Although he valued the opinion of his family, friends and staff, he did not seek their advice on his decision to run. In Governor Breathitt's oral history for the University of Kentucky, he observed that Henry would have made a great governor, acknowledging that at the same time "He would have made everyone mad."

During his conversation with Breathitt, Henry confirmed he intended to run his own campaign, and Breathitt remembered, "Well, the trouble is, Ward did run his own campaign. And he's such a strong person, he ran his own campaign, and that's always a mistake for a candidate."

It triggered a cascade of mistakes, but Breathitt was unaware of how Ward's association with the circus of corruption during the Barkley-Chandler campaign of 1937 hardened his view about maintaining tight control of a campaign to protect his reputation.

Ward's conviction that truth, principles and qualifications mattered were admirable, but they collided with a nation in turmoil over civil rights and the Viet Nam War. It marked the end of an era of courthouse politics and political campaigning dominated by stump speeches delivered at county fairs or standing on a wagon in the middle of a tobacco field.

Just as television enlightened and entertained viewers, it also transformed the political landscape. A powerful tool for molding and polishing a candidate's image, it created new job opportunities for overworked, underpaid journalists who accepted better pay and working conditions in a more prestigious field—public relations and political consulting.

The visual power of broadcast television focused attention on a candidate's physical image or attractiveness. Television was entertainment—and a snappy slogan or catchy theme song that appealed to viewers carried more weight with voters than a candidate's detailed explanation of the advantages of concrete over asphalt for a road bed. As Ward organized his campaign, he gambled on the way politics and government should work—and he lost.

## 22 Flashing Yellow Lights

In late 1966, Governor Edward "Ned" Breathitt's administration earned national acclaim for Kentucky's progress in civil rights, but politicians eyeing the next election faced discontent and resentment over the new law.

As Highway Commissioner Ward signed maps and scrutinized purchase orders, Louisville and Jefferson County civil rights advocates led a wave of protest marches and boycotts.

National television broadcasts featured large crowds marching for equality or an end to the Vietnam war. That social and political fault line divided Americans demanding law and order from courageous protesters seeking equality under the law, and Ward believed the tension and anxiety spilled over into his campaign in 1967.

In Governor Edward "Ned" Breathitt's oral history for the University of Kentucky, he recalls that turbulent period in state politics. As Kentucky's vibrant social justice movement strengthened, the mostly white, middle aged male cohort of Democrats once again jockeyed for factional control for the party nomination.

The Combs administration passed one of the toughest civil rights laws in the country in 1964, and Henry supported it, but the election of 1967 would test the skill of even the most seasoned politician. According to Kentucky historian

George Humphreys, the "Democratic brand was becoming tarnished...folks were fatigued by the failures from the Vietnam War and Great Society."

Breathitt recalled Henry was weighed down by too many negatives—"He got all the negatives that I had, which were plenty." Breathitt admired Henry for staying "tough and committed" to meaningful strip-mining legislation, but it came at a cost. Coal operators backed Republican Louie B. Nunn, and "were mad at me, and distrustful of Ward." When he growled that he "didn't give a damn whether someone agreed with him or not," he made some powerful enemies.

He promoted himself as an honest and effective public administrator who measured progress by the number of state park lodges, county roads or new interstates or bridges he built. He backed bills improving the lives of Blacks throughout his career, and as Conservation Commissioner, ordered the desegregation of state parks following U.S. Supreme Court and Kentucky Court of Appeals rulings overturning legal challenges to integration laws.

But to tie his defeat to his honesty or independent streak is misleading. "The Sound Builder for Kentucky," who supported civil rights, viewed support for open housing laws as a bridge too far to cross. The controversy over equality ignited during the Combs and Breathitt administrations, and in 1967, open housing laws were a critical flashpoint.

The next step forward was a ban against housing discrimination, but every Democratic candidate for the primary that year -ten in total, including Lieutenant Governor Harry Lee Waterfield and Henry Ward, opposed the law. That blanket opposition early in the race cost him the support of an emerging and powerful block of Jefferson County Black voters.

After Henry won the May primary, Ned Breathitt remembered Ward distanced himself from his administration. "But I-I was then-Ward didn't want me out front. He thought I was so cut up over civil rights, he was afraid of it. He was from down in the Purchase and-although he was for what I did, it was not a burning philosophical sort of thing. And he knew I-I was damaged over that and that Nunn would-he didn't want Nunn making a big issue..."

The discontent that Henry sensed did not happen overnight. A decade after the end of World War II, the U.S. Supreme Court decision in *Brown vs. Board of Education of Topeka* overturned segregation in the schools. In 1956, *The New York Times* noted that Louisville's school desegregation plan unfolded without incident, and that "Integration of public schools passed its second day here today without incident. The children and their teachers apparently have taken the change in stride." In 1963, Governor Combs issued an Executive Order desegregating state licensed business.

On July 2, 1966, *The New York Times* reported "the old South's only state civil rights act [barring employment discrimination], in respects stronger than the Federal Civil Rights Act of 1964, went into effect in Kentucky today."

Yet rising young Republican star Louie Nunn portrayed the Combs-Breathitt faction and the new laws as a threat to individual freedom. Running against 39-year-old Hopkinsville attorney Edward "Ned" Breathitt in 1963, Nunn openly appealed to the festering white anger and resentment over racial progress, losing to Breathitt by just over 13,000 votes.

The tally confirmed the strength of Nunn's cynical and self-serving strategy. His emphasis on white privilege ignored the educational, social and financial damage endured by generations of Kentucky Blacks, resigned to living in a nation paying lip service to "equal opportunity for all." Blacks who served in World War II, the Korean War and Vietnam, bitterly accepted no amount of patriotism or sacrifice was good enough to secure their equality in their own country.

Breathitt and Nunn shared similar backgrounds. They served in World War II and earned law degrees. Both became active in state politics early in their career; Breathitt volunteered for the campaigns of candidates Adlai Stevenson, Alben Barkley and Bert Combs; Nunn worked in the field for John Sherman Cooper, Thurston Morton and Dwight D. Eisenhower.

Breathitt defeated Happy Chandler in the May, 1963 primary. On June 26, Governor Combs signed the executive order barring racial discrimination in any business licensed by the state. In a state distinguished more by its "Old South" tourism image promoting bourbon, Bluegrass, thoroughbred horses and hospitality, and less for progressive social reform, the Congress for Racial Equality called the order the "most significant stride accomplished so far in the fight for civil rights." It ignited a controversy that nearly overwhelmed Combs' successor—Breathitt, a young and earnest newcomer to Kentucky politics.

In Governor Breathitt's oral history, he described Louie Nunn's television broadcast condemning the order the following evening:

Nunn "...made a direct appeal to the people of Kentucky on the issue of the executive order. And he had the Kentucky flag, and the American flag, and the Constitution of Kentucky, and the biggest Bible I ever saw...and he just said that we're not gonna have dictatorship in Kentucky and 'We're not gonna have executive—government by executive decree by a governor on a matter as sensitive as this one is, and my first act as governor will be to rescind that executive order. This is a matter for the legislature, my friends, and you and I know, my fellow Kentuckians, that legislature will know how to deal with this issue.'"

Breathitt remembers that while listening to Nunn's broadcast, he "...got a knot in the pit of my stomach, and it didn't leave 'til the last vote was counted and I was declared the winner, because it was a tough race."

"The issue was racism, inherent racism in Kentucky and it was there. And even though from Governor Clements, Governor Wetherby, Governor Chandler, Governor Combs had all taken positive steps to deal with the issue-and to integrate Kentucky the feelings were there. And once somebody made the issue—and then Governor Nunn campaigned over the state. I mean he really did, And-and some of his supporters put out bogus handbills. Some of 'em showed me marching with Martin Luther King and-and then had miscegenation...they weren't signed, they were just scattered out at stockyards and places. That-that-that Breathitt thinks that the only way to really solve the-the racial issue is intermarriage. Well, you know how that went over. And boy, I really was-I was in deep trouble over that issue. And-but you see, that then gave the Republican Party hope...and that gave them the feeling that if they really worked hard on the campaign, they could win the governorship."

Nunn's narrow margin of defeat in 1963 defeat deepened his determination to win in 1967. Henry remembered that "...by the end of 1965 interest was stirring in the next governor's race. Because things looked good for Democrats, the woods were full of candidates." Six people, including Happy Chandler, planned to run for the nomination.

By the fall of 1966, Henry's high-profile performance as Highway Commissioner put him in a favorable position, at least until Bert Combs got back into the race. Henry remembered how quickly Democrats withdrew their support, "running him down" in front of anyone who would listen. "I'd be silly to get in the race [in] a situation like that."

It was a pattern Ward grew accustomed to. During each election cycle, Henry's name stayed at the top as a potential nominee. Party insiders praised his administrative skill and honesty, then rejected him—Hammerin' Hank was too independent, unpredictable and boring to attract votes. Close associates who knew him best insisted he was a warm, loyal and caring friend—a side of him familiar to a small inner circle that Ned Breathitt described as members of the Kentucky press, Barry and Mary Bingham, and all the "do-gooders" inside state government.

For the majority of Kentuckians, Henry Ward was a face or name in the newspaper, a stocky, middle-aged bureaucrat dressed in a dark suit, white shirt and narrow tie, slapping his hat impatiently against his leg or puffing on a cigar as he delivered a mind-numbing lecture to some newspaper reporter explaining the pros and cons of paving a road with asphalt or concrete.

*Commissioner Ward at work*

The average Kentuckian knew little about laws he passed and the hell he raised fighting for public power, modernizing the park system, or protecting schoolchildren and landowners from overreach by the Army Corp of Engineers. Henry shrugged off his disappointment. If there was a more popular candidate, so be it, until Bert Combs dropped out of contention.

Combs recently separated from his wife Mabel. Initially she agreed to join his campaign, but changed her mind. Henry recalled "Because one of the stories was Mabel said 'If you file – I'll file,' which meant 'I'm going to file for divorce.'... "So Bert figured if he got involved and his wife filed a suit for divorce right in the middle of his campaign and the scandal came out, it'd be harmful, so he couldn't actually run." The couple later divorced.

But again, this was no ordinary time in history or Kentucky politics. The pragmatic partnership between Dr. Martin Luther King and Lyndon Johnson, strengthened by King's vision and Lyndon Johnson's determination to build not just a "Great Society" but an equal one, marked an exceptional period of social progress haunted by tragedy.

Another pair of influential Kentuckians weighed in on their choice for the nominee, and Breathitt agreed to honor that request. He recalled that "...then Barry Bingham [Sr.] and Mary Bingham came to see me in the governor's mansion. I don't think they ever did that in their life," but in late 1966, they did. "[B]ut they came to see me, and says, for the good of Kentucky we can't have Nunn...And-and-because of the-he had played the race card, and they thought he would be a reactionary. I think history proved differently...And-well, it did prove dif-di-differently as far as I'm concerned. But...I didn't know that. And-and-But they said 'There is no choice, but Henry Ward. And if you will back him all out, we will back him all out with the paper.'"

"And-but they were so afraid that I was going to go with somebody not of Henry Ward's stature, and they felt that he would be an outstanding governor. And I -I think he would have been. He would have made everybody mad, but he'd been an outstanding governor."

Without the Binghams' editorial support, "I could never have passed both the civil rights and the strip mine bill, because they built the climate of support for strip mine control, and they were a strong voice to get rid of the-the incubus of the-of segregation in Kentucky, always. So I had to make the choice to go with Ward."

Breathitt and Combs met with Henry, presuming he would agree to run. "I'll be damned if I will!" Ward snapped. "You ruined me. You got out here and encouraged your friends to promote you, and in the process in promoting you—you've been running me down. What a weak candidate I'd made, how many enemies I've made in the state—I don't know about it." Breathitt wanted to make amends, and Henry remembered he "half facetiously" suggested they could make it up to him if Combs would agree to run his campaign.

Henry called their bluff: "If you will manage the campaign, I will run," I said. This will be the best proof to your friends that you not only are supporting me, but you think I can win. This is important, for in their campaign to draft you they chopped me down as a potential candidate with the argument that I could not win. Every time my name has been mentioned, those favoring someone else have used this argument against me, especially declaring that I could not win the support of the court house crowd because they do not consider me that kind of politician. I consider that a compliment, but I have no illusions about winning without the full support of the administration and a reasonable portion of the local politicians commonly known as the court house crowd. Combs surprised and gratified both me and Breathitt by agreeing that he would be the campaign manager."

Henry resigned as Highway Commissioner in late November 1966, but soon after, so did his new campaign manager—Bert Combs. President Johnson appointed Combs to the United States Court of Appeals for the Sixth Circuit, and Lexington attorney Foster Ockerman agreed to replace Combs.

Ockerman served as assistant manager of Ned Breathitt's campaign in 1963. A World War II Navy Lieutenant who skippered several torpedo boats, he returned to Kentucky to practice law and served in the Kentucky House of Representatives for 3 terms in the mid-1950s.

A devout Methodist, and a tall and accomplished family man, he earned praise for his super human ability to put in long days at his law practice and in Frankfort, as a valued Democratic party volunteer and strategist, except on Sundays, when he rushed back to Lexington to take his family to church.

Ockerman planned Henry's first major event, a rally attended by over 1,000 people at Ward's campaign headquarters at the Sheraton Hotel in Louisville.

*Gladys Ward (left) and supporters at 1967 campaign event*

"Any doubts about the extent to which the Breathitt administration is backing Ward were dispelled at the headquarters opening yesterday," the *Courier-Journal* reported.

Breathitt, Combs and Ward shared the platform, and Combs predicted that "Louie will languish and Cookie will crumble. It doesn't matter which of them gets the nomination. It doesn't matter which one of them loses in November."

"Ward "Blasts GOP," declaring "I view with alarm evidence that some of these people hold Kentucky voters in contempt, and think they can get away with confusing, bemuddling or deceiving the people of Kentucky with reckless and irresponsible statements, distortions of the truth and slick propaganda."

On the Republican side, that primary was much uglier. Louie Nunn, running against Jefferson County Judge/Executive Marlow Cook, achieved two objectives: he won the nomination, and factional control of the Kentucky Republican party, by blasting Cook's background, public record, character, and his religion.

"Mr. Nunn vigorously opposed the open housing proposal [in Louisville] and openly attacked Mr. Cook and a 'triumvirate' of rich Louisville Jews supporting him for 'coddling' civil rights leaders here," *The New York Times* reported.

The smear prompted widespread condemnation from Democrats, Republicans, and the Republican candidate for Lieutenant Governor, Thomas B. Ratliff. "The Nunn campaign is one of the worst campaigns of religious bigotry racial prejudice and downright muck-raking in the history of our state," Ratliff declared.

Kentucky's popular Republican U.S. Senator, John Sherman Cooper "...accused Nunn of having 'stirred appeals to racial prejudice' against Mr. Cook. He publicly declared his support of Mr. Cook."

Following Cooper's stern rebuke, (Cooper eventually endorsed Nunn) Nunn vehemently denied accusations of bigotry, right up to the night in November he triumphantly ended 24 years of Democratic party control of state government.

On May 23, Ward won the primary in a landslide. "I'm jubilant!" he exclaimed to the crowd as they chanted "Tell it like it is!" To another reporter he bragged "I got plenty of votes and I got 'em on my own," Ward said in the interview. "They said I couldn't get the courthouse crowd and yet I had a great majority."

*The New York Times* reported that "The Republicans' division and distress appeared to have markedly enhanced the election prospects of Henry Ward, the Democrats' overwhelming choice for Governor. Mr. Ward...ran up an unexpectedly heavy vote of 187,000, or 54 per cent of the vote cast for the five top Democratic contenders. Altogether where were 10 Democratic contenders for the nomination. Mr. Ward, the 57-year-old former State Highway Commissioner, overwhelmed them all with a bigger vote than the total of his nine opponents."

But there were warning signs Henry later acknowledged he ignored. 200,000 Democrats who voted in the '63 primary did not vote in May of '67. November was six months away, a long stretch of time for Nunn to validate, over and over again, Kentucky voters' fear and anger over "urban rioting, a decline of law and order, "welfareism and the war in Vietnam..." Nunn promised to maintain law and order, and apply common sense solutions to problems in state government.

Henry won by such a large margin—over 100,000 votes—that he recalled "...everybody was so damned optimistic that I couldn't get anything done—all summer clear up to September, nobody would do a damn thing. I went home, and practically closed headquarters down."

John Ed Pearce asked "What do you remember about that campaign? A lot, probably."

"Very frustrating," Henry replied.

During an interview with this writer, Foster Ockerman expressed *his* frustration, except for very different reasons—trying to tell Henry Ward how to campaign was futile. The "man who made Kentucky modern," and scored so highly on the scale for integrity and competence, simply could not adapt to running a modern political campaign.

# 23 End of Damn Story

"He is honest," wrote a national newspaper columnist, Joseph Kraft, in a column about Ward and the governor's race. "The only trouble is that he has no rapport with the electorate. He is short, unglamorous. He snarls when he speaks. On television he projects about like Ed Sullivan."

Participants in the Ward Oral History project came from a variety of backgrounds and experience, many distinguished leaders in their fields, including Thomas L. Preston, founder and CEO of ForeseeNow, a consulting firm, and the first recipient of University of Kentucky's Lifetime Achievement Award for Public Relations.

Preston campaigned enthusiastically for Henry, and drafted a detailed administration plan, modeled after the reorganization in the Highway Department, to streamline and modernize state government.

Preston declared "this man was absolutely brilliant—so thorough in details…a voracious reader with great recall and memory." A lifelong learner, "He was honest to a fault, but it cost him the election. He was too blunt with the people who wanted favors. 'Hell no! That's not the way I'm going to have my administration work,' he would say."

Prodding by his campaign manager and friends to shake more hands and greet more voters, drew his irritation and his ire. They need to "Take me as I am," he insisted, "If not, I'll move on."

He *did* move on, after voters compared Henry, a middle-aged bureaucrat who scowled more often than he smiled, to his tall and photogenic Republican opponent, the 43-year-old Louie B. Nunn. In 1967, they either stayed home or voted for Nunn.

The candidates relied on the traditional methods of persuasion: newsletters, pamphlets, hats, and bumper stickers. Ward supporters passed out a tiny metal lapel pin in the shape of a hammer. The "Committee of Responsible Republicans" endorsed Henry, distributing bumper stickers that read "Fooey on Louie." Nunn punched back with "Tired of the War? Vote Nunn," and "Time for a Change— Vote the Nunn Team."

Television ownership increased, and candidates purchased airtime to broadcast catchy songs and slogans alongside commercials for "Diet Delight Artificially Sweetened Fruit Cocktail" or a Philco Vivid Vision Town and Country television set.

On those broadcasts Nunn looked and sounded polished and businesslike; in comparison, Henry's appearance, mannerisms, and growling baritone made him look like old news. As Kentuckians tuned into their favorite TV programs in the comfort of their living rooms, the era of stump speeches delivered on the courthouse steps or during country ham dinners inside packed school gymnasiums or church basements faded away.

During Nunn's campaign against Breathitt in 1963, he framed the contest as a referendum on civil rights legislation that trampled on individual rights. In 1967, Ward played it safe, and distanced himself from Breathitt's record. Instead, he promoted his successful record as parks and highway commissioner. His public administration experience easily surpassed Nunn's, who served as Glasgow city attorney, then was elected Barren County Judge Executive.

Henry's combined term of service in state government totaled 13 years. A public record Nunn conveniently used against him; it was a risky strategy due to the sheer weight of Ward's state wide impact. It was painfully obvious Henry could not fire up a crowd, but on the other hand, Hammerin' Hank *did things*—a legacy you could drink (clean water), light your home or farm with (cheaper electricity), drive over ( interstate highway or new bridge) or enjoy (a boat ride or fishing tournament at Kentucky Lake).

More notably, he did it without breaking any laws or skirting ethics rules, a sterling reputation that Nunn turned against him, by sarcastically referring to him "Mr. Clean." Governor Combs declared that Nunn could sneer at Henry's reputation all he wanted, but his integrity was an achievement in the colorful and cut-throat arena of Kentucky politics.

Nunn's early involvement in Kentucky politics began when he volunteered for John Sherman Cooper's campaign. Engaged and energized by politics, he became a fierce competitor who nearly surpassed Earle Clements' skill at forging strong political alliances.

U.S. Senator John S. Cooper, Beula Nunn, and Louie Nunn (1967). Courtesy of University of Kentucky Special Collections, James E. Weddle Photographic Collection

Despite the heated campaign rhetoric, Nunn and Ward shared much in common on the issues, offering a moderate to conservative vision for Kentucky's future. After the election, Nunn proved to be more moderate than opponents feared, and decades later, he was affectionately remembered for his wit and storytelling ability.

In contrast, Henry grew most animated reciting statistics or boring policy details. Reserved and awkward in front of large crowds, his dry sense of humor often registered as an insult. "If Henry could have been *appointed* Governor, the state would have been *fine!*" Foster Ockerman sighed in exasperation.

While Ockerman organized schedules, publicity, and press releases, Henry remembered the team prepared "position papers that they thought I would issue, which didn't appeal to me."

At one point during his interview, Foster paused at length and sighed as he recalled watching Henry smile, thank him, then stuff the material into a bulging briefcase he carried everywhere. The team gave up trying to persuade Ward to include those talking points during appearances, and the sight of that overstuffed briefcase became an inside joke among the staff.

That inflexibility could be traced to the U.S. Senate campaign of 1938. Ward concluded Barkley and Chandler ceded control to overzealous supporters, a choice Henry refused to consider. Proud of his reputation for being honest, he intended to protect his good name.

Every four years, Happy Chandler declared he was running for *something*. In 1967, Ward beat Chandler for the nomination by a considerable margin, so Happy jumped at the chance to strike back.

Chandler's poor showing signaled he might wish to consider a graceful exit from politics. Yet what he did next proved time had not mellowed his need to remain relevant in the circus of Kentucky politics. Chandler endorsed Nunn. Henry lost by 29 thousand votes; Ward later calculated that Chandler's bolt cost him around 15,000 votes out of that total.

While Ockerman monitored the polls and Henry ignored his advice, a *Courier-Journal* feature titled "Electorate Seems Bored by Kentucky Campaign," was distributed nationally by *The Los Angeles Times* and *Washington Post*. "It is awfully hard," a bemused Democratic organizer observed, "to stir up any enthusiasm for a candidate who calls himself 'the builder' and recites the Eighth Commandment (Thou shalt not steal) a dozen times a day."

The Nunn campaign painted the opposition as entrenched and corrupt. "Ward," the Republicans assert, "is another handpicked candidate chosen by the group of consultants and contractors that have been getting nearly a billion dollars in state contracts, mainly without open public competitive bidding."

The charge was a lie. Ward enforced wide open, competitive bidding, and signed off on every major purchase order until the day he resigned. The "young and hungry" contractors previously locked out from bidding praised Ward for treating them fairly; the contractors who benefited from rigged bids vowed to get even during the next election.

The *Courier-Journal* published a feature titled "Conversations with the Candidates," and Nunn and Ward shared thoughtful, informed answers. Each supported the Kentucky Education Association's 19-point legislative plan, pledged not to increase taxes, and agreed it was important to reform the legislative process to restrict the power of the governor's office.

Strip mining regulation however, revealed sharp disagreement. Kentucky coal operators exerted strong influence over the General Assembly. In 1934 and 1942, Henry pushed back against the intimidation and pressure exerted by payday lenders and the utility industry.

The hostility between the coal industry and Henry stretched back to the early 1950s. "I know I remember we had a fight with one outfit claimed it—that it owned the mineral rights to Pine Mountain State Park. Pine Mountain State Forest. And determined to exercise their rights to strip. We took them to court and won the battle, that was way back in when I became commissioner of conservation."

In 1950, Lawrence Wetherby, then Lieutenant Governor and chair of the Legislative Research Commission, organized a tour of strip-mining sites to investigate its environmental impact. Strip mining scarred the landscape, polluted the water and soil, and triggered flooding or sinkholes. Overweight coal trucks damaged roads and caused accidents or fatalities, dangers too serious to ignore any longer.

When Wetherby became Governor, he asked Ward to draft a bill enforcing reclamation standards. "I wrote the first state strip mining law in nineteen and fifty-two...we didn't get it passed." Calling it a "hot battle," it failed Henry remembered, because "the coal interests were too strong..." Yet Wetherby refused to give up, putting the bill at the top of his agenda for the next session. In 1954, the bill passed, but *The Courier-Journal* observed the Governor risked the bill's success by keeping Henry in the forefront of the action.

"When Mr. Ward arose in the Senate chamber last Thursday to defend the strip-mine bill, he readily admitted what every legislator in Frankfort had been saying for days: the strip-mine bill could be passed with relatively little trouble if the Governor would delegate the responsibility for its enforcement to someone other than Henry Ward. For opponents of the bill, the strip- miners who will be forced to reclaim stripped lands, know that Mr. Ward, as one of the several men for enforcement of the reclamation regulations, will insist that the law is followed."

In Governor Wetherby's oral history for the University of Kentucky, Wetherby described the process. "I, uh, I had Dick Moloney, as I mentioned, who was my floor leader and he had introduced the bill. He had prepared well for the hearings on it. Then he had a perfect witness, and that was Henry Ward, who was the commissioner of conservation, and Henry came up as a witness, and he had the facts about what it would cost the coal operators to, uh, restore the land as we had proposed in our bill, and he discounted all of the coal operators' testimony." Henry stayed involved, and the Breathitt administration passed an even tougher law in 1966.

Henry's stand on strip mining long a matter of public record, during a speech in Harlan County, Nunn complained that the coal industry "has been treated by the last two administrations as an embarrassing and unwanted stepchild... We propose to give the coal industry the sincere help it deserves-and in helping it we will help all Kentucky."

Henry continued "telling it like it is," but he alienated two critical voting blocs—the coal industry and urban Blacks supporting open housing laws in Jefferson County.

In April, 1967, Henry released a written statement that he believed "...every person is created equal –in the sight of God. But each person is not born with equal opportunities, and it is the obligation of society to seek a remedy to this problem, particularly in the field of education and in the protection of the individual to his just rights in his 'pursuit of happiness,'...I am opposed to bigotry, prejudice or oppression in any form."

Yet he opposed local or state law banning housing discrimination. While Louie Nunn touted "self-reliance" and "personal accountability" as the way to overcome racial oppression, Henry defended individual rights—"the right to sell a house to anyone of his choice, or to refuse to sell it to anyone not of his choice," over laws banning "block busting" and discrimination denying Blacks their right to buy or rent property of their choosing.

In late April, Mrs. Harry McAlpin, a Black voter who chaired the Kentucky Council on Human Relations, resigned from Ward's women's advisory committee. In her letter of resignation, she stated "I thought you were keen and thorough," Mrs. McAlpin said. "But you either have misread and misinterpreted the proposed open housing legislation, or you haven't even read it." Referring to Ward as a candidate with a "deep sense of moral decency...You have made clear that the moral rights of Negroes, as citizens of our commonwealth are less important than their legal rights...I am through...as one of your supporters."

As November approached, Kentucky college students who chanted "half an oaf is better than Nunn," seemed to pinpoint the mood in Kentucky.

Nunn cited an independent study by the Midwest Research Institute documenting Kentucky's slide in education, agriculture, health and welfare. Ward responded that the study was "all wet." Nunn fired back that Kentucky's highway statistics lagged in comparison to adjoining states in completed mileage and interstate construction.

A newspaperman who out researched researchers, Ward pulled statistics from "official records" contradicting the Research Institute, helpfully adding the records confirmed a nearly 30% increase in personal income since 1960.

When the facts turned against him, Nunn resorted to cruelty instead. Ned Breathitt recalled Nunn related a story about a campaign stop in Adair County, and the photos of the candidates inside the courthouse. "They did this, of the candidates, one of Louie Nunn, and Louie looked handsome, you know, and-and there was Henry Ward scowling...and a pock marked faced (*sic*). You know, he had a pock marked face."

Chandler was there too. "And he bragged on Louie, and talked about what a great county judge he was, and how close he was to John Sherman Cooper, that 'sainted' Kentuckian...But he said, 'Now look at that picture of that fellow. Louie Nunn is a distinguished Kentuckian. He looks like a governor. Look at that other fellow. He doesn't look like a governor. He got a face like a late summer pumpkin...And everybody just roarin' and laugh (*sic*). And he did that at courthouses and he-he made fun of-of Henry Ward...But I stayed with Henry. Right at the end the polls showed Henry getting in trouble."

Henry and his supporters continued working 18-hour days. In photographs he appears smiling happily, surrounded by enthusiastic "Win with Ward" crowds of over 2,000 men, women, children at rallies. He cut the ribbon celebrating "Henry Ward Day in Pulaski County," and attended teas and receptions sponsored by county Democratic women's clubs. Working an overflow crowd in the Crystal Ballroom of the Hotel Beecher, he promoted a nine-point plan for prosperity and progress.

Two weeks before the election, Henry confided to John Witt that he "had a bad feeling," and polls showed his lead slipping away. Yet he refused to trade favors for votes. During one meeting, supporters promised Ward they would carry the county for him in exchange for a favor. "You'd be crazy as hell to think I could do that," Ward retorted.

In late October, Breathitt was on a ship headed to the Caribbean for a governor's conference, when "Foster called me on marine radio. He says, 'You get on back here. This-this campaign's in trouble.'" Breathitt was joined by Earle Clements, who as usual, surfaced at the last possible minute. They doubled down, but Nunn cut in fast, winning by 29, 449 votes.

After his defeat, "with a set jaw, an effort at humor and a display of resignation," Henry met with campaign workers and thanked them for their support. He blamed himself, the national mood, and the fact the campaign lacked a unity of purpose. "I'm not kidding myself [sic] if I was a poor candidate. I'm not a good candidate. I'm not a glad-hander, back slapper. I'm -I-I'm all right, congenial enough if I felt I needed to. But I...I'm not...I haven't got that old charisma..."

Supporters and close friends expressed regret Kentuckians never got a chance to see the warm and caring side of "Hammerin' Hank." His sole motivation to run for governor reflected a sincere desire to serve the people of his state.

Eventually his disappointment faded. During his oral history, Ward often mentioned how "lucky" he was—lucky to have discovered his true vocation as a newspaperman, to serve in the General Assembly, to shape conservation policy. According to Henry, he just happened to be in the right place at the right time to step up and make a difference. "I was a nobody...just a damned kid who had to work for a living and couldn't even go to college. I think the opportunities I have had go beyond what I had any reasonable right to expect," he said.

Henry retired from public life. The Paxton family offered him job as publisher of the newspaper, now called *The Paducah Sun*. But he encountered difficulty and unhappiness adjusting to the hometown he'd been away from for over twenty years, and disliked attending to the "business side" of running the paper. He briefly served as Director of Kentucky Independent College Foundation, then he and Gladys moved to Florida. After she died from a heart ailment, he remarried, traveled and was widowed again. He moved to Lexington and enjoyed spending time with his daughter and grandchildren.

Looking back over his career, he appreciated the honors he received: Kentucky's Outstanding Young Man, and the Kentucky Press Association's Man of the Year. The first inductee into the Kentucky Transportation Hall of Fame, he was also named to the Journalism Hall of Fame.

He never sought that recognition; he was too busy moving on to the next job that needed doing. In his memoirs, he acknowledged that he was most gratified when someone walked up to him and shared a story about how a column he wrote or a bill he voted for was meaningful to them or helped improve their lives.

Ward reluctantly returned to visit Kentucky from Florida in 1978. Parks Commissioner Bruce Montgomery, against Henry's wishes, planned a ceremony re naming the Village Inn, the main lodge of Kentucky Dam Village State Resort Park, in his honor. Initially, Henry refused to accept and scolded Montgomery for the idea. During his tenure in the Conservation and Highway Departments, Ward initiated a policy prohibiting the naming of public buildings for people still living.

Bill Powell, a *Courier-Journal* reporter who worked with Henry at the *Sun-Democrat* and knew him well, covered the occasion. "No one paid any attention yesterday to the man walking alone among the early-rising tourists on the shore of Kentucky Lake. If they had, they might have heard him say something about the need for parking closer to the new boat dock at Kentucky Lake State Resort Park. Or they might have seen him study the park cottages and grounds and run his fingers over picnic tables to see if they were clean. Anyone asking would have learned that Henry Ward was back home—where he started Kentucky's modern park system, now a national model, 32 years ago."

Addressing the small crowd gathered, including Governor Julian Carroll and former Governor Ned Breathitt, Ward's voice "...choked. He paused, several moments, fighting tears. But he reverted quickly to the slugger style that earned him the nickname "Hammerin' Hank." He said the lodge stone with his name carved on it 'will at least save my family the expense of buying me a monument.'"

In 1992, Kentucky Education Television broadcast a one-hour documentary *'Hammerin' Hank, Henry Ward: A Kentucky Original,* that introduced the crusading reporter known as "the father of Kentucky parks" to a new generation of Kentuckians. Up until his death, reporters, historians, and students of government contacted him for observations or opinions, which he happily shared.

Often they returned to the same question—what would a 4 year term under Governor Henry Ward have been like? Would he have kept his promises? Henry replied "I don't have to answer that. You didn't give me a chance to show you I was telling the truth."

The "rough lookin' fella," the "triple-threat man" in journalism, the legislature and state government, believed deeply in the ideas and ideals he memorized in his high school civics class. During a long stretch of unselfish public service, he was untainted by corruption, motivated by progress, not power. For this reason alone, his life is instructive.

His early adventures resemble the fictional lives of those idealistic Frank Capra movie heroes—Longfellow Deeds and Jefferson Smith. As the villains and cynics in those Hollywood films sneered these do gooders were "saps," Henry's story proves there is still honor in standing up for simple human decency and the truth.

# 24 Notes on Sources

**Henry T. Ward Files/Personal & Professional Documents**: Newspaper articles, columns, state and federal correspondence, reports, photographs, personal letters, precinct returns, research, campaign, policy and broadcast materials written for Senators Alben Barkley and Earle Clements, and miscellaneous documents from Henry Ward's personal/professional files provided to author by permission of Patricia Ward Willis.

**Original Manuscript**: "Recollections of 45 Years in Government and Politics" by Henry Ward

**Original Manuscript**: "Some Recollections of Family and Events of the Past" by Henry Ward

**Author Research Interviews**: (audio cassette/transcribed by author) Preston Kennedy, Retired Executive Editor of the *Paducah Sun,* October 10, 2003, Nicholasville, Ky. Foster Ockerman, attorney and former campaign manager for Henry Ward, October 14, 2003, Lexington, Kentucky

## Oral History projects:

**Henry Ward Oral History Project**: (abbreviated as Ward Project) John Ed Pearce, for the Kentucky Oral History Commission March 21-22, 1986, Howey in the Hills, Florida, Kentucky History Center Call Number: 1985OH05 Interviewee: Henry T. Ward, from typewritten transcript.

**Henry Ward Colleagues Oral History Project**: (abbreviated as Ward Colleagues Project) S. Roggenkamp, for the Kentucky Oral History Commission, Kentucky History Center Call No. 2005OH12 Interviewees: Calvin Grayson, 2/11/04, Lexington Ky.; Billy Joe Hall, 2/3/04, Mt. Sterling, Ky.; Preston Kennedy, 3/29/04, Nicholasville, Ky.; Fred Paxton, 6/28/2004, Paducah, Ky.; Tom Preston, 4/17/04, Lexington, Ky.; B.L. Stamper, 5/6/04, Owenton, Ky.; Pat Willis, 7/22/04, Frankfort, Ky.; John Witt, 2/4/04, Frankfort, Ky; Julian Carroll, 12/21/2004 Frankfort, Kentucky

**Oral History Interviews: Nunn Center for Oral History, University of Kentucky**

*Barkley, Alben W.*, interview by Sidney Shalett, Alben W. Barkley Oral History Project, 2006oh052_bark018, October 18, 1953, Louie B. Nunn Center for Oral History, University of Kentucky Libraries.

*Hampson, Catherine*, interview by Terry L. Birdwhistell, November 11, 1975, Earle C. Clements Oral History Project, Louie B. Nunn Center for Oral History, University of Kentucky Libraries.

*Pearce, John Ed*, interview by L. Elisabeth Beattie. January 09, 1993, Kentucky Writers Oral History Project, Louie B. Nunn Center for Oral History, University of Kentucky Libraries.

*Breathitt, Edward T., Jr.*, interview by Terry L. Birdwhistell. February 06, 1997, Edward T. "Ned" Breathitt, Jr. Oral History Project, Louie B. Nunn Center for Oral History, University of Kentucky Libraries

*Wetherby, Lawrence,* interview by John Kleber, August 30, 1979, Lawrence Wetherby Oral History Project, Louie B. Nunn Center for Oral History, University of Kentucky Library

**Newspapers**

*Bozeman Daily-Chronicle · The New Dealer · The State Journal
The Corbin Daily-Tribune · The New York Times · The Paducah Sun-Democrat
The Paducah Sun · The Courier-Journal · The New York World-Telegram
Lexington Herald-Leader · The Sentinel-Echo Whitley Republican
Louisville Times*

## Bibliography

Edward J. Cleary *The Orsanco Story Water Quality Management in the Ohio Valley Under an Interstate Compact,* (Baltimore Maryland: The John Hopkins Press, 1967)

George H. Douglas *The Golden Age of the Newspaper* (Westport, Connecticut: Greenwood Press, 1999)

Ira Katznelson *Fear Itself The New Deal and the Origins of our Time* (New York: Liveright Publishing Corporation, 2013)

Harry L. Hopkins, *Spending to Save, The Complete Story of Relief* (W.W. & Norton Co., New York, 1936)

Richard Lowitt and Maurine Beasley, *One Third of a Nation Lorena Hickock Reports on the Great Depression,* (University of Illinois Press, Chicago & Urbana, 1983)

Alfred Runte, *National Parks: The American Experience,* (University of Nebraska Press, Lincoln, 1979)

Willard Rouse Jillson, *Kentucky State Parks,* (Kentucky Geological Survey, Frankfort, Ky., 1924)

Harry Schacter, *Kentucky on the March* (Harper & Brothers, New York, 1949)

Thomas K. McCraw, *TVA & The Power Fight 1933-1939,* (J.P. Lippincott Company, Philadelphia, New York, Toronto, 1971)

Harry McPherson, *A Political Education A Washington Memoir,* (University of Texas Press, Austin, 1995)

E. Kenneth Burger, Managing Editor, C.G. Wyckoff, Publisher, *Magazine of Wall Street,* Volume 60, April 24-October 9, 1937

Tracy E. K'Meyer, *Civil Rights in the Gateway to the South, Louisville, Kentucky, 1945-1980* (The University Press of Kentucky, Lexington, 2009)

Griffith Borgeson, *The Golden Age of the Racing Car,* (W.W. Norton Co., New York, 1966)

Leonard Mosley, *Blood Relations The Rise & Fall of the du Ponts of Delaware,* (Atheneum, New York, 1980)

John H. Fenton, *Politics in the Border States,* (The Hauser Press, New Orleans, Louisiana, 1957)

Robert Shankland, *Steve Mather of the National Parks* (Alfred A. Knopf, New York, 1970)

Grant Milnor Hyde, *Handbook for Newspaper Workers,* (D. Appleton & Co., New York, 1926)

William E. O'Brien, *Landscapes of Exclusion, State Parks and Jim Crow in the American South,* (University of Massachusetts Press, Amherst & Boston, 2016)

C.E. Blee, Chief Engineer, *The Kentucky Project, A Comprehensive Report on the Planning, Design, Construction, and Initial Operations of the Kentucky Project, Technical Report, No.* 13 (United States Government Printing Office, Washington, D.C., 1951)

Oliver Gramling, *AP The Story of News,* (Farrar and Rinehart, Inc., N.Y. Toronto 1940)

## Chapter 1 End of Damn Story

1 *"Henry was a"* Senator Marlow Cook, letter to author, dated September 1, 2004

2 *"praised him as the man who" The Courier Journal,* October 13, 2002

3 *"the last dinosaur in the swamp" The Courier-Journal,* May 16, 2017

4 *"...treated like small puddles of water" The Louisville Times,* 6/25/1974

5 *"Johnson wanted to ask me"* Ward Oral History Project, for the Kentucky Oral History Commission, Interviewer: John Ed Pearce, Interviewee: Henry T. Ward, March 21, 1985 Howey in the Hills, Florida, Repository: Kentucky History Center, 1985OHO5, transcript P. 123 (hereinafter cited as Ward Project)

6 *"...a colorless organization Democrat" The New York Times,* November 5, 1967

7 *"Let's get this damn place organized"* Henry Ward Colleagues Oral History Project, (hereinafter cited as Ward Colleagues Project) conducted by S. Roggenkamp, for the Kentucky Oral History Commission, Kentucky History Center Call No. 2005OH12 Ward Colleagues, John Witt

8 *"One of the things I learned"* Ward Colleagues, Billy Joe Hall

9 *"...rubbing people the wrong way" The Courier-Journal,* September 9, 1962

10 *"His smile was forced"* Ward Colleagues, B.J. Stamper

11 *"...fleet of beat-up"* "Recollections of 45 Years in Government and Politics" by Henry Ward, P. 38

12 *"Bert you're in trouble"* Ward Project, P. 66

13 *"Henry Ward was incorruptible" The Courier-Journal,* October 8, 2002

14 *"Henry Ward was no charmer"* Ward Colleagues, Fred Paxton

15 *"I would go to hell and back"* Interview, Preston Kennedy, transcript, P. 40

16 *"You just knew"* Ward Colleagues, Preston Kennedy

17 *"the Blackstone Hotel in Chicago"* Ward Project, P. 133

18 *"There I had a chance to learn" The Sun-Democrat,* August 19, 1935
19 *"they were at the finish neck and neck" The Courier-Journal,* undated clipping
20 *"Henry Ward was a"* Author interview, Preston Kennedy October 7, 2003
21 *"End of damn story"* Ward Project, P. 121

**Chapter 2 Explosion and Tears**

1 *"When I was a boy in Lone Oak" The Sun-Democrat,* May 1, 1934
2 *"I was a nobody...just a damned kid who had to work" The Courier-Journal,* June 25, 1974
3 *"A fine philosophy about what the"* Ward Project, P. 5
4 *"My father believed in education"* Ward Project, P. 2
5 *"I can see my father"* Ward Colleagues, Patricia Willis
6 *"until his death two weeks later" The Sun-Democrat,* November 16, 1915, December 4, 1915
7 *"You can imagine how desolated"* "Some Recollections of Family and Events of the Past" by Henry Ward, P. 3
8 *"The first bottle of soda pop" The Sun-Democrat,* September 18, 1940
9 *"Those trips to Paducah"* "Some Recollections" P. 3
10 *"I set traps for rabbits"* "Some Recollections" P. 4
11 *"I learned early how to"* Ward Project, transcript, P. 2
12 *"I delivered a lot of prescriptions"* "Some Recollections" P. 4
13 *"I did that with enthusiasm"* "Some Recollections" p. 5
14 *"..the only job I got I could find"* Ward Project, P. 3
15 *"...I had a little experience"* Ward Project, P. 4
16 *"more life into the paper" The Sun-Democrat,* February 21, 1996
17 *"I'd only been through the 8th grade"* ibid
18 *"Remember that criminals,"* Grant Hyde, *Handbook for Newspaper Workers,* Grant Hyde, (D. Appleton & Co., New York, 1926), P. 209
19 *"Mr. Cobb, what would you say" The Paducah Sun,* February 20, 1996
20 *"I had a lonely childhood"* "Some Recollections", P. 4
21 *"Libraries raised me" The New York Times,* December 9, 2009
22 *"Looking back, I do not consider"* "Recollections of 45 Years", P. 1
23 *"Journalistic structure" Handbook,* Hyde, Title Page
24 *"The length of a story"* Interview, Preston Kennedy, P. 48
25 *"How did this happen?" The New York Times,* August 1, 2009
26 *"...one of the bad turns journalism took"*, Interview, Preston Kennedy, transcript, P. 20

27 *"The most valuable people who ever"* Ibid., P. 20
28 *"And I said, 'No'"*, Interview Preston Kennedy, P. 13
29 *"...if you don't think,"* *The Sun-Democrat*, April 29, 1938
30 *"...happy madhouse of commerce"*, *The Sun-Democrat*, February 21, 1996
31 *"A gal rushed into"* *The Sun-Democrat*, March 22, 1934
32 *"Now the Depression was"* Ward Project, P. 6
33 *"...whatever small share of prosperity"*, George Blakey, *Hard Times and New Deal in Kentucky, 1929-1939*, (University Press of Kentucky, Lexington, Ky., 1986), P. 6
34 *"It was merged with the Sun"* "Some Recollections", P. 5
35 *"that old Ford barely made it..."* Ward Project, P. 5

## Chapter 3 A Crusader Goes to Frankfort

1 *"Calling town officials scheming crooks"* *The Sun-Democrat*, January 23, 1933
2 *"I learned later on that was his first chore"* Preston Kennedy Interview, P. 10
3 *"You see, these people were people of character*, Preston Kennedy Interview, P. 43
4 *"I never saw a man of any age"* Testimonial letter, Edwin J. Paxton, Sr., 1942
5 *"Either you change or die."* Ward Colleagues, Fred Paxton
6 *"WPSD-TV went on the air in 1957"* Fred Paxton, letter to Henry Ward, March 14, 1997
7 *"That boy [Edwin J. Paxton] was and is a live wire"* "The Good Old Days, Being Some Reminiscences, With a Little Salt of Kentucky Journalism in the last Century Address Delivered by Urey Woodson At Sixty-second Annual Meeting of the Kentucky Press Association, June 25-27, 1931, Paducah, Ky. (Privately Printed)
8 *"...that began with a winning lottery ticket"* *The Paducah Sun* February 20, 1996
9 *"I stayed with it so long that I could close my eyes"* Ibid.
10 *"Many are the problems"* Testimonial letter, Edwin J. Paxton, Sr., 1942
11 *"The Paducah Sun was an evening paper"* Ward Project, P. 5
12 *"I have seen 19 men executed"* *The Sun-Democrat*, December 9, 1934
13 *"...'Ramblers Rambling by the Ramblers"* Ward Project, P. 7
14 *"'The smaller the town, the tougher that kind of"* Herald-Leader, August 20,1978
15 *"They'd raid places that had slot machines"* Ward Project, P. 7
16 *"Can you explain the difference..."* *The Sun Democrat*, May 24, 1933
17 *"So I used a fellow who was a notorious drunk"* Ward Project, P. 8

18 *"And they were reluctant to do so..." Ibid.*, P. 8
19 *"You're kind of stupid writing about all that stuff"* Ward Project, P. 7
20 *"the magistrate inside his office" The Sun Democrat* July 16, 1933
21 *"You may notice there is a new byline" The Sun Democrat*, July 14, 1933
22 *"Paducah was then a big railroad center"* "Recollections" P. 3-4
23 *"couldn't get the fellow who was now the representative"* Ward Project, P. 9
24 *"cease complaining and lift up their chins" The Sun Democrat* January 4, 1932
25 *"2,246 industries operating with approximately"* George T. Blakey, *Hard Times and New Deal in Kentucky:1929-1939* (University Press of Kentucky, Lexington, Ky., 1986) P. 10-11
26 *"One of the earliest eyesores of the Depression"* Harry L. Hopkins, *Spending to Save, The Complete Story of Relief* (W.W. Norton & Co., New York 1936) P. 127
27 *"By January, 1933, whole sections of business" Ibid.* P. 115
28 *"as the numbers jumped from" Ibid.* P. 95
29 *"the man had been only stopping" "I'm a married man, but I can't make enough" The Sun Democrat*, February 17, 1933
30 *"Our common difficulties"* Franklin D. Roosevelt, Inaugural Address, March 4, 1933, https://avalon.law.yale.edu/20th_century/froos1.asp
31 *"by merely talking about it. We must act. We must act quickly. Ibid.*
32 *"I shall never vote for F.D. Roosevelt"* Undated letter of Dexter T. Barrett, to Alben W. Barkley, Barkley Collection, Political File Series (1938-1940), Box 14, Margaret I. King Library, Special Collections & Archives, University of Kentucky, Lexington, Ky.
33 *"Millions of men and women were" The New Dealer*, June 10, 1938, Louisville, Kentucky
34 *"The housing on the entire western portion"* "Working Files of County Planning Survey" Crittenden to Laurel County, Crittenden County Report, Box 28, 2, (1934-1937), Kentucky Department of Libraries and Archives.
35 *"...a little cleaning to do"* Edited by Richard Lowitt and Maurine Beasely, *One Third of a Nation, Lorena Hickock Reports on the Great Depression*, (University of Illinois Press, Urbana and Chicago1981) P. x
36 *"...go out around the country" Ibid.*, ix
37 *"poured out in near record-breaking..." The Sun Democrat*, August 6, 1933 August 7, 1933
38 *"Ward Captures Seat In House" The Sun Democrat*, August 11, 1933
39 *"nobody heard of a family of five" One Third of a Nation*, P. 25

40 *"Pasted up on the doors" Ibid.*, P. 25
41 *"You travel as far as you can" Ibid.*, P. 28
42 *"Kentucky Must Not Fail" Kentucky House Journal*, Governor's Message, February 15, 1934, P. 46
43 *"accept the votes and influence of any clique, clan" The Sun Democrat*, undated, original clipping, 1933
44 *"At 24, I was too young, inexperienced, naïve"* "Recollections" P. 5

### Chapter 4 Rip Roaring Speeches and the Sales Tax Revolt

1 *"Is it not a hard matter to tell" Kentucky House Journal*, Governor's Address to the Joint Assembly of the Session, May 9,1934, P. 13-14
2 *"Shall we put you down" The Sun Democrat*, April 15, 1934
3 *"I'll go even further than that" The Sun Democrat*, January 25, 1934
4 *"Ward Compels Reading of" Ibid.*, February 16, 1934
5 *"Now comes Representative Chris Gottachalk" Ibid.* February 7, 1934
6 *"Chairman Rhodes Myers interrupted Henry" Ibid.*, February 15, 1934
7 *"the trouble was, without records or witnesses"* "Recollections" P. 3
8 *"the centers of the small loan business " The Sun Democrat* March 31, 1934
9 *"a chance meeting in a downtown restaurant" ibid.*
10 *"these young fellows in the House" The Sun Democrat*, February 12, 1934
11 *"started howling" Ibid.*, March 4, 1934
12 *"Murphy's bill was 'putrid'" Ibid.*
13 *"Are we going to be dictated to" Ibid.*, March 24, 1934
14 *"cut my throat from ear to ear" Ibid.*, March 15, 1934
15 *"Henry Ward, raised here, acquiring his knowledge" Ibid.*, March 14, 1923
16 *"was a major issue in Kentucky politics"* "Recollections" P. 7
17 *"I'd say not more than ten percent of them"* Ward Project, P. 19
18 *"hard and fast administration boys" The Sun Democrat*, March 19, 1934
19 *"Why don't you get some action on" Ibid.*, January 24, 1934
20 *"What is actually done, not what is said" Ibid.*, March 24, 1934
22 *"Personally, I am not in favor of" Ibid.*, February 28, 1934
23 *"Do you want a sales tax" Ibid.*
24 *"He says for God's sake"*, *"I haven't had time to sleep or eat"*, *"I have bragged on this Legislature"*, *"They can call you wild jackasses"*, *"So my friends, you see it is whose ox" Kentucky House Journal*, Governor's Address, May 9, 1934, pages 18, 21, 24, 27
25 *"House Passes Income Tax, Capitol Guarded" The Sun Democrat*, May 16, 1934

24 NOTES ON SOURCES    233

26 *"blow the old governor to hell"*, *"Last night the jobless rode"* The Sun Democrat, May 17, 1934
27 *"Many of the legislators"* Ibid., May 22, 1934
28 *"fired the daughter of a legislator"* Ibid., May 29, 1934
29 *"He filed an amendment"* Kentucky House Journal, May 29, 1934 Record of Proceedings to Amend HB 11
30 *"or any other appliance used in the game of baseball"* Ibid., June 7, 1934, P. 473
31 *"I have heard it rumored"* The Sun Democrat, June 8, 1934
32 *"are heaping bitter criticisms"* Ibid., July 2, 1934

## Chapter 5 Reformer Reformed

1 *"I made a vigorous fight"* The Sun Democrat, undated original clipping, full page campaign ad
2 *"You won't find out"* The Herald-Leader, January 31, 1988
3 *"I felt like I knew him from the articles he wrote"* The State Journal, July 21, 1967
4 *"is 21 years of age and resides"* original undated clipping, The Sun Democrat, 1934
5 *"By the time we got back to Paducah"* Ward Project, P. 22
6 *"The marriage, which comes as a surprise"* original undated clipping, Ibid. 1934
7 *"Three Governors Confuse Kentucky"* The New York Times, February 8, 1935
8 *"I was among them. We insisted that once a call"* "Recollections" P.5
9 *"When I first went to Frankfort"* The Sun-Democrat, October 26, 1935
10 *"Opponents accused me of getting a new car"* "Recollections" P.6
11 *"a quiet, kindly able, Southern judge"* Time Magazine, October 16, 1939
12 *"...bungling..."*Ibid., Time Magazine
13 *"...Kentucky's happy man is no mere country clown."* Ibid., Time Magazine
14 *"the Rural Electrification Administration measure,"* 77m1: Letter from Henry Ward to Gov. A.B. Chandler, A.B. Happy Chandler papers, 1900-1985, August 4, 1936 University of Kentucky Special Collections Research Collection, Margaret King Library.

## Chapter 6 Dousing the Kerosene Lanterns

1 *"at the rate of progress shown"* Records of the Rural Electrification Administration [REA], 1934-73, Record Group 221, 1937 Report of the Rural Electrification Administration, p. 14.
2 *"the charred remains of an owl and possum"* Ibid., p. 63

3 *"I wonder if the gentleman knows that in New Zealand"* Marquis Childs *The Farmer Takes a Hand: The Electric Power Revolution in Rural America,* (Doubleday, New York, 1952) P. 26-27

4 *"In one county in which I worked"* Records of the REA, 1937 Report, P. 79

5 *"the greatest extent of the farmers of America"* Record of proceedings at the National Rural Electric Cooperative 1st Annual Convention, St. Louis, Mo., 1943, NREC newspaper, Kentucky Utilities Co. Archive, Lexington, Ky.

6 *"to the moral uplifting of the nation"* Ibid, P. 5

7 *"Everything Roosevelt did he was opposed to it,"* Author interview, Robert Watt III, Lexington, Kentucky, April 10, 2006.

8 *"the most vicious piece of legislation every passed"* The Courier-Journal, March 27, 1934

9 *"Henry, some representatives of the utilities"* The Sun-Democrat, February 20, 1936

10 *"I got the bills referred to the committee"* Ward Project, P. 15

11 *"Our inability to secure an enabling act"* 77m1: Letter from Ben Kilgore, to Gov. A.B. Chandler, A.B. Happy Chandler papers, 1900-1985, September 8, 1936, University of Kentucky Special Collections Research Collection, Margaret King Library

12 *"so that you see a good deal hangs on"* Ibid. Letter from Morris L. Cooke to Gov. A.B. Chandler, December 22, 1936

13 *"had been more concerned with building and controlling"* James C. Klotter, *Kentucky: Portrait in Paradox, 1900-1950,* (Kentucky Historical Society, Frankfort, Kentucky, 1996)

14 *"RESOLVED – THAT WHEREAS RADICAL, unusual, unnotified"* A.B. Chandler Collection *77m1: copy of October 13, 1936 resolution from B.N. Gordon, Mayor, Hopkins County, Ky., to Governor Chandler*

15 *"If you give things to people you must first take them away"* Interview, R. Watt, III.

16 *"Rural electrification, through low-cost projects sponsored"* Appendix B: Opinion of The Public Service Commission of Kentucky, Administrative Order No. 22, May 15, 1937.

17 *"The Kentucky Public Service Commission has done more to aid"* A.B. Chandler Collection, 77m1: undated report "Work of the Public Service Commission, 1937

18 *"might well serve as a model for other state commissions"* Ibid., Telegram from John Carmody to A.B. Chandler, May 18, 1937

19 *"The first benefit we received from the REA was lights"* Scearce, Rose Dudley, *What REA Service Means To Our Farm Home,* Rural Electrification NEWS, Publisher: Rural Electrification Administration, Franklin D. Roosevelt Library, Carmody Papers (March, 939), http://newdeal.feri.org/tva/tva23.htm. New Deal Network, http://newdeal.feri.org (September 19, 2014)
20 *"I gained a reputation as an advocate"* *The Sun-Democrat,* May 16, 1936

## Chapter 7 A Deplorable Situation

1 *"One word more...you have heard charges"* Franklin D. Roosevelt: *The Public Papers and Addresses of Franklin D. Roosevelt, 1938* (New York: Russell & Russell), 1938 1950, Item 165
2 *"The Sheriff of the county told me"* 63m143: Report from County No. 8 Adair, Undated, Political File Series, Alben W. Barkley papers, 1893-1966, University of Kentucky Special Collections Research Center, Margaret I. King Library.
3 *"a grand political racket in which the taxpayer"* *The New York Times,* July 2, 1938
4 *"National Interests Backing Chandler in Kentucky Fight"* *The New York World-Telegram,* June 14, 1938
5 *"a fair-haired boy among the anti-New Deal elements"* Ibid.
6 *"agitation toward freeing the toll bridges"* *The Sun-Democrat* January 6, 1938
7 *"taking the crack at me."* Ibid., 1/6/1938
8 *"a very brilliant man"* Barkley, Alben W., interview by Sidney Shalett, Alben W. Barkley Oral History Project, 2006oh052_bark018, October 18, 1953, Louie B. Nunn Center for Oral History, University of Kentucky Libraries.
9 *"...created a very desperate and ticklish situation"* Ibid., Shalett
10 *"the fellow who won the nomination in the first compulsory"* Ibid., Shalett
11 *"I made no request of the President or his son"* *The Sun-Democrat,* January 25, 1938
12 *"How did you handle that?"* Alben Barkley Oral History Interview, Shalett, 10/18/53
13 *"Some of us were for Barkley and decided to do"* Ward Project, P. 17-18
14 *"It's going to be a bitter, nasty sort of campaign"* Ward Files, Undated letter from Ed Paxton, Jr. to Edwin Paxton, Sr.
15 *"They got to talking in rather loud tones"* *The Sun-Democrat,* February 12, 1938
16 *"may be the Gettysburg of the party's internecine strife"* *The New York Times,* February 12, 1938

17 *"Well, he said, that's it,"* Alben Barkley Oral History, Shalett, 10/18/53
18 *"Many big businessmen not only feared"* James Burns, Susan Dunn, *The Three Roosevelts: Patrician Leaders Who Transformed America*, (Grove Atlantic Press, New York., N.Y., 2002) P. 308.
19 *"Fiscal policy of the administration is in a mess." Happening In Wall Street by E.K.T., The Magazine of Wall Street*, C.G. Wyckoff, Publisher, Vol. 60, Apr 24-Oct 9, 1937, P. 23
20 *"The Courier-Journal does not customarily taken an editorial position" The Sun Democrat*, July 1, 1938
21 *"100% for Barkley"* Ward Files, Letter from Ed Paxton, Jr. to George Goodman, February 18, 1938
22 *"make a monkey of himself" The Sun-Democrat*, February 28, 1938
23 *"At one time in the session it was suggested by some administration leaders" Ibid*.

## Chapter 8 Victors and Victim

1 *"Stokes defended his series, stating" The New York Times*, July 2, 1938
2 *"My name is Chandler, Governor of Kentucky," The Sun-Democrat*, December 1, 1938
3 *"a grand political racket in which the taxpayer" The New York Times*, July 2, 1938
4 *"the deplorable situation in Kentucky" The New York Times*, August 3, 1938
5 *"Vote Buying Bared in Kentucky" The New York World-Telegram*, June 6, 1938
6 *"a reliable, disinterested reporter"* 1939 newspaper column, *Fourth Estate, Stokes and the WPA Congressional Findings Support Exposes of Intimidation*, Columbia University Libraries, Pulitzer Prize Committee News Reels, 1939, Reel ID: Columbia University Libraries MRR FN 3881 1936 1939 and 1940.
7 *"an amiable, vigorous, ruddy-cheeked," New York World-Telegram*, June 6, 1938
8 *"from top to bottom...the word has gone out" Ibid*.
9 *"started the Barkley publicity office"* "Recollections" P. 12
10 *"If you can get us your speech"* Alben W. Barkley Papers, Political File Series, 1938 undated letter from Henry Ward to Alben Barkley
11 *"A political machine that desired to win"* Undated newspaper column, "Today in Kentucky" by Henry Ward, *Ibid*.
12 *"As the campaign gets hotter -and it will be the hottest in years" New York World Telegram*, June 6, 1938

13 *"a slender gentleman", "They're putting on people in this county", "There was a federal investigator through here", "Well, I've got a right to wear half of it" New York World Telegram,* June 10, 1938

14 *"The Kentucky mountaineers are not often considered of great importance" Investigation of Senatorial Campaign Expenditures and Use of Governmental Funds Report of the Special Committee to Investigate Senatorial Campaign Expenditures And Use of Governmental Funds in 1938, Summary of Cases by States and Miscellaneous Cases, Part II,* January 3, 1939, U.S. Government Printing Office, Washington, 1939, Report No. 1, Part II, p. 65

15 *"I took an active part as an official" The Sun-Democrat,* September 9, 1938

16 *"Barkley Has Earned Splendid Record"* 63m143: *The New Dealer,* undated copy, edited by Henry Ward, Alben W. Barkley papers, Political File Series

17 *"removed our unfortunates from their dungeons" Ibid.,* Newspaper ad, May 13, 1938 Section 2. Page 3.

18 *"As yet, no one will accept the statement", Ibid.,* Letter from Ben Johnson to Alben Barkley, June 2, 1938

19 *"a throng that filled the grandstand" The Sun-Democrat* June 18, 1938

20 *"Barkley was interrupted in the middle of"* Harry McPherson, *A Political Education, A Washington Memoir,* (University of Texas Press, Austin 1972), P. 66

21 *"written in mud by the migratory feet of a weasel" The Sun-Democrat,* July 17, 1940

22 *"The record I have made", "Every pensioner, every WPA worker" The Sun-Democrat,* June 18, 1938

23 *"laid bare as cynical a picture of democracy"* 1939 *Cynical on Democracy,* Raymond Clapper, Scripps-Howard newspaper columnist, 6/6/38, Columbia University Libraries, Pulitzer Prize Committee News Reels, 1939, Reel ID: Columbia University Libraries MRR FN 38811936 1939 and 1940.

24 *"I had no instructions other than to write the facts as I found them" The New York World Telegram,* July 18, 1938

25 *"in a far flung organization", Summary of Cases by States and Miscellaneous Cases, Part II,* January 3, 1939, U.S. Government Printing Office, Washington, 1939, Report No. 1, Part II

26 *"It is only human for them to say" New York World Telegram* July 1, 1938

27 *"the biggest man in the U.S. Congress" "for the truth of the matter" "Chandler is making a play" "a real government 'of the people, by the people, and for the people'" The Paducah Sun-Democrat* July 17, 1938

### Chapter 9 A "Decent Fella"

1 *"funds were so tight I didn't feel like charging everything I'd spent"* Ward Project, P. 26
2 *"There are many persons in this country"* The New York Times, January 4, 1939
3 *"During that election cycle"* Investigation of Senatorial Campaign Expenditures and Use of Governmental Funds. Report of the Special Committee to Investigate Senatorial Campaign Contributions and Expenditures and Use of Governmental Funds in 1938. Part 1-3, Part I, p. 53, 1939, U.S. Government Printing Office, Washington, D.C., 1939
4 *"And Tom Rhea said 'I've got to have $100,000 dollars"* Ward Project, P. 26
5 *"I haven't the faintest idea what my intention was"* The Paducah Sun-Democrat, August 8, 1936
6 *"It's always been my ambition to"* The Paducah Sun-Democrat, February 5, 1938
7 *"the businessmen who voiced their opinions"* The Paducah Sun-Democrat, September 4, 1940
8 *"my first love and one [in] which I had"* Ward Project, P. 86
9 *"was the equivalent of 720 dead horses"* "The Ohio River Valley Water Sanitation Commission and Its Activities" Englebrecht, Vicory, Jr., Tennant, Presentation at the International Conference on Environmental Pollution, Lisbon, Portugal, 15-19, April 1991
10 *"New Era on Ohio River"* The New York Times, July 17, 1966
11 *"To re-draft a bill 71 pages in length"* The Paducah Sun-Democrat, February 8, 1938
12 *"a fellow craftsman now turned organization politician"* The Courier-Journal Undated Column, J. Howard Henderson, 1942
13 *"The power industry grew from two mutually hostile"* Thomas K. McCraw, TVA and the Power Fight, 1933-1939, (J.P. Lippincott, Philadelphia, Pa., 1971) P. vii
14 *"Howard you may be right, but there's one thing I've learned"* Ward Project, P. 27

### Chapter 10 "They'll Build that Dam or Bust"

1 *"Do you have to make four or five arguments"* The Courier-Journal, February 4, 1922

## 24 NOTES ON SOURCES

2 *"like blown smoke through the floodgates of Wilson Dam" TVA The Great Experiment,* Tennessee Valley Authority, TVA Heritage Series, https://www.tva.com/about-tva/our-history/tva-heritage

3 *"the large reservoir with more than 4,000,000 acre-feet" The Kentucky Project A Comprehensive Report on the Planning, Design Construction, and Initial Operations of the Kentucky Project, Technical Report No. 13* U.S. Government Printing Office, Washington: 1951

4 *"In the summer of 1933, if a flyer had climbed into his plane at Paducah" TVA Program in Text and Pictures from the Architectural Forum,* Reprinted by permission of the Tennessee Valley Authority, Knoxville, Ky., August, 1939, P. 2

5 *"One range or line of holes drilled across the river" The Kentucky Project,* p. 29 *"Because of its unusual size" Ibid.,* P. 545

6 *"I have to work to make a living for myself and my family" The Paducah Sun-Democrat* advertisement, August, 1940

7 *"Kentucky was once regarded as a detour state" The Paducah Sun-Democrat,* March 11, 1941

8 *"The Kentucky rate thus established" The Courier-Journal,* February 8, 1942

9 *"Under the TVA Act, a state had first claim"* Gary Luhr, unpublished history of rural electrification in Kentucky, (1991), Provided to author by permission of G. Luhr, VP, KAEC.

10 *"Ward Bill 146, because it demands special privilege legislation" The Paducah Sun-Democrat,* Undated ad

11 *"As I see it, the issue is reaching such importance" The Paducah Sun-Democrat,* March 18, 1942

12 *"It could be argued that he and his western Kentucky colleagues"* George Humpheys e mail to author, April 18, 2021

13 *"When you are in trouble, it seems that more trouble" The Paducah Sun-Democrat,* September 12, 1941

14 *"That Representative Ward has been and is the leader" Ibid.,* January 14, 1932

15 *"copperhead type of opposition against the bill" Kentucky Accepts T.V.A. Power,* Alex T. Edelmann *The Journal of Land & Public Utility Economics* Vol. 18, No. 4 (Nov., 1942), (University of Wisconsin Press, Madison, Wisconsin)

16 *"We shall say goodbye to all privately owned" The Paducah Sun-Democrat,* February 19, 1942

17 *"little men with large ambitions" The Sentinel-Echo,* undated editorial, 1942

18 *"the prejudices and emotions of" The Paducah Sun-Democrat,* January 21, 1942

19 *"We shall say goodbye to all privately owned" The Paducah Sun-Democrat,* February 19, 1942
20 *"If you don't want TVA, it is not my business to sell it to you"* Gary Luhr, unpublished history of Kentucky rural electrification, P. 4,
21 *"And now, Mr. Ward, I have finished my speech" "You have shown..." "...and the two men shook with anger..." "Look here sir, I represent... "Your time is up, Mr. Blakely, sit down." The Courier-Journal* February 3, 1942
22 *"I can testify that the head of another" The Paducah Sun-Democrat,* February 21, 1942
23 *"Do you want to appear for the bill" "I am sure you can't come here in opposition"The Courier-Journal,* February 3, 1942
24 *"He has fought public ownership at every turn" Ibid.,* February 4, 1942
25 *"with cold, cutting fury" Ibid.,* February 7, 1942
26 *"should not be taken by anyone as representing" Ibid.,* February 6, 1942
27 *"I implore you in the name of the inarticulate masses"* Frederick D. Ogden, Editor, *The Public Papers of Keen Johnson 1939-1943,* (The University Press of Kentucky, Lexington, Kentucky, 1982) Pages 60-67
28 *"The straps are around my ankles" The Paducah Sun-Democrat,* February 19, 1942
29 *"If this amendment is passed, TVA will never see the light of day" Ibid.*

## Chapter 11 First Rate Candidate - Third Place Finish

1 *"And because Keen encouraged me, I ran for Lieutenant Governor"* Ward Project, P. 28
2 *"the longest in American history"* Ira Katznelson, *Fear Itself The New Deal and the Origins of our Time* (Liveright Publishing, New York, 2013) P. 281
3 *"made all the difference. Ever since World War I" Ibid.,* Pages 280-281
4 *"...fears of many of their German," "...the key foreign relations and military" Ibid.,* Pages 280-281
5 *"77.1% still opposed the New Deal" The Paducah Sun-Democrat,* September 9, 1940
6 *"Hitlerized trading bloc in post-war Europe" Ibid.*
7 *"She answered the telephone" The Paducah Sun-Democrat,* July 13, 1942
8 *"City's First Blackout is Excellent" Ibid.,* September 29, 1942
9 *"They are loaded and the years have about covered them" Ibid.*
10 *"... during the war" Ibid.,* February 25, 1996
11 *"Ward's force as a speaker does not rest" Ibid.,* January 7, 1942
12 *"For ten years as a member of the state legislature" Ibid.,* May 31, 1942

13 *"But after Rhea's boy got in the race, Barkley told me"* Ward Project, P. 28
14 *"I aided in bringing about the passage"* The Courier-Journal, July 13, 1942
15 *"For weeks, they have been riding"* The Paducah Sun-Democrat, May 31, 1942
16 *"Vote for Ward or We'll Bolt, Unions Say"* The Courier-Journal, August 4, 1942

## Chapter 12 Following in Their Footsteps

1 *"Ward was brash enough to think"* Falcon O. Baker, "Kentucky Strikes It Rich", The Saturday Evening Post, August 17, 1955 P. 33
2 *"After the Barkley election, I took Gladys and Pat"* Ward Project, P. 36
3 *"Do you think of yourself as a conservation man"* Ward Project, P. 112
4 *"Old-fashioned parks wouldn't do for post war America"* Saturday Evening Post, P. 74
5 *"the champion liars...molten brimstone, bubbling hot pools and a river"* Bozeman Daily Chronicle, April 10, 2011
6 *"a canyon so deep that a man could shout into it at night"* The National Parks: America's Best Idea: Parks -Yellowstone-PBS http://www.pbs.org/national-parks/yellowstone
7 *"editors in the East refused to publish what they deemed"* Ibid.
8 *" The period of speculation began as the gold seekers"* Alfred Runte, National Parks: The American Experience, (The University of Nebraska Press, Lincoln, 1979) P. 34-35
9 *"A region rich with scenic effects and interest"* International Photography and Hall of Fame Profile: *William Henry Jackson (1843-1942)* (https://iphf.org/inductees/william-henry-Jackson)
10 *"These grand panoramic paintings and photos"* Dr. Julie Aronson, Director of Interpretation, Cincinnati Museum of Art, telephone conversation with author, 5/2017
11 *"disorders of the Blood; rheumatism, Gout, Scrofula, Syphilis,"* Brochure, Hotel Arlington, University of Louisville Libraries, UNIV. ARCH. GB 1198.3 .K4 A75, 1886, P. 15
12 *"Wholly unclassable, almost impassible"* Richard F. Weingroff, Highway Existence: -100 Years and Beyond A Peaceful Campaign of Progress and Reform: The Federal Highway Administration at 100, U.S. Department of Transportation, Federal Highway Administration, Vol. 57, No. 2 Autumn, 1993 P. 1
13 *"Of 3,462,522 km (2,252,570 mi) of rural public roads,"* Ibid. P. 2

14 "...*It was not until after World War I and its accompanying lessons of the military*" Griffeth Borgeson, *The Golden Age of the Racing Car*, (W.W. Norton & Company, Inc., New York, 1966) P. 14

15 "*Except for urban centers the United States was devoid of roads*" Ibid.

16 "*the official pathfinder for the National Organization*" The New York Times, June 16, 1912

17 "*Mammoth Cave is to be on the route*" Automobile Topics Illustrated, A Weekly Journal Devoted to the Interests of American Automobilists, Published by Automobile Topics (Incorp.), New York, N.Y., E.E. Schwarzkopf, President, Vol. 27, August 17, 1912, P. 39

18 "*blazed the way for the all southern transcontinental*" The New York Times, November 9, 1913

19 "*a motion picture man and Lord Branston of England*" Ibid.

20 "*both sensationally uncombed*" Robert Shankland, *Steve Mather of the National Parks, A Biography*, (Alfred A. Knopf, New York, 1970) P. 30

21 "*His was a lightning fast brain with an electric nervous energy*" Horace M. Albright and Marian Albright Schenck, *Creating the National Park Service The Missing Years* (University of Oklahoma Press, 1999) P. 37

22 "*grappled with a host of issues that came up*" Rebecca Conard, *The National Conference On State Parks: Reflections on Organizational Genealogy*, (The George Wright Society Hancock, Michigan 1997) The George Wright Forum, Vol. 14, No. 4 (1997) P. 31

23 "*a state park every hundred miles*" Ibid. P. 34

24 "*Kentucky has ceased to be a detour state*" The New York Times, October 8, 1925

25 "*260 feet long and 25 feet high*) Jeannie McConnell, *The History of Cumberland Falls*, (Kentucky State Parks, Frankfort, 1982) P. 11-12

## Chapter 13 The Beautiful Old House and the Moonbow

1 "*You are also privileged and invited to join with*" Willard R. Jillson, *The Old Kentucky Home*, The Register of the Kentucky State Historical Society, (Frankfort, Kentucky, 1921) Volume 19, No. 56 May, 1921, P. 7

2 " *advanced ideals and inspirations of our time*" Ibid., P. 4

3 "*We drove out to Federal Hill and found it a complete wreck.*" Catherine Connor, *From My Old Kentucky Home to the White House: The Political Journey of Catherine Connor*" (The University Press of Kentucky, Lexington, Kentucky 2009), P. 34

4 *"To Every Expatriate From Kentucky in All the World"* Jillson, *The Old Kentucky Home, Ibid.*, P. 6

5 *"knew very little firsthand of the old south"* *The New York Times*, January 12, 1934

6 *"the great spectacle of African slavery at 'close-ups'"* Young Allison, *The Old Kentucky Home, Immortalized by Stephen C. Foster, Its Song and the Story* (Published Under the Auspices of Kentucky Department of Parks, Frankfort, Ky 1959) P. 28

7 *"She insisted that Foster had written his plaintive and sentimental"* Catherine Connor, *From My Old Kentucky Home, Ibid.*, P. 35

8 *"We thought it was a fine idea"* Ibid., P. 36

9 *"in tangible form the sentiment of Kentuckians"* *The New York Times*, July 5, 1923

10 *"This song has touched the hearts of the world"* Catherine Conner, *From My Old Kentucky Home, Ibid.*, P. 36

11 *"A State Park with adequate up-to-date hotel accommodations"* Kentucky State Parks, Kentucky Geological Survey, Frankfort, Ky. 1924, State Journal Company, Printer to the Commonwealth Frankfort, Ky., *A Brief Presentation of the Geology and Topography of Some Proposed State Park Areas Based Upon Original Field Investigation*, Willard Rouse Jillson, Sc.D., State Geologist of Kentucky and Chairman of the Kentucky State Park Commission, P. 84

12 *"broad recreational areas rich in historic dignity"* Ibid., P. 2-3

13 *"...or industrial and commercial interests will creep"* Ibid., P. 2-3

14 *"beautiful resort in the heart of the Kentucky mountains"* Jeannie McConnell, *Ibid.*, P. 7

15 *"The waters fall like a finely woven medieval lace"* Huffman, Noah Garland 1981-, *"Hanging the Moonbow : Tom Wallace and the Cumberland Falls Fight, 1926-1931."* (2005). Electronic Theses and Dissertations. Paper 648 https://doi.org/10.18297/etd/648, P. 23

16 *"sewer for mining camps"* Ibid., P. 28

17 *"I am almost detached from my regular job"* Ibid., P. 18

18 *"In 1926, Arkansas Democrat Thaddeus H. Caraway accused Insull"* U.S. Senate Historical Office, "Election Case of Frank L. Smith of Illinois, 1928," Senate.gov, https://www.senate.gov/about/origins-foundations/electing-appointing- Senators/contested-senate-elections/110Frank Smith.htm, (Accessed on 12/16/22)

19 *"...but one more example of a 'battle royal of the millionaires.'"* Ibid.

20 *"two dozen lobbyists had been indicted"* Noah Huffman, *Hanging The Moonbow*, Ibid., P.70

21 *"under the necromantic name of 'development'"* Tom Wallace, *Caught in the Power Net, The Survey Graphic,* (Survey Associates, Inc., N.Y. 1929) Volume LXII, No. 7, July 1, 1929, P. 390

22 *"tumbling waters and pillars of bloom...its foundations registering"* Ibid., P. 390

23 *"a great revenue-producing heritage"* Ibid., P. 417

24 *"Why should Kentucky, in an era of road-making"* Ibid., P. 417

25 *"she said, 'I wish there was something I could do for you, Dad"* Leonard Mosley, *Blood Relations The Rise & Fall of the du Ponts of Delaware*, (Atheneum, New York, 1980) P. 336

## Chapter 14 Roosevelt's Tree Army

1 *"Although we now look back upon the depression"* Henry Ward, "The Kentucky State Park System" Unpublished history, for the Spindletop Research Institute for the Kentucky Department of Parks, November 8, 1968, P. 1

2 *"at its peak, there were 2635 CCC camps"* Ibid. P. 6

3 *"Scenery a Cash Cow"* Kentucky State Park Commission, *Report and Recommendations of the Kentucky State Park Commission for the Biennial Period 1926-1928* (Frankfort, Kentucky) January 4, 1926, P. 26

4 *"I want to complement the Commission"* Kentucky Progress Commission, *Kentucky Progress Magazine,* (Publication Office, Louisville, Kentucky) November, 1929, Volume 2, No. 3, P. 9

5 *"on a recent visit to Kentucky"* Ibid., P. 32

6 *"The Glamour of Kentucky"* Kentucky Progress Commission, *Kentucky Progress Magazine,* June 1931, Vol. III, No. 10, P. 9

7 *"The Motion Picture Kentucky"* Kentucky Progress Commission, *First Report of the Kentucky Progress Commission to the 1930 General Assembly of Kentucky,* (Frankfort, Kentucky), December 6, 1929, P. 14

8 *"To Anchor and Chain"* The Paducah Sun-Democrat, August 27, 1935

9 *"When the money of the taxpayers is used"* Ibid., September 5, 1936

10 *"Thousands of motorist drive through the village"* Ibid., undated column, 1941

11 *"thousands of tourists annually to this state"* Ibid., June 7, 1940

12 *"only 2.7 per cent of out of state visitors stopped"* Ibid., June 7, 1940

13 *"The Division of parks has had to scrimp, beg, borrow"* Bailey Wootton, *Yearly Report, 1940,* Division of State Parks, (Department of Conservation, Frankfort, Ky), P. 6
14 *"a number of so-called state parks" "and the doing away with wood railings"* Ibid., P. 6, 8
15 *"Henry has been giving more time and thought"* University of Kentucky, Special Collections, Earle C. Clements, Gubernatorial Series, Conservation—Forestry, (1948-1950) Box 74
16 *"I had adopted promotion of an effective state park program"* "Recollections" P. 19
17 *"fret about things not going the way they should"* The Courier-Journal, undate newspaper column
18 *"Kentucky's industrial payroll ranked second to last"* Thomas Syvertsen, "Dissertation" P. vi
19 *"Yeah, I had been interested in conservation"* Ward Project, P. 86-87
20 *"We felt that something needed to be done to help the economy"* "Recollections" P. 19

## Chapter 15 Ready, Set, Go...

1 *"so we kept on working"* "Recollections" P. 20
2 *"simply fed up with the high-handed operations in the state house band"* James C. Klotter, Editor, Edmund D. Lyon and C. David Dalton, Assistant Editors, *The Public Papers of Governor Simeon Willis, 1943-1947,* (The University Press of Kentucky, Lexington, 1988), P. 24
3 *"concerned about future load growth, approved five generating units"* Tennessee ValleyAuthority, A Monument to Man's Will, https://www.tva.com/energy/our-power-system/hydroelectric/tva-s-mightiest-work, Accessed 12/30/2022
4 *"The 1943 election convinced me"* "Recollections" P. 18
5 *"We knew the legislature could not be persuaded to provide funds"* Ibid., P. 20
6 *"He was a bare-knuckle politician"* The New York Times, March 14, 1985
7 *"He's fearless, you know"* Hampson, Catherine, interview by Terry L. Birdwhistell, November 11, 1975, Earle C. Clements Oral History Project, Louie B. Nunn Center for Oral History, University of Kentucky Libraries.
8 *"emerged far more powerful than he had ever been"* Thomas Syvertsen, "Dissertation" P. 121
9 *"pushed the state party much closer to the mainstream"* Ibid., P. viii
10 *"But I had become interested in the parks and realized"* Ward Project, P. 36, 91-92

11 *"The notion of World War II as 'the Good War'"* https://www.nps.gov/subjects/Nationalhistoriclandmarks/upload/WWII_and_the_American_Home_Front-508.pdf , P. 36 Accessed 12/30/2022

12 *"Parks Popular With Troops" In Kentucky*, Official Publication of the Commonwealth Of Kentucky, (Publication Office, Louisville, Kentucky), 1943 Volume 6, Winter Issue No. 4 P. 35

13 *"Even in the midst of the world's most catastrophic war"* Ibid., 1944 Volume 7, Winter Issue Number 4, P. 7

14 *"new high point in modern pioneering in America"* The New York Times, October 11, 1945

15 *"like this for them when they come home"* Ibid. October 11, 1945

16 *"We created the greatest production machine"* Ibid. October 11, 1945

17 *"I'm not going to run for re-election in 1945"* Ward Project, P. 30

18 *"I was not aligned with Clements"* "Recollections" P. 19

19 *"His [Earle's] position was understandable"* Thomas Syvertsen, "Dissertation", P. 83

20 *"I didn't come to the Senate just to make trouble."* "Recollections" P. 19

21 *"Another fine old judge who found a place in the Governor's office."* Ward Project, P. 30-31

22 *"an outdated constitution which obstructed the financing of new services"* Thomas Syvertsen, "Dissertation", P. vii

23 *"Back room man, an embracer and understander"* Harry McPherson, *A Political Education A Washington Memoir*, (University of Texas Press, Austin, 1972) P. 30

24 *"the greatest humanitarian this nation ever knew"* Thomas Syvertsen, "Dissertation", P. 10

25 *"Can you get Mr. Paxton to meet with me?"* Ward Project, P. 37

26 *"The roads we build today will build the Kentucky of tomorrow."* In Kentucky, Official Publication of the Commonwealth of Kentucky, (Publication Office, Louisville, Kentucky) 1947 Volume 11, Fall Issue, Number 3, P. 9, 35

## Chapter 16 Let's Make a Deal

1 *"I have been authorized by TVA to say"* "Recollections" P. 20

2 *"not compromise with principle"* *"the resources we have..."* In Kentucky, Official Publication of the Commonwealth of Kentucky, Publication Office, Louisville, Kentucky, 1948 Volume 11, Winter Issue, Number 4, P. 19.

3 *"guests danced on all three marble floors of the spacious State Capitol"* Ibid., P. 50

4 *"Clements was a man of terrific intellect"* Pearce, John Ed, interview by L. Elisabeth Beattie. January 09, 1993, Kentucky Writers Oral History Project, Louie B. Nunn Center for Oral History, University of Kentucky Libraries.
5 *"It was a famed cultural and world-trade center."* Harry Schacter, *Kentucky on the March*, (Harper & Brothers Publishers, New York, 1949), P. 4
6 *"If you wanted something done, you better be right with Earle Clements"* Ward Colleagues Project, Fred Paxton.
7 *"80 counties in Kentucky are without industrial development of any significance."* Kentucky Senate Journal, Regular Session of 1948, Volume 1, (January 6 – March 19, 1948) Documents Department, Perry Publishing Co., Frankfort, Kentucky, P. 24-25
8 *"You're kidding," Ward recalled having told the Governor"* The Courier-Journal November 27 1955
9 *"'The Kentuckian boldly retorted'"* "Dissertation", Syvertsen, P. 388
10 *"shotgun appraisal, of all the purchasable properties"* Ibid., P. 388
11 *"I expected, of course, we'd make another effort"* Ward Project, P. 32
12 *"that I would not do anything for the utilities"* Ward Project, P. 33
13 *"I had been working with the Tennessee Valley Authority"* "Recollections" P. 20
14 *"Governor Clements commented, 'Well, all I can say is'"* Ward Project, P. 92-93
15 *"You and your friends worked to get me committed" "It came as a shock..."* Ibid., P. 20-21
16 *"Mr. Paxton wasn't the type to try to persuade"* Ibid., P. 21
17 *"It has proven suicidal to turn over the operation"* Commonwealth of Kentucky, Frankfort, Kentucky, *Annual Report, 1945-46* Division of State Parks, Department of Conservation
18 *"Everyone wanted a seat on the patronage train"* Falcon O. Baker, Kentucky Strikes It Rich, *The Saturday Evening Post*, August 17, 1955 P. 33
19 *"A county chairman who had produced"* Ibid., P. 33
20 *"I'm not a patronage man, I don't believe in it"* Ward Project, P. 38
21 *"If you will take the job, I will put it this way:"* "Recollections" P. 21
22 *"If I am given the job, I do not mind accepting full responsibility" "So I agreed to become Commissioner..."* Ibid., P. 21

## Chapter 17 No More Pioneer Stuff

1 *"For years I hooted at Frank's fishing trips"* Falcon O. Baker, "Kentucky Strikes It Rich", *The Saturday Evening Post*, August 17, 1955 P. 74

2 *"Some people might think this appointment is a bad one"* The Courier-Journal, March 31, 1948

3 *"The Governor didn't even mention..." Ibid.,* March 31, 1948

4 *"I had some credentials beyond my interest in state parks"* "Recollections" P. 21-22

5 *"I still think water is Kentucky's most..."* Recollections, Ward, P. 22

6 *"I am going to have to arrange for some form of motor"* "University of Kentucky, Special Collections, Earle C. Clements Collection, Gubernatorial Series, Conservation—Forestry, (1948-1950) Box 74 Letter from Conservation Commissioner, Henry Ward to Governor Earle Clements, April 17, 1958

7 *"All over the world they sing"* Falcon O. Baker, "Kentucky Strikes it Rich", P. 74

8 *"And I raised hell, but it didn't do any good"* Ward Project, P. 39-40

9 *"Pure drinking water and better health protection"* The Courier-Journal, June 30, 1948

10 *"is not as far-reaching as I would have desired" Ibid.*

11 *"... literally speaking, overhangs Cumberland Falls State Park"* Whitley Republican, December 4, 1947

12 *"accumulated neglect of years"* In Kentucky, *Official Publication of the Commonwealth of Kentucky,* Publication Office, Louisville, Kentucky, 1948 Volume 12, Summer Issue, Number 2, P. 9, 12

13 *"ranked second in tourism"* Thomas Syvertsen, "Dissertation", P. 391

## Chapter 18 A Firebug's Playground

1 *"Was negligence an unwitting ally of arson"* Whitley Republican, March 17, 1949

2 *"various rules and restrictions" "some relief from" "Governor Clements told me before and after the election"* University of Kentucky, Special Collections, Earle C. Clements Collection, Gubernatorial Series, Conservation—Forestry, (1948-1950) Box 74 Letter from E.M. Gatliff to Henry Ward.

3 *"In many ways restore to the hotels the good name" Ibid.* Box 74, Letter from Gatliff to Ward

4 *"The gentleman from Harvard is a total misfit" Ibid.* Box 74, Letter from Gatliff to Ward.

5 *"about fifty years old and very dissipated"* "Mr. Hardin was very much worried about his wife, Elizabeth," *Ibid.,* Box 74, unsigned report titled "RE: M.P. Hardin" P. 2

6 *"Mr. Hardin and Mr. Masters were very cagey about describing"* Ibid., Box 74, "RE: Mr. Lanham" P. 5
7 *"had a little gift to give them to take with them"* Ibid., Box 74, "RE: M.P. Hardin" P. 4
8 *"but with single reservations where they should be doubles"* Ibid., Box 74, "RE: Eve Sparrow" P. 9
9 *"We took over operation of the village July 1"* Ibid., Box 74, Letter from Ward to Clements, July 7, 1948
10 *"one fourth of State Park hotels in U.S. are located there"* Unpublished "Report by W.T. Ammerman, National Park Service on Survey of Kentucky State Parks" September 24, 1948, P. 44
11 *"The State of Kentucky acting through its authorized representatives"* Ibid., P. 45
12 *"I explained to Mr. Graham and Mr. Cregor that this is a new administration"* "University of Kentucky, Special Collections, Earle C. Clements Collection, Gubernatorial Series, Conservation—Forestry, (1948-1950) Box 74, Letter from Henry Ward to Earle Clements, May 27, 1948
13 *"because most everyone I talk with, volunteers to the effect"* Ibid., Box 74, Letter from W.E. Martin to Henry Ward, August 24, 1948
14 *"The Division of Parks does not have either $10,000 or $25,000"* *"Mr. Curtis is entitled consideration by the state because he has devoted"* Ibid., Box 7 letter from Henry Ward to Earle Clements, October 27, 1948
15 *"He will do anything that Mr. Hardin asks him to do"* Ibid., "RE: Mr. and Mrs. Masters" Box 74, P. 10
16 *"While this may be a technical violation"* *"discharge any employee"* Ibid., Box 74, Letter from Henry Ward to Judge E.B. Johnson, October 15, 1948
17 *"Moonbow Inn at Cumberland Falls Park Burns to Ground"* The Corbin Daily Tribune March 14, 1949

## Chapter 19 Speeding Backward

1 *"The Chandler second administration was an undistinguished one."* "Recollections" P. 31
2 *"We are finding that as advertisers learn"* University of Kentucky, Special Collections, Earle C. Clements Collection, Gubernatorial Series, Conservation—Forestry, (1948-1950) Box 74, Letter from Henry Ward to Earle Clements, March 10, 1949
3 *"The State of Kentucky provides separate facilities"* Ibid., Letter from Henry Ward to Lincoln Hale, November 1, 1949

4 *"Do you not think that since our boys faught [sic]" Ibid.,* Letter from Reverend J. E. Bowen to Henry Ward, August, 13, 1949
5 *"to be fair minded and in possesion[sic] of some facts. Ibid.,* Letter from Reverend J.E. Gillis to Henry Ward, May 25, 1950
6 *"That whereas the white citizenry have more than three pools..." Ibid.,* 5/25/50
7 *"In the context of 1940 this was..."* Henry Ward – Record on Civil Rights, Ward Files, undated statement.
8 *"There'd been a push, with the black population"* Ward Project, P. 93-94
9 *"I'm a person who speaks straight from the shoulder" The Courier Journal,* May 31, 1951
10 *"directed that all State Park facilities be opened to..."* Ward, Record on Civil Rights
11 *"The Kentucky Democratic party was more unified"* "Dissertation", Thomas Hamilton Syvertsen, The Graduate School, University of Kentucky, 1982, P. 487
12 *"Brawls in the House of Factions" Divide and Dissent, Kentucky Politics 1930-1963* (University Press of Kentucky, Lexington, Kentucky, 1987) P. 60
13 *"It has been said, and with considerable truth, Ibid.,* P. 59
14 *"...without a doubt, one of the most popular..."* Recollections, P. 30
15 *"I had my share of support for governor"* Recollections, P. 30
16 *"the worst candidate the state had seen" Ibid.,* P. 30
17 *"in asking the people something for myself"* Ward Files, "Statement by Henry Ward, Commissioner of Conservation, For Release Monday Afternoon, May 9, 1955"
18 *"better government, more goodies"* "Recollections", P. 31
19 *"Chandler had been aiming some barbs against me..." Ibid.,* P. 31
20 *"Instead of an explanation, he gave a glowing account"* John Ed Pearce, *Divide and Dissent,* P. 65
21 *"quite possibly one of the biggest upsets in the political history"* Marshall County Daily, *The Life of H.H. Lovett Part 10: Circuit Judge,* Justin Lamb, December 22, 2018
22 *"'a team man,' not an individual star, not a great speaker" The New York Times,* July 3, 1955
23 *"It really twisted my heart to give up"* "Recollections" P. 32
24 *"It did not take me long to find that my Washington assignments"* "Recollections" *Ibid.* P.32
25 *"A 30-minute program was developed for television..." Ibid.,* P. 33
26 *"a whole battery of automatic typewriters that could grind out" Ibid.* P. 32

27 *"Well, Lawrence talked to me about it"* Ward Project, P. 50
28 *"Kentucky lost a great asset"* "Recollections" P. 33
29 *"In less than a year I had changed my mind"* "Recollections" P.33
30 *"I accepted because it meant"* Ibid., P. 33

## Chapter 20 Run Down Dump Trucks

1 *"I am not a candidate"* The Courier-Journal, August 19, 1960
2 *"New Highway Commissioner Ward confirmed"* Ibid., September 1, 1960
3 *"Did you know that one of the smartest politicians"* Henry Ward Colleagues Oral History Project, Repository: Kentucky History Center, Call No. 2005OH12, Calvin Grayson, Interviewee, February 11 2004
4 *"He spends more money on building"* The Courier-Journal, August 27, 1960
5 *"a vitally interested throng [that] includes state employees"* Ibid.
6 *"the presence of Old Pro Clements in the politically sensitive"* The Courier-Journal, August 19, 1960
7 *"I never heard of anyone getting into trouble for"* Thomas Syvertsen, "Dissertation", P. 22
8 *"found a practical use for trucks as heavy"* Courier-Journal, April 13, 1960
9 *"It also called for exactly defined tires and tubes,"* Ibid., April 13, 1960
10 *"Cooke Automobile Empire Collapses"* The Lexington Herald, May 22, 1960
11 *"A number of counties are spending hundreds of thousands."* Louisville-Courier Journal, August 5, 1960
12 *"We can't afford to meddle in the affairs of"* Ibid.
13 *"the letter and spirit of the law"* The Courier-Journal, August 8, 1960
14 *"That was the last anyone heard of it."* "Recollections" Henry Ward, P. 34
15 *"In Louisville, everyone was an expert,"* Ibid., P. 34
16 *"So I went to Frankfort to see him,"* "Recollections" Henry Ward, P. 35
17 *"In fact he called me – Clements called me"* Ward Project, P. 54
18 *"Hell, I'm working on canceling it"'* Ward Project, P. 55-56
19 *"Bert, you're in trouble"* Ward Project, P. 64
20 *"There was a feeling expressed"* The Courier-Journal August 28, 1960
21 *"From now on, by God,"* Patricia Ward to author.

## Chapter 21 Stranger in the Kingdom

1 *"Ward said that his experience taught him"* Paducah Sun-Democrat, September 1, 1960
2 *"I'll take care of the politics"* Ward Colleagues Project, Calvin Grayson
3 *"Kentuckians for Better Transportation,"* Member Letter, Louisville, Ky., 2/2/1987, P.8

4 *"Aside from the outside appearance of him being a rough fella"* Ward Colleagues Project, John Witt
5 *"The public doesn't know how much he did"* Ibid., John Witt
6 *"I had the privilege of acquiring the first rights of way"* Ibid., John Witt
8 *"It wasn't a nice place for someone to come in"* Ibid., John Witt
9 *"Out in the districts they... oh, hell they were housed"* Ward Project, P. 68
10 *"Believe me, I felt the pressure of that"* Ibid., John Witt
11 *"I don't give a damn if you do or not"* Ibid., John Witt
12 *"He said we – the engineers – don't inform the public enough"* Ward Colleagues Project, Calvin Grayson
13 *"go to UK or any other university and ask for an economic impact study"* Ibid.
14 *"I don't want to go back again – I'll tell you what"* Ibid
15 *"It came to his attention that school kids"* Ibid., John Witt
16 *"Planning? We had no planning"* Ward Project, P. 69
17 *"We need urban planning and we need a young grad"* Ward Colleagues Project, Calvin Grayson
18 *"I was scared of Ward, by the way, he had everybody scared of him"* Ibid.
19 *"I was convinced that I had to get on top of purchasing"* Ward Project, P. 64
20 *"There were protests that this hampered"* "Recollections" Henry Ward, P. 40
21 *"This produced the biggest difficulty I had as Commissioner,"* Ibid., P. 41
22 *"particularly in connection with the purchase of scrapers"* Ward Project, P. 65
23 *"I was determined to bust this up"* Ward Project, P. 65
24 *"So I think Bert was in complete agreement"* Ward Project, P. 67
25 *"You have to be sure of the facts"* Ward Colleagues Project, John Witt
26 *"I took the job as commissioner of highways"* The Courier-Journal, September 8, 1962
27 *"Finally, Ward broke up the old political practice"* Ibid.
28 *"qualified Kentucky as the second state in the nation for"* Ibid.
29 *"Previously, beginning in 1952, the diversion of highway money"*, Ibid.
30 *"I won't stay if you put Bert's cousin"* Ward Project, P. 81
31 *"After Henry took over, he informed Combs"* Ward Project, P. 81
33 *"I just completely bypassed Marcum"* Ward Project, P. 83
34 *"They wouldn't give any money for planning"* The Louisville Times, June 25, 1974
35 *"I don't want to make 128 county judges mad"* Ward Colleagues Project, Calvin Grayson
36 *"He would have made everyone mad"* *"Well the trouble is, Ward did run his own"* Breathitt, Edward T., Jr., interview by Terry L. Birdwhistell. February

06, 1997, Edward T. "Ned" Breathitt, Jr. Oral History Project, Louie B. Nunn Center for Oral History, University of Kentucky Libraries

**Chapter 22 Flashing Yellow Lights**

1 *"The Democratic brand was becoming tarnished"* George Humphreys, e mail to author, July 23, 2022
2 *"He got all the negatives that I had, which were plenty."* Edward T. "Ned" Breathitt, Oral History, February 6, 1997
3 *"were mad at me, and distrustful of Ward."* Ibid.
4 *"But I-I was then-Ward didn't want me out front."* Ibid.
5 *"Integration of public schools passed its second day"* The New York Times, September 12, 1956
6 *"The old South's only state civil rights act"* The New York Times, July 2, 1966
7 *"most significant stride accomplished so far"* The New York Times, June 29, 1963
8 *"made a direct appeal to the people of Kentucky"* Edward T. "Ned" Breathitt, Oral History, February 6, 1997
9 *"The issue was racism, inherent racism,"* Ibid.
10 *"by the end of 1965 interest was stirring"* "Recollections" Henry Ward, P. 47
11 *"I'd be silly to get in the race in a situation like that"* Ward Project, P. 116
12 *"Because one of the stories was Mabel said"* Ward Project, P. 115-16
13 *"then Barry Bingham [Sr.] and Mary Bingham came to see me"* Edward T. "Ned" Breathitt Oral History, February 6, 1997
14 *"I could never have passed both the civil rights and"* Ibid., Breathitt Oral History
15 *"I'll be damned if I will!"* Ward Project, P. 116
16 *"If you will manage the campaign, I will run"* "Recollections" Henry Ward, P. 49
17 *"Any doubts about the extent to which the Breathitt administration"* The Courier-Journal, November 11, 1966
18 *"Ward Blasts GOP"* Ibid.
19 *"Mr. Nunn vigorously opposed the open housing"* The New York Times, May 14, 1967
20 *"The Nunn campaign is one of the worst"* Ward Election Poster, "What Leading Republicans say about Louie Nunn"
21 *"accused Nunn of having stirred appeals to racial prejudice"* Ibid., May 24 1967.
22 *"I'm Jubilant!"* The State Journal, May 24, 1967

23 *"The Republicans' division and distress"* The New York Times, May 25, 1967
24 *"Everybody was so damned optimistic"* Ward Project, P. 79
25 *"What do you remember about that campaign?"* Ward Project, P. 117

**Chapter 23 End of Damn Story**

1 *"He is honest, wrote a national newspaper columnist"* The Louisville Times, June 25, 1974
2 *"This man was absolutely brilliant"* Ward Colleagues Project, Thomas Preston, April 17, 2004
3 *" Take me as I am, if not, I'll move on"* Ibid.
4 *"If Henry could have been appointed governor"* Author Interview, Foster Ockerman, 10/14/2003, Lexington, Kentucky.
5 *"position papers that they thought I would issue"* Ward Project, P. 117
6 *"Electorate Seems Bored by Kentucky Campaign"* The Courier-Journal, October 7, 1967
7 *"Ward,"the Republicans assert,"* Ibid.
8 *"I know I remember we had a fight with"* Ward Project, P. 76
9 *"I wrote the first state strip mining law"* Ward Project, P. 74
10 *"the coal interests were too strong"* "Recollections" Henry Ward, P. 23
11 *"When Mr. Ward arose in the Senate chamber"* The Courier-Journal, undated clipping
12 *"I uh, had Dick Moloney, as I mentioned"* Wetherby, Lawrence W., interview by John Kleber. August 30, 1979, Lawrence W. Wetherby Oral History Project, Louie B. Nunn Center for Oral History, University of Kentucky Libraries.
13 *"has been treated by the last two administrations"* The Courier-Journal, undated, "Conversations with the Candidates" Kathleen Arnold
14 *"that every person is created equal"* Campaign Statement by Henry Ward, Democratic Candidate for Governor, April 19, 1967, Ward Files
15 *"The right to sell a house to anyone of his choice"* The Courier-Journal, October 7, 1967
16 *"I thought you were keen and thorough"* The Courier-Journal, April 27, 1967
17 *" half an oaf is better than Nunn"* The New York Times, November 4, 1967
18 *"all wet" "rigged and trumped up"* The Courier-Journal, October 18, 1967
19 *"They did this, of the candidates, one of Louie Nunn"* Breathitt Oral History Project
20 *"And he bragged on Louie, and talked about what a great"* Breathitt Oral History Project

24 NOTES ON SOURCES

21 *"You'd be crazy as hell to think I could do that," The Paducah Sun-Democrat*, April 17, 1974
22 *"Foster called me on marine radio"* Breathitt Oral History Project
23 *"with a set jaw, an effort at humor and a display of resignation" The Courier-Journal* undated original clipping, James S. Tunnell
24 *"I'm not kidding myself [sic] if I was a poor candidate"* Ward Project, P. 119
25 *"I was a nobody...just a damned kid who had to work" The Courier-Journal*, June 25, 1974
26 *"No one paid any attention yesterday to" The Courier-Journal*, August 20, 1978
27 *"I don't have to answer that. You didn't give me a chance" The Paducah-Sun* April 17, 1974

**Photo Sources**

Unless otherwise noted, photos from personal collection of Henry T. Ward, by permission of Patricia Ward Willis.

P. 52 Beall, Lester, Artist. *Here it Comes Rural Electrification Administration, U.S. Department of Agriculture // Beall*. United States, . [193] Photograph. https://www.loc.gov/item/2010650609/.

P. 63 Harris & Ewing, photographer. *Senator A.B. 'Happy' Chandler, Democrat of Ky*. United States District of Columbia Washington D.C. Washington D.C, 1940. Photograph. https://www.loc.gov/item/2016877579/.

P. 63 Harris & Ewing, photographer. *Senator Alben Barkley, New Majority Leader of the Senate* United States District of Columbia Washington D.C. Washington D.C, 1937. Photograph. https://www.loc.gov/item/2016872039/.

P. 84 TVA https://www.loc.gov/resource/fsa.8e00586/ *Kentucky Dam Lock Building* Farm Security Administration - Office of War Information photograph collection (Library of Congress)

P. 105 Jackson, William Henry, photographer. *Hot Springs, on Gardiner's River, Upper Basins*. , 1871. Washington, D.C.: W.H. Jackson. Photograph. https://www.loc.gov/item/2005685072/.

P. 108 Harris & Ewing, photographer. *Stephen Mather.*, None. [Between 1910 and 1920] Photograph. https://www.loc.gov/item/2016855394/.

P. 116 Postcard, collection of author.

P. 121 "The Survey Graphic," July 1929, Volume 7, The Hathi Trust Digital Collection https://babel.hathitrust.org/cgi/ls?q1=The%20Survey%20Graphic;field1=ocr;a=srchls;lmt=ft&facet=bothPublishDateRange:%221920-1929%22

## About the Author

Sharon Roggenkamp, a native of Springfield, Ohio, worked as a part-time columnist and community reporter for *The Lexington (Kentucky) Herald-Leader*, then joined the staff at Scott County Public Library, Georgetown as Media Coordinator from 2012 until 2019. She currently serves as a volunteer docent and social media coordinator for the National Voice of America Museum of Broadcasting in West Chester, Ohio. This book is based on an oral history grant she was awarded from the Kentucky Historical Society, and the personal and professional archive of Henry Ward.

www.ingramcontent.com/pod-product-compliance
Lightning Source LLC
Chambersburg PA
CBHW042127160426
43198CB00021B/2934